WRITING IN COLLABORATIVE THEATRE-MAKING

D1145618

Writing in Collaborative Theatre-Making

Sarah Sigal

 macmillan
education

palgrave

First published 2017 by
PALGRAVE

Palgrave in the UK is an imprint of Macmillan Publishers Limited, registered in England, company number 785998, of 4 Crinan Street, London, N1 9XW.

Palgrave® and Macmillan® are registered trademarks in the United States, the United Kingdom, Europe and other countries.

ISBN 978–1–137–33169–4 hardback
ISBN 978–1–137–33168–7 paperback

This book is printed on paper suitable for recycling and made from fully managed and sustained forest sources. Logging, pulping and manufacturing processes are expected to conform to the environmental regulations of the country of origin.

A catalogue record for this book is available from the British Library.

A catalog record for this book is available from the Library of Congress.

For my father

Contents

List of Illustrations

Acknowledgements

I would like to thank the following people for their generosity:

For the generous cooperation and of the following practitioners who agreed to be interviewed: Sophie Austin, Sebastian Born, Stephen Brown, Vic Bryson, Oliver Dimsdale, David Farr, Helen Edmundson, Scott Graham, Carl Grose, Theo Herdman, Steven Hoggett, Samuel James, Dawn King, Bryony Lavery, Stuart McLaughlin, Nancy Meckler, Anna Maria Murphy, Tim Phillips, Ben Power, Liz Ranken, Peter Rankin, Guy Retallack, Emma Rice, Ferdy Roberts, Angela Simpson, Mark Stevenson, Polly Teale and Michael Wagg.

For the friendly and helpful administrative assistance in arranging for interviews of the aforementioned practitioners, as well as the viewing of archival material: the staff of the offices of Filter Theatre, Frantic Assembly, Kneehigh, Shared Experience and Teatro Vivo.

For rich and wonderful rehearsal room collaborations: Jessica Beck, James Bounds, Linda Campbell, Amelia Cavallo, Rebecca Dunn, Jason Eddy, Susanna Fiore, Katharine Fry, Giles Gartrell-Mills, Theo Herdman, Erin Hunter, Ailsa Ilot, Emily Jones, Penny Lisle, David Luff, Ellie McRea, Fiona Putnam, Katharina Reinthaller, Andrew Shepherd, Helen Tennison, Hannah Thompson, Geraldine Timmins, Anna Westlake, Jennifer Williams, Alex Woolnough and many, many others.

Finally, I am eternally grateful for the love and support of my parents, Kass and Michael Sigal.

Section 1

Understanding the Practice: key elements and early examples

Introduction

When I began working as a young writer, I was curious about the possible interactions between the play text, the performers' input and the director's ideas in both the workshop and the rehearsal room. I had the pleasure of working with directors who employed improvisation to develop the script and performers who were adept not only at devising through speech and physicality but also at finding ways into a rough draft of a text, uncovering what could be lifted, highlighted, changed, deleted or incorporated into a physical sequence. I have continued to pursue this practice in my own work as a writer and director and also in my academic research in order to better understand the ways in which different companies and practitioners position the text and how writers position themselves in the collaborative process. The process of theatre-making is alchemic. It is imprecise, unscientific. The very nature of live performance is ephemeral, temporary and intangible, and the process of creating it is born of a combination of instinct, experience, knowledge, negotiation and, most importantly, collaboration. A production can be changed by an insertion or deletion of a line or two, a discovery in rehearsal or a conversation. There are trials and experiments, the inclusion and exclusion of certain constants and variables to achieve a particular result. And thus we reach what can often seem like a dilemma of the seeming permanence of text versus the seeming ephemerality of performance, or what theatre-maker/writer/deviser Chris Goode has referred to as a 'phoney war' between writing and devising.[1] A text can exist without the act of performing it live and performance can exist without a text to inform or guide it, but what are the ways in which the two can be integrated into the same collaborative process? What are the possibilities for a writer and a text in collaborative theatre-making? How can this alchemic process form and re-form to accommodate practitioners and companies who want to commission writers and writers who want to work with companies and collectives?

My intention for *Writing in Collaborative Theatre-Making* is to provide writers, companies who want to collaborate with them and practitioners who want to make the transition into becoming writers themselves with a series of strategies that incorporate practical, theoretical and historical approaches to making work so that they may be better placed to negotiate a mutually beneficial process and build on these legacies within their own approaches to working. I am going to deconstruct several different collaborative processes, focusing on the intersection of the process of the writer and that of the company, taking examples from the work of and interviews with writers, directors, dramaturgs and companies, as well as a project in which I was involved as a writer. In the past two decades, the field of the kind of collaboration that involves text and writers has expanded and gained a higher profile across the UK in the form of an increased number of productions, higher education courses, conferences, workshops and articles; writers and writer/directors today use a variety of methods to make devised, site-specific, physical theatre and adaptations. *Writing in Collaborative Theatre-Making* will investigate the processes used by Filter Theatre, Frantic Assembly, Kneehigh, Shared Experience, Teatro Vivo and the in-house and commissioned writers and writer/directors with whom they have worked in order to answer a number of questions. What is the role of the writer in new collaborative theatre-making in the UK? How can texts be produced in different processes that involve a commissioned writer? How is authorship negotiated by practice between writers and other creative collaborators? What can we learn from historical collaborative practice?

While *Writing and Collaborative Theatre-Making* offers a number of possible models of working, of course I do not intend to say that these are the *only* approaches to writer–company collaboration or even that there are models consciously put forward by the practitioners from the case studies themselves.[2] The purpose of this book is to provide a number of possibilities for writer–company collaboration by analysing the practices of a number of writers, writer/directors, directors and companies, then offer a series of strategies that can be used to generate and develop work in a workshop or rehearsal-room setting, loosely based on these collaborative practices. This book will outline different configurations of relationships between writers and their collaborators, examining the practicalities of making work, such as the complex and often problematic issues of hierarchy and negotiation, combining both practical and theoretical aspects of writing and collaboration. While doing so, I will attempt to address issues of best practice for collaborators when working with text and writing – how to discuss the work, how to navigate company hierarchy and how to respect different spheres of authorship and authority within a project.

The companies

There are numerous companies working in the UK who could be described as working collaboratively, but this book is particularly concerned with the work of five companies that choose to commission writers and writer/directors, each representing a distinct strand of writer–company collaborative practice: Shared Experience, Frantic Assembly, Filter Theatre, Kneehigh and Teatro Vivo. Each company serves as an example of a particular process of collaboration with a distinct interpretation of the writer's role, authorship and company hierarchy. Founded in 1975 by Mike Alfreds and now run by Artistic Director Polly Teale, Shared Experience works primarily by adapting canonical texts such as *War and Peace* and *Anna Karenina* and provides an example of a company that works with writers, particularly in order to adapt extant non-dramatic texts. Founded by co-directors Scott Graham and Steven Hoggett in 1994 and now run by Hoggett, Frantic Assembly incorporates text and movement by working simultaneously with writers and performers to create a three-dimensional narrative; it provides an example of a company that juxtaposes written texts with movement scores through improvisational choreography. Established in 2001 by Oliver Dimsdale, Ferdy Roberts and Tim Phillips, Filter Theatre's work is predominantly sound driven, using sound effects and soundscapes in conjunction with projections and moving sets, creating original work, adaptations of non-dramatic extant texts and the radical reworking of classic performance texts, such as plays by Shakespeare and Chekhov. Kneehigh, originally a theatre-in-education company founded by Mike Shepherd in 1983, is based in Cornwall, working with adaptation and original material through dance, song, acrobatics and music. Teatro Vivo was founded in 2005 by Sophie Austin as a company focused on creating devised, written and scripted work for non-theatre spaces, working for and with local communities, in order to make live performance accessible to a wide variety of audiences of different ages and backgrounds.

The context

In the UK, within the first two decades of the twenty-first century, the nature of the dramatic text has shifted in relation to changing under-standings of authorship and the writer's role, and as a result, it has the potential to be not only a product of the writer's creative input but a result of the shared creative agency of an entire production team.[3] The changing status of the writer and the text have come to be emblem-atic of the way in which British theatre-makers have positioned them-selves within the rapidly shifting cultural and economic climate of the early twenty-first century. Describing how writing for performance in the new millennium is becoming an ever-more varied practice, John Freeman writes in *New Performance/New Writing*, 'Have we reached the point where we no longer ask, "What can we write?" so much as "What can we do with writing?"'.[4] The term 'writing for performance' has expanded to include not only singly authored written work but a variety of approaches, such as the co-authorship of two writers or more; adaptations; collaborations between writers and companies; and writ-ing as scripting within a devising process. In *Dramaturgy in the Making*, Katalin Trencsényi writes that in the emergence of new theatre- and performance-making such as 'performance art, devised theatre, com-munity theatre, site-specific performances' and 'dance theatre',

> New relationships have been explored with the text and its relation-ship to the rest of the elements of the performance…. These changes have all influenced and shaped new ways of thinking of and making theatre, as well as pushing the boundaries of dramaturgy. The tradi-tional 'two-steps process' – the writer writes a play and the director stages it in collaboration with the dramaturg – has dissolved into myriad new ways of working, with more and more stress on the pro-cesses through which a performance is created.[5]

The evolution of this field has had implications with respect to notions of authorship and creative identity – especially in an environment in which the text is the product of layers of different creative influences from a number of practitioners, in addition to the writer. As a result of the flexible and varying nature of the collaborative process, the role of an individual writer can change from company to company and pro-duction to production, and, depending on the process, the author or authors of the piece might include the director, performers, the designer and/or the dramaturg, in addition to the writer.

Since the late 1990s and early 2000s, what has been come to be known as collaborative theatre has flourished in the UK in a way not seen since the days of the political theatre of the 1970s, in which companies such as Joint Stock (1974–1989), Monstrous Regiment (1975–1993), Gay Sweatshop (1975) and 7:84 (1971–2008) emerged. However, the reasons why this particular practice has become so prominent are complex. Writer Clare Bayley explains that the late 1980s and early 1990s 'was a time of formal experiment and a stirring for new approaches to break down the formality of the roles of playwright and director, to develop a more collaborative, workshop-based practice and to incorporate devising work into a finished text', citing the emergence of writers such as, for example, Carl Grose and Tim Crouch, as well as the influence of directors such as Tom Morris during his tenure at the Battersea Arts Centre and Sue Emmas at the Young Vic Theatre in placing a new emphasis on workshopping and devising in new theatre development.[6] The new millennium saw the emergence of British companies like (but not limited to) Filter Theatre, Punchdrunk (2000), Sound and Fury (2000), Gecko (2001) and 1927 (2005), as well as the growth of companies established in the previous decade, such as Told by an Idiot (1993), Hoipolloi (1994), Frantic Assembly, Third Angel (1995), Improbable (1996) and the Shunt collective (1998). What sets this category of companies apart from others is that they prioritize the use of collaborative (and often devised, or partially devised) approaches to theatre-making in order to integrate text with other elements of production such as performance, design, use of performance space and the director's concept, as well as using text in original and unusual ways, in order to find fresh possibilities for performance. Some of these companies, such as Frantic Assembly and Gecko, focus on devising movement, some such as Punchdrunk and the Shunt collective are interested primarily in the appropriation of unconventional, alternative performance spaces and the experience and participation of spectators, while others like Sound and Fury and 1927 engage with media such as sound and video. The roles of the text and the writer (if a specifically designated writer is used) have evolved in order to meet the distinct needs of these companies, whether to act as a scripting writer within the devising process; a writer/dramaturg in the rehearsal room who works not only with performers and a director but also designers; a writer/director who shapes both the production and text; or a writer or dramaturg who scripts a text for a particular performance space. Many companies seek the help of writers external to the company, while some use internal or external writer/directors in order to create or adapt a text for a project; for example, Sound and Fury commissioned writer Bryony Lavery to write the text for *Kursk* (2009) and Hoipolloi employed company writer/director Shôn Dale-Jones to adapt Edward Gorey's *The Doubtful Guest* (2009).

One reason for the growth of new companies in the new millennium is that Arts Council funding benefited greatly from increased subsidy under Prime Minister Tony Blair's New Labour government (1997–2007), which fostered innovation within companies, growth within the field of new theatre-making and also the development of new audiences. In an article on 18 February 2012, *The Economist* noted that 'Under Labour, central-government support for the sector through Arts Council England (ACE), the principal funding conduit, more than doubled, from £179m in 1998–99 to £453m in 2009–2010.'[7] During this period, an increasingly wide variety of theatre companies were being funded and encouraged to develop a more expansive and innovative programme of work than in previous years in order to promote innovation, to change the face of the arts in general and theatre specifically and to bring a new demographic into British theatres who had not previously been target audience members. As *Guardian* theatre critic Michael Billington comments,

> once Blair and Brown shed the cautious financial pragmatism of 1997–99, theatre ... experienced a sense of renewal. New money changed the cultural climate and had many positive effects: the regional survival, the expansion of the repertory, the quest for new audiences through cheap tickets. ... As Blairism reached its twilight period, it was possible to detect ways in which theatre had become both more socially inclusive and more artistically inquisitive.[8]

In this period, a variety of different theatre companies with distinct objectives were encouraged to apply for funding – such as companies that were formed to produce work by artists of particular ethnic backgrounds, like the British East-Asian company Yellow Earth (1995) and the British African company Tiata Fahodzi (1997). Likewise, collaborative theatre companies with claims to new processes of theatre-making received public subsidy at a level not seen since before stringent funding cuts for the arts under Margaret Thatcher's Conservative government in the 1980s. As funding grew, more companies with a wide variety of different agendas began to emerge and produce new work that often challenged the status quo and experimented with innovative approaches to theatre-making. As Bristol Old Vic Theatre Artistic Director Tom Morris said in 2012, when this funding started to be cut under David Cameron's government, increased public subsidy allowed theatre-makers to 'escape the strictures of the marketplace' by allowing them not only to 'invest in truly unpredictable work' but also to encourage new audiences that might not otherwise come to the theatre to see this work through inexpensive, subsidized play tickets.[9] Increased public subsidy for the arts helped both new and established companies develop their practice, make new productions and commission external writers. As these companies became more numerous and influential, gaining a higher public profile throughout the late 1990s and into the new millennium, more practitioners felt encouraged to develop their own collaborating practices.

With the increase of Arts Council funding for theatre, there was also a proliferation in the number of new plays and new writers, effectively enlarging the pool of talent from which companies could select when deciding to collaborate with a writer, as well as increasing the possibility that a percentage of these new writers would be interested in collaboration. Aleks Sierz explains this 'renaissance of new writing' in the UK: 'In the past decade, more than 300 playwrights have made their debuts. It has also been calculated that between 500 and 700 writers make a living out of stage plays, radio plays and TV drama in Britain'.[10] In 2009, the Theatre sector of Arts Council England commissioned an investigation into the state of new writing for performance – surveying, discussing and interviewing a number of new writing theatres, companies and practitioners across the country to gain an understanding of the state of new writing from 2003 to 2009, to understand the impact of the additional £25 million in funding secured under the 2003 Theatre Review and to assess whether further investment would be fruitful.[11] The report demonstrated that during this period, the 'overwhelming majority' of tickets sold were for new plays, that 42 per cent of work produced in the theatres and companies surveyed consisted of new plays and that there was a significant growth in audiences for new plays, between 2003 and 2004 and between 2007 and 2008.[12] As Emma Dunton, Roger Nelson and Hetty Shand wrote in 2009,

New writing in theatre at a grassroots level appears to have undergone a period of renaissance over the past six years. Additional funding has enabled a wider variety of new writing/new work to take place in an extraordinary mix of venues across the country. A new more diverse generation of voices is emerging into a culture of experimentation and change. ... The period since 2003 was mostly viewed as one of growth, inspiration and diversification.[13]

Dunton, Nelson and Shand found in an Arts Council-commissioned survey that 55 per cent of practitioners surveyed agreed with the following statement: 'There is a wider variety of work seen on stage under the banner of new writing/new work now than there was six years ago', and thus, they sought to investigate in discussion groups how practitioners believed the term 'new writing' could be defined and what the roles of the writer and text were considered to be.[14] The majority believed that not only 'an individual writing a play' but also 'a writer collaborating with other artists' could be included in the definition of new writing or new work, and a third of the group suggested that new writing/new work could be defined as 'a company devising work', 'a devising process which results in a text-based piece of theatre', 'a group devised piece which has been crafted by a writer/ director' and 'a theatre text that emerges from an artistic exploration of ideas, either individually or collectively'.[15] Not only had new writing grown in the UK during the noughties and had indeed been encouraged to grow through Arts Council initiatives, but the definition of new writing had expanded in the eyes of practitioners throughout the country, encompassing not only the work of a single writer or author, but also the collaborative composition of multiple writers, authors, practitioners and companies. The possibilities for new approaches to theatre-making, and specifically, collaborative writing, seemed to be opening up as quickly as the theatre-makers themselves could conceive of them.

Although there are many variations of the definition of 'new writing', there are even more variations of companies' and writers' approaches to collaborative composition; each company tailors the collaborative process to its own needs and aesthetics, and each writer has his/her approach to composition and collaboration. In 2007, Ruth Little (at the time, literary manager for the Royal Court Theatre) remarked on the ways in which collaboration has influenced new performance writing:

We are now regularly making work which takes the dramatic script as a 'theatrical score'; where the playwright participates alongside director, designer, composer, choreographer, puppeteer, performer, drawing on live resources in action to produce a text. ... Writers are developing new confidence in the languages of theatre, and in the dramatic potential of their own language.[16]

The rise of collaborative performance-making in the UK has encouraged writers to broaden their concept of the creative process and consider new ways of working which rely upon the involvement of collaborators within a production. Authorship in this context is bound up with the 'live resources' of the other company members, so the dramaturgical process of a collaborative piece becomes an ongoing dialogue between the writer and the rest of the company. If we are to understand the possibilities for writers and companies alike in the collaborative composition of this theatrical score, it is important to examine different writers' and companies' processes and the motivations behind them – aesthetic, ideological and practical.

Definition of terms

Terms such as 'writing,' 'collaboration,' 'devising,' and 'authorship' have a particular meaning within different writer–company collaborative practices. Although some definitions of terms overlap in meaning from company to company or practitioner to practitioner, others differ within the context of the work being made. I believe it is important to discern which terms have unique meanings within the context of each practitioner's work, or whether different practitioners and companies have shared definitions for specific aspects of their creative process. In this way, I can try to construct an understanding of how collaborative and devised practices have disrupted traditional definitions within theatre-making practice.

Collaboration. The definition of this particular term is important because the way in which each artistic director and writer defines the word illuminates the way in which they work and how they view the field of collaborative theatre as a whole, as well as their experiences of collaboration. Collaborative theatre is complex because there are many different processes that are considered collaborative and many variables within the practice that often change from project to project in order to suit the needs of the hierarchy, aesthetics and ethos of the company, in addition to the timeline, budget and nature of the production. The companies included in this book not only work with writers and writer/directors internal and external to the permanent artistic directorship but also make particular demands in terms of the kind of work that they commission, and they therefore look for writers with particular skills and creative philosophies, engaging with the development of commissioned texts through a number of stages that encourage a process of continual adjustment between the company and the writer; as a result, there is a significant period of time between the moment when the writer is commissioned and the final performance of the production when the script is not a fixed entity but rather subject to development and negotiation. Although many people say that all theatre is collaborative, for the purposes of this book the way in which I will define collaborative theatre-making will be a process involving creative contributions from a writer, director(s), performers, designers (set, costume and lighting), a producer and possibly a movement director; the script does not exist in any substantial form prior to the workshops, research and development and/or rehearsal period, and the company works together in dialogue with one another to create a production, sharing the creative responsibility.

Collaborative creation. I will use 'collaborative creation' as an umbrella term used to signify a method of working designed to create material, not simply written work but also physical scenes, methods of staging and sometimes design. For Shared Experience, 'collaborative creation' can be taken to mean the process of creating the script, the physical sequences devised by the movement director with the performers or the staging created with the performers and directors. For Frantic Assembly, collaborative creation can be taken to mean the process used to create the text with the writer, the devised movement sequences with the performers and also the process that melds the two elements together, led by the directors. In the case of Filter, the term is slightly different and will be used to signify a process whereby original material is created (by actors, writers, directors or designers) without regard as to whether or not it will be kept in the final production; the act of collaborative creation is the basis for the entire collaborative process in that the script is being created roughly at the same time as the staging and soundscape. In the case of Teatro Vivo, collaborative creation is dependent upon the process used for each individual production and can range from director-led devising to devising inspired by an extant text to work created by writers and also through director-led devising.

Devising. A definition of the term that I have found helpful in this context comes from Deirdre Heddon and Jane Milling, who define it as, 'a set of strategies that emerged within a variety of theatrical and cultural fields'.[17] When the word 'devising' is used with regard to Filter, it refers to a process wherein material (generally scenes, with or without dialogue) is created by the performers in the company specifically through dialogic (rather than physical) improvisation guided by a director present in the rehearsal room; the writer may then edit and incorporate the scenes devised by the performers into the text that is being developed. For Frantic Assembly, devising is used not to create the written text but rather the physical sequences with the performers. In the case of Shared Experience, devising will be used less frequently than in the case of the other two companies, as improvisation is more commonly used as a director's technique to unlock previously written material; the physicality is partially devised by the performers, but the process is more tightly controlled by the movement director and artistic directors than in the case of Frantic Assembly, who allow their performers more creative agency. In the case of Teatro Vivo, like collaboration, devising takes on a different role for each production, depending on the parallel role of the writer(s) and the text that may also be incorporated.

Writing. I use the term 'writing' in order to signify the creation of material through the act of written or notated verbal composition, generally the task of the designated writer.[18] For Shared Experience and Frantic Assembly, all writing is carried out by the commissioned writer, but within the context of Filter, this person may also be more specifically referred to as the 'scripting writer', which signifies that their job is not only to compose new material but also to incorporate annotated scenes devised by the performers into the script. In Filter's process, other collaborators such as the performers and company artistic directors partake in the writing process by contributing to the text scenes and monologues they have written themselves. Similarly, as we have a specific phrase to indicate which member of the company is in charge of the writing (scripting writer and not playwright), we also refer specifically to the 'text' when we mean the script for performance (including lines and stage directions) and 'production' or 'project' when we mean the work as a whole (including music, directorial decisions, blocking, gesture and proxemics). In Andy Field's article 'All theatre is devised and text-based', he defines text as 'a blueprint for performance and a basis for making something happen', which feels usefully open and flexible in this context, rather than the more conventional term 'play', which feels like a different kind of text for performance, one more likely to be born of a singly authored creative process.[19] Whether one says 'text' or 'play' might seem both arbitrary and also pedantic to some, it is my hope that the particular use of this more neutral word might lend itself to a wider variety of theatre-making contexts. Additionally, within writing falls the subcategory of adaptation, which is distinct from writing an original work (for instance, *Stockholm*) and writing an adaptation of a novel (*War and Peace*), a work of nonfiction (*Faster*) or a myth (*The Odyssey*).

Writer. I will use the term 'writer' throughout, rather than 'playwright'. Firstly, the writers themselves in the study often self-reference (and are credited in programmes) 'writer' rather than 'playwright'. Secondly, within the context of collaborative and devised theatre, the term writer is often used more frequently than playwright because the term playwright can often bring with it connotations of a kind of distance from the company, of a playwright who writes the script separately from the director, designers and performers, rather than one who works directly with the company, possibly scripting alongside a devising process or creating fragments of text as inspiration for a workshop. Ben Payne explains this conundrum in an article written in 1998:

> There is a spectrum of approaches to theatre which, though text-based, may not fit conventional notions of playwright. For instance, writing text for theatre ... providing structures, 'stimulus text' or fragments of text for a company to devise from or devise around ... writing as part of a collective process of devising....One attraction of the term 'writing for performance' is that it appears to allow the writer to directly engage with other performance art forms, free from the historical and ideological associations of 'plays' and 'playwrights'.[20]

Although Payne is also referring to writers who work within the context of performance art, his explanation helps us understand the possible associations with the word 'playwright' – a person who writes plays in a solo-authored process rather than, for example, works alongside a collaborative or devising process. Like using 'text' instead of 'play' or 'writing' instead of 'playwriting', rather than creating distance from the practice of playwriting qua playwriting, in using the term 'writer' I hope to encourage readers to consider the practice of writing for performance a responsive and flexible practice, open to collaborative interventions.

Dramaturgy. When I use the term 'dramaturgy', I will be referring to the editing and overseeing of the material, both the devised work created by the performers (if applicable) and the scripted work by the writer or writers. The dramaturg in this case is more limited in terms of creative capacity – shaping material at hand rather than producing new material – than the scripting writer. I will examine the ways in which composition and authorship are constructed and isolate the variables and constants in each different case study by recognizing the drama-turgy of each company's process – that is to say, the overview of the production of the piece with regard to the overall conceptual, thematic and narrative objectives. Cathy Turner and Synne K. Behrndt define the purpose of dramaturgy as that which 'describe[s] the composition of the work, whether read as a script or viewed in performance', link-ing dramaturgy to the practice of musical arrangement or the visual composition of a painting.[21] They define the practice of dramaturgy as 'an observation of the play in production, the entire context of the performance event, the structuring of the artwork in all its elements'.[22] Bertolt Brecht explains the dramaturg as 'a critical facilitator with an inherently collaborative sensibility, driven by an ideological commit-ment to realize the ideas of the philosopher in practical terms'.[23] Using Turner and Behrndt's definition of dramaturgy as a process and Brecht's definition of the dramaturg as a role, I will frame the collaborative pro-cess within the function of authorship in relation to the company's intentions for the production. It is useful to observe and compare how different companies compose their material dramaturgically for the per-formance (and later, the finished dramatic) text; for the purpose of this study, these models of working are structured with regard to the nature of the writer's involvement in the project.

Structure and function

Writing in Collaborative Theatre-Making is divided into two sections: the first being composed of this Introduction and Chapter 1, 'A Brief History of the Writer in Collaboration', aiming to give the reader an understanding of the history of the practice; and the second being composed of the five proposed models of writer–company collaborative practice: The writer as co-creator, the writer as company scribe, the writer/director, the writer as poet and multiple writers. Each model will be explored in a different chapter, some of which presents one case study (Chapters 3, 5 and 6), some of which presents more than one case study (Chapters 2 and 4). I have structured the book in this way in order to help the reader understand the role of the writer and the text in collaborative practice by examining the way in which it functions from company to company and alters with the different nature of each writer's involvement. Each model is informed by interviews with practitioners, company archival material, analysis of the dramatic texts (and, in some cases, drafts of texts), study of the final production, investigation of each company's hierarchy and also a historical examination of writer–company collaborative processes to build these different models.

In Chapter 1, I placed the work of these five contemporary companies into the context of the pioneering work of previous generations of practitioners, giving a short history of the different ways in which the roles of the writer, writer/director and writer/dramaturg have evolved throughout the twentieth century. Each historical example demonstrates not only different examples of writer–company collaboration but also how and why they evolved and how they were ultimately connected, giving a revisionist overview of the historical origins of new collaborative theatre-making practices, specifically categorizing each production according to the role that the writer, writer/director and text played in each.

Chapter 2 examines the model of writer as co-creator, looking at the ways in which companies have worked with both of them in-house and commissioned writers to create both a production and a published text, with the writer serving a highly significant authorial function in the process. I look at the work of Helen Edmundson on *War and Peace* (1996, 2008) for Shared Experience, whom I have defined as an in-house writer, as Edmundson has written many plays for the company, although she is commissioned to do so each time and is not strictly a fixture of the permanent artistic directorship of Shared Experience. I compare this process to the work of Bryony Lavery on *Stockholm* (2007) for Frantic Assembly, to whom I refer as a commissioned writer, as she is one of many writers with whom the company has worked. Chapter 3 investigates the model of writer as company scribe, using as an example the text that Stephen Brown scripted for Filter Theatre's *Faster* (2003), looking at the ways in which Brown incorporated material written and devised by the performers, previous scratch performances and previous texts scripted by other writers. Chapter 4 examines the model of the writer/director, looking at the ways in which both an in-house writer/director and a commissioned writer/director created a production and a text in collaboration with a company. I analyse the work that writer/artistic director Polly Teale has made for Shared Experience, using *Brontë* (2005, 2010) as an example, and compare it to the work that writer/commissioned director David Farr has made for Filter, using *Water* (2007) as a case study. Chapter 5 will explain the model of the writer as poet, exploring the ways in which a commissioned writer can collaboratively produce texts for performance through poetry, acting as a part of a team of creative artists rather than the primary creative force in a collaborative process. I will examine the work of Carl Grose and Anna Maria Murphy for Kneehigh and their collaboration on *Tristan and Yseult* (2003, 2014). Chapter 6 considers the ways in which the multiple-writers model can operate within the collaborative process, looking at the role I played as a commissioned writer alongside my fellow writers Vic Bryson and Michael Wagg for Teatro Vivo in creating *The Odyssey* (2012).

Each chapter will provide details for a model of working. While the first section will explore the process whereby the production was created and the ways in which the text was positioned throughout, the second, shorter section will be comprised of a series of practical strategies that I have created, inspired by and designed to complement the processes used within each model. It is important to note that these strategies are creations of my own; although they have been inspired by the exercises and practical approaches that writers, directors and movement directors from each company have developed, I have reimagined them in order to give the reader the opportunity to find they own way into each model presented in the book. These practical strategies are open to interpretation and modification, and they can be altered to suit the needs of the reader and the size and nature of the company with whom they are working. They can be followed directly, as exercises, or as guidelines, appropriated and altered as required to suit the needs of those using them.

1   A Brief History of Writing, Writers and Text in Twentieth-Century Collaborative Theatre

This study of twentieth-century collaborative ways of working is significant because many of the approaches to collaborative writing used by
the contemporary companies in this book can be considered, to borrow
some terminology from the field of ethnology, what Jared Diamond
refers to as either 'blueprint copying' – conscious copying or modification of an extant practice – or 'idea diffusion' – accidental imitations
which arose from similar cultural circumstances but embodied the same
basic idea of an extant practice.[1] Much of these five companies' work
with writers and attitudes towards the text stem – either directly or
indirectly – from a series of historical tendencies, debates and practices.
Developments in twentieth-century collaborative theatre-making generated new possibilities for the creation of performance material and the
manipulation of language (written, spoken, gestural and visual), as well
as new ways of thinking about the role of the writer or writer/director
and the concept of authorship. This chapter will discuss four significant
historical examples which relate to the ways in which the roles of the
text and writers have shifted over time: Erwin Piscator's dramaturgical
collective and multi-authored work, Theatre Workshop and the practice of partially devised scripting, The Open Theater's writer/director
co-creation and Joint Stock's writer's workshop. My intention for this
chapter is to examine the role of the writer in each historical example,
the role of the text and how it was created, how authorship was negotiated and the extent to which each tendency influenced later writers and
companies.

I have chosen this selection of writers, directors and companies to
demonstrate the ways in which writing in collaborative theatre-making
originated and subsequently evolved within a particular span of time.

I will begin with the work of Piscator in Germany in the 1920s and finish with the productions created by Joint Stock in England in the 1970s in order to present what I believe is the most fruitful period regarding collaboration and writing in the years predating the early work of Shared Experience (beginning with their first production in 1975). This is only a small selection of practitioners' collaborative methods, and there are further significant examples of collaborative theatre in general and writer–company collaboration specifically, such as The Federal Theatre Project, The Living Theatre, Monstrous Regiment, Théâtre du Soleil, The Women's Theatre Group and The Wooster Group, to name but a few. I have chosen each permutation of writer–company collaboration in this chapter in order to represent a discrete approach to the development of the role of the writer and the text that resulted from a process of making work with the purpose of either creating an original production or adapting an extant text for performance.

Erwin Piscator and the dramaturgical collective

The work director Erwin Piscator (1893–1966) pioneered in Berlin from 1920–1929 marks the beginning of writer–company collaboration as a definable, documented practice in the twentieth century. Disillusioned with the capitalist system after witnessing first-hand the carnage of the First World War, Piscator approached theatre-making from a Marxist perspective by focusing on the economic determination of social forces on the worker rather than the personal psychologies and individual motivations of 'bourgeois' plays, but he believed that there were few existing plays that would suit his purpose and thus needed to find writers with whom he could work.[2] As a director who soon became commissioned by the Communist Party, Piscator was sometimes assigned writers for specific projects designed to convey the aims of the Party. As C.D. Innes concludes,

> Established authors were frequently unable to comprehend his aims and uncooperative when asked to revise their work … so Piscator wrote his own scripts with the help of his dramaturge, or, when possible, worked in close association with a dramatist instead of accepting finished plays.[3]

Influenced by Soviet directors such as Vsevolod Meyerhold and Sergei Eisenstein, Piscator felt an urgency to develop a new way of creating texts and working with writers in order to incorporate factual documents such as statistics, photographic images and current news stories, inciting audiences to political revolt by providing answers to the big political questions of the time. This approach to dramatic writing was new and unfamiliar to many writers who struggled with Piscator's vision and subsequent needs for a dramatic text that would accommodate these new technologies.

As a result, Piscator developed skills as a writer and a dramaturg, pioneering collaborative methods of scripting both as an artistic application to a political ideology and also as a practical solution to problems regarding the convergence of new forms and new subject matter in performance. In addition to Marxist ideology, Piscator's dramaturgical methods were also influenced by Dadaists artists' usage of randomness and chance in their work. Cathy Turner and Synne K. Behrndt note that 'according to Piscator, contemporary theatre did not offer scripts that exemplified this dramaturgy', that 'drew on montage techniques and mobilised all the technical resources of the stage', so his own creative intervention became necessary.[4] Piscator was not interested in texts commonly written throughout Europe at the time, dealing with the journey of an individual character and his or her emotional, psychological dilemmas; he wanted to stage productions that represented everyday problems experienced by real people, that connected politics, history and economics to the human experience.[5] Turner and Behrndt continue, explaining that Piscator found that 'conventional dramatic structures were too compressed and too closely focused on the individual experience', so through the use of montage, 'he was able to present a layered, loosely knit presentation of the action as a series of clearly historicized events – using, for example, filmed interludes, projected text or documentary material'.[6] Additionally, the director was able to expand the structure of his project to encompass the multiple voices of his collaborators, incorporating the work of designers, artists and dramaturgs – a development which would prove vital in his later work. In order to achieve his goals, Piscator expanded his role as a director to that of writer and dramaturg who arranged the different fictional, documentary and visual materials necessary to dramatize the stories he wanted to tell and in the style in which he wanted to stage them. Piscator opened up the channels of production to encompass the notion of 'author' as more than one single writer, as being embodied by a collective – himself leading a group of collaborators who could contribute to the writing, presentation, staging and design of his productions. Most importantly, this collaborative approach to production allowed for greater flexibility in terms of the kind of script with which Piscator worked.

Early experiments with multi-authored work

Working with writer Felix Gasbarra, sent to Piscator by the Communist Party on his first production *Revue Roter Rummel* (1924), he utilized collaborative methods in order to script politically relevant work in a limited amount of time. Piscator found a means of working with Gasbarra as a director and dramaturg to shape the script and the production, while depicting the political events and ideas in which he was interested in a theatrical fashion within the flexible but structured format of the revue. *Revue Roter Rummel* used a series of loosely connected sketches and songs to bring together the most current information, ideas and images in order to engage the audience in a new way. Depicting the 'triumph of communism', the production was designed to provide both entertainment and information for a politically undecided, and thus valuable, audience.[7] Piscator noted that in compiling the text, he and Gasbarra 'put together old material and wrote new material to go with it. Much of it was crudely assembled to add up-to-the-minute material right to the end'.[8] Together, Piscator and Gasbarra devised a method of collaborative scripting that allowed them to co-author a series of scenes, giving Piscator more control over the project in order to make the style and content of the piece theatrically exciting while disseminating political propaganda for the Party.

While working on *Sturmflut* (*Tidal Wave*, 1926), Piscator found that the use of new technologies, such as projections, was necessary to facilitate collaboration with writers to create productions that could illustrate rapidly changing political ideologies. Piscator believed that theatre was not as 'up to date' as the newspapers in terms of political events and opinions because it was 'still too much of a rigid art form, predetermined and with a limited effect', and he wanted to create productions that were much more journalistic in that they could be updated regularly in order to keep up with current events.[9] Piscator's work on

Sturmflut grew from his experience working with Gasbarra on *Revue Roter Rummel* and exemplifies his emerging role as a director-dramaturg who guides the collaborative process in order to work with a writer on a commissioned script. *Sturmflut* was a play about the Russian Revolution which the Communist Party had commissioned from playwright Alfons Paquet, with whom Piscator had worked two years previously in the successful *Fahnen* (*Flags*, 1924). Since they had worked together before, Piscator was surprised when Paquet delivered a script which, in his eyes, was overly symbolic, inconsistent, lacking in factual information and a step back from the progress they had made with *Fahnen*.[10] While Piscator wanted Paquet to stage the Revolution by capturing a single moment of it, Paquet was more interested in a poetical depiction of the zeitgeist of the Revolution in order to induce audiences to relate to the political events not only intellectually but emotionally as well.[11]

Sturmflut was ultimately a seminal moment in the development of the writer's role in collaboration from the writer's perspective as well as the director's; it marked a moment in which it was necessary for a writer to collaborate closely with a director on the text in order to meet his demands, thus sharing the authorship of the production. Piscator filmed images and scenes to be projected during the play to tell the story of the Russian Revolution in the epic style in which he wanted to tell it, but he found that the dynamics and style of the staging (his vision) were at odds with the structure of the script (Paquet's vision). Piscator found a solution in working together with Paquet and the performers during rehearsals to guide the writer in making alterations to the script in order to meet the demands of his elaborate staging and projections. In 1926, Piscator explained the process, saying they worked to create 'a complete reconstruction' of the text in a new kind of process for his company, where he, Paquet, the designers and the performers often had to improvise in the moment to edit, rewrite and stage the script, using 'their imagination to fill out new avenues and new twists as they occurred' in rehearsal.[12] Piscator and Paquet discovered that working on a text in rehearsal allowed the writer to capitalize on the creative input from the company, rewriting the script with the director and reconciling the differing visions of the writer and director for the production. The director noted that Paquet 'had the experience of seeing important new connections emerge in the moments of intuitive cooperation by all concerned'.[13] Piscator learned that if he wished to be a pioneer in the development of agitprop theatre and work with writers to do so, he had to find a way of approaching each production anew, relying on collaboration with the writer and the company to inform the dramaturgical process.[14]

The Adventures of the Good Soldier Schwejk and stage design as an element of composition

Die Abenteuer des braven Soldaten Schwejk (*The Adventures of the Good Soldier Schwejk*, 1928) is an example of the way in which Piscator adapted a novel to the stage himself as a writer/director with the help of a dramaturgical collective.[15] Piscator adapted Jaroslav Hašek's unfinished novel of the same name, about Schwejk, a Czech soldier in the Austro-Hungarian Army and the absurdity of his wartime experiences, in collaboration with Brecht, Gasbarra, Leo Lania, designer Traugott Müller, stage manager Otto Richter and cartoonist George Grosz. The group struggled to find a way of compressing the lengthy novel into a two-and-a-half-hour play, and because Hašek had died five years before, the group could neither commission him as the adaptor of his own novel nor consult him on the adaptation they were creating.

Piscator had found an alternative to either having to rely on the work of a single writer or having to work on the text alone that allowed him adapt Hašek's novel, by utilizing the skills of his collaborators who helped him realize his vision for the production. As a writer/director, Piscator discovered a way of writing through scenographic innovation, compressing the lengthy novel into a two-and-a-half-hour play. Piscator used projections of Grosz's animations of the people and places that Schwejk encounters in his travels and also a treadmill on which Schwejk could walk continuously as a dramaturgical problem-solving device, allowing the performers to move physically without necessitating lengthy exposition – what Piscator had begun to call 'Total Theatre'.[16] These two inclusions symbolized both Schwejk journey and the seeming endlessness of the First World War, drawing the audience's attention to the greater historical, political and economic forces at work in the main character's life.[17] Gasbarra noted that Piscator's decision to use the treadmill meant that Piscator and his dramaturgical collective 'no longer needed a framework other than the original story' and 'strictly avoided using any material other than Hašek's original text', and it meant that 'once the staging had been decided upon, the writer had only to compress the essentials of the novel'.[18] Piscator's dissatisfaction with the plays available to him led him to rely on these new dramaturgical approaches not only in collaboration with writers but also as a writer/director in order to shape his ideas and resources into cohesive productions which suited the needs of the epic. The production was what historian John Willett called, 'the most radical and successful of all Piscator's productions', as Piscator's major accomplishment was finding a way of keeping 'so episodic and picturesque a narrative uninterruptedly on the move'.[19]

Piscator's legacy

The processes that Piscator pioneered in developing these three productions is unique in that they were the first significant examples of using a collaborative approach to scripting with a writer in the rehearsal room and as a writer/director working with a dramaturgical collective. Piscator is an important figure because he developed new ways of making performance which involved the process of working with writers, dramaturgs, performers and designers as integral to the creation of the text and, as a result, reconceptualized the notion of authorship and generated new possibilities for the creation of material through collaborative writing and dramaturgy. Piscator's wife, Maria-Ley Piscator, noted in 1967 when reflecting on her husband's work that 'The artistic value of a production ... may well depend on modern dramaturgy opening new dimensions'.[20] His approach to working with a writer in the rehearsal room in order to alter the text in an immediate fashion was a significant development in collaborative practice that continues today, not only in the contemporary companies examined in this study but in numerous other collaborating companies around the world. Piscator also discovered a unique way of approaching adaptation, which we will explore further with the productions of Shared Experience and Filter's *Faster*. Piscator created a legacy for himself by establishing the Dramatic Workshop with his wife at the New School for Social Research in New York in 1940 where he trained performers such as Living Theatre director Judith Malina (who later pioneered approaches to collaborating with text with her own company, inspired by the techniques she learned at the Dramatic Workshop's Studio).[21] The development of Piscator's authorial vision and the way in which he as a director worked with writers and as a writer/director worked with the text significantly influenced the development of writer–company collaborative practice in the twentieth century.

Theatre Workshop, Joan Littlewood and partially devised scripting

Piscator's legacy of the writer/director-led approach to collaboration is demonstrated most significantly in the UK in the productions of The Theatre Workshop (1945–1974), an ensemble started in Manchester and later based in London at the Theatre Royal Stratford East. Artistic Director Joan Littlewood (1914–2002) not only worked with writers to produce plays that she believed were truthful to working-class lifestyles (little-represented in West End productions at the time) but also acted as an auteur, incorporating the tropes of popular entertainment traditions like cabaret, Pierrot shows and music hall into her productions to pioneer a more inventive, physical approach to theatre-making. Littlewood produced new writing and helped to develop writers such as Brendan Behan, Shelagh Delaney and Ewan MacColl, and after producing Behan's *The Quare Fellow* (1956), she focused the efforts of the company with the intention of 'looking for texts with a spark of life, an original subject matter or grasp of everyday speech patterns from which the company could improvise'.[22] The director grounded Theatre Workshop's productions in text, whether classics such as Shakespeare's *Richard II* (1955), original texts by new writers such as Delaney's *A Taste of Honey* (1958) or her own work as a writer/director such as *Oh! What a Lovely War* (1963), varying the approach to suit the project in question. Like Piscator, Littlewood believed that she needed to take an artistic stand against established 'old guard' realism and also a political one against the conservative politics of plays such as those seen in the West End at the time.[23] She was greatly influenced by the work that she and her partner writer Ewan MacColl made in the 1930s by using living newspaper and agitprop techniques (inexpensive, mobile sets and costumes) to create theatrically innovative, political productions with limited resources. Littlewood was the acknowledged foremost creative agent in the company and made most of the major decisions that affected their process, but she believed that it was important to collaborate with other practitioners to make work that questioned the standards of contemporary British playwriting: 'My objective in life ... is to work with other artists – actors, writers, designers, composers – and in collaboration with them, and by means of argument, experimentation and research, to keep the English theatre alive and contemporary'.[24] This section will explore the writer/director-driven, partially devised scripting process that Littlewood developed while making *Oh! What a Lovely War*, using work devised by the performers of Theatre Workshop, extant historical texts and music hall songs. Although Littlewood collaborated with a number of writers on productions for The Theatre Workshop, the writer/director model which she used in creating *Oh! What a Lovely War* serves a number of functions: it provides a bridge between Piscator's dramaturgical collective and the following sections on The Open Theater and Joint Stock; it offers a useful historical precedent for the writer/director model explored in Chapter 4; and it also illuminates the possibilities of a partially scripted, partially devised collaborative process, further detailed in Chapter 3 (*Faster*) and Chapter 6 (*The Odyssey*).

Oh! What a Lovely War

Littlewood ended up creating *Oh! What a Lovely War* in collaboration with Theatre Workshop performers as a writer/director out of what she came to believe was necessity. Before rehearsals started, Theatre Workshop Producer Gerry Raffles presented Littlewood with a BBC recording of a series of popular music hall songs sung by soldiers in the trenches during the First World War, compiled by Charles Chilton, and he suggested that she direct a play with a similar subject. When presented with two scripts about the war, the first by Gwyn Thomas and the second by Ted Allen, Littlewood ended up rejecting both; she believed that Gwyn's play was too obvious[25] and Allen's too pro-military and anti-German.[26] The director found the previous writers' attempts to dramatize the First World War lacking in truth and believed there was potential in using songs from the era to develop an emotional connection with the historical material for a modern audience.[27] Littlewood was looking for something that would both keep audiences entertained in the kind of old-fashioned, populist tradition of music hall and tell the story of the life of the common soldier in the trenches, which was rarely explored at the time; this vision drove Littlewood to take the helm of the project not only as the director, who guided the devising process, but also acting as the scripting writer in charge of the text.

Littlewood came to be not only the director but also the writer on *Oh! What a Lovely War* because she believed in a participatory, collaborative process insofar as it benefited her system of working with practitioners with different skills. After deciding on her vision for the production, the director decided that acting as her own writer while devising material with the performers in rehearsals would be the most practical route forward. (I will explore this approach to collaboration via the writer/director model in Chapter 4, when I break down David Farr's role in creating *Water*.) Although the director maintained, 'I do not believe in the supremacy of the director, designer, actor or even the writer. It is through collaboration that this knockabout theatre survives and kicks'.[28] Peter Rankin (Littlewood's personal assistant from 1964 until the end of her life in 2002) notes that Littlewood preferred to be firmly in control of decisions.[29] He explained that the problem with collaboration and the democratic process of devising theatre was that 'if people really are all set on having their say, it's very slow'.[30] Rankin continues, 'when they started Theatre Workshop ... they did call it a cooperative and they did have meetings, but I think people began to find they had a function.'[31] Although Littlewood facilitated a process within which everyone was allowed an opinion and was able to contribute to the production, she also believed that the process was more efficient when each person had a specific role and when she herself was in charge of the overall vision of the piece.

The writer/director–performer collaboration

Littlewood alternated between guiding the performers through a series of highly structured, improvised scenes in the daytime (which were noted in rehearsal) and scripting scenes in the text as inspired by these improvisations in the evening. Rankin describes the process by explaining that Littlewood would guide the source material from which the company would devise work by bringing in research material on the First World War for them to read; additionally, performers interviewed war veterans and were led through a series of military drills by an army sergeant whom Raffles invited to the rehearsal.[32] Then, having absorbed this research material, the performers would improvise scenes under Littlewood's direction during rehearsals in the daytime, while the director would take whatever was scripted home in the evenings and 'put order into it and read and write it out'.[33] In the mornings before rehearsal, Littlewood would edit what she had scripted the night before from the devising process with what Rankin called a 'secretary' and then go over the new scenes with the performers before devising more material, repeating the process all over again.[34] Littlewood scripted the work by using a variety of material, such as improvisations, anecdotes and interjections from the company – whatever she thought helped develop the text, moving the production forward. The process was systematic and methodical and also allowed Littlewood a maximum of control over the material, but it was often frustrating and sometimes evening worrisome for a group of performers who were used to performing with pre-written scripts rather than devising their own material and thus having to navigate their way through a wilderness of discussion, experimentation and constant adjustment. The idea of starting without a script was not common practice for Theatre Workshop; although they had used improvisation and devising techniques to explore classical texts and make dramaturgical changes to new work, they had not produced an entire show in this way before. Littlewood recalled that during one rehearsal, actress Ann Beach came to her in tears crying, 'We're all lost. We're getting nowhere. Can't we just do a straightforward play?'[35] Littlewood retorted, 'If we don't get lost, we'll never find a new route'.[36] This episode, small and anecdotal as it is, is a reminder that combining devising with scripting in a collaborative process that relies on material generated by performers but controlled and organized by a single figure such as a writer/director has the potential to be inspiring but also difficult and frustrating, especially if the company in question has not worked in this way before and does not have a shared language for working and a shared understanding of the ultimate goal.

Littlewood drew from traditions not only of epic theatre but also from music hall in order to inform a dramaturgical structure for the script. Like Piscator and his revue, Littlewood decided that a flexible, episodic structure would allow for a variety of different scenes and musical numbers; as a result, the shape of the production was a modern interpretation of a music hall show – short comedic scenes patched together between song-and-dance numbers. Using the flexible, episodic dramaturgical structure of music hall and allowing her dramaturgy to be influenced by scenography like Piscator, Littlewood drew on the agitprop techniques that she had learned while working with MacColl in the 1930s, such as projections of images and statistics from the period into the production's design, and incorporated songs from the First World War into the text. As a result, the statistics of the deaths from the war undercut the glib, patriotic propaganda of the songs and gave the production an element of political commentary. *Oh! What a Lovely War* met with great critical and commercial success, being a production rarely seen before by critics and audiences – meticulously researched and nostalgic in its form but contemporary in its political message.

Littlewood's legacy

Oh! What a Lovely War not only represents an example of engagement with the writer/director model of working involving a partially devised, partially scripted collaborative process, it is also an example of the inherent complexity of authorship of this kind of work. Littlewood once told a story of sitting in a restaurant with Gerry Raffles after the play's opening; someone asked why her name was not on the programme (as the writer) and Raffles responded, 'She's ashamed of us.'[37] Littlewood immediately wrote her name on the programme and then added, 'For Gerry Raffles, the only begetter of *Oh! What a Lovely War*'.[38] This seemingly incidental anecdote betrays an attitude regarding the production's authorship; although it was important for Littlewood to have full artistic control over the play and the process used to devise and script it, it was less important to her to have public recognition as a writer, as it is likely that Littlewood did not see herself as a writer, per se. The creation of a play text was not her primary motivation for engaging in the scripting process, but rather a necessary element in the production of *Oh! What a Lovely War* – a means to an end. As we will see in the section on Joint Stock Theatre, the elements of The Theatre Workshop approach that influenced subsequent generations of British practitioners throughout the 1960s and beyond were the experimentation with traditional, popular or folk modes of performance, the politically charged, left-wing ethos inherent in the productions and also the way in which Littlewood's particular brand of collaboration that incorporated the work of performer/deviser as well as scripted text.[39] Littlewood's engagement with devising has left a legacy for contemporary companies in terms of her approach to dramaturgical structures and developing material with performers.

The Open Theater: working towards writer–director co-creation

New York City-based company The Open Theater (1963–1973) was founded by director Joseph Chaikin (1935–2003) as a committed to working directly with commissioned writers to create a text alongside the performers, under Chaikin's supervision. Working with writers like Megan Terry, Jean-Claude van Itallie and Sam Shepard, Chaikin used hundreds of different improvisation exercises in order to encourage his company of performers to create pieces that embodied a variety of distinct voices and unique visual motifs created physically. Productions such as *Viet Rock* (1968), *The Serpent* (1968) and *Terminal* (1970) dealt with themes such as politics, death and the emotionally crippling limitations of societal norms by establishing their own language, a mix of physicality, gesture, spoken words, wordless sounds and song, collated and organized into a text by the company writer. In 1966, Richard Schechner said, 'Playwrights are an important part of The Open Theater,' and cited Chaikin as saying: 'These pieces are inspired by the actors' work ... there's a give-and-take. After the writer has suggested a form ... we begin to improvise with them. ... [T]he mode of language depends on the form of the improvisation, its goals, and our own warm-up'.[40] The company relied on a system guided by Chaikin's own direction; a writer would suggest an idea to the performers on which they could expand through structured improvisations, led by the director. The Open Theater is, in many ways, emblematic of a whole generation of collaborative, experimental companies that sprang up in the United States in the 1960s and '70s, such as The Living Theatre, The San Francisco Mime Troupe, Bread and Puppet Theatre and El Teatro Campesino, with the intention of exploring the notion of approaches to collective creation for artistic and also political purposes:

> In the 1960s and 1970s – decades marked in so many Western nations by utopic yearning – the theatre, as elsewhere, became a site of social building, and, in the alternative theatres of North America.... [T]he group was ascendant. Collective creation ... rose

to prominence, not simply as a performance-making method, but as an institutional model.[41]

I have chosen to focus on The Open Theater, particularly Chaikin's collaboration with writer Terry on *Viet Rock*, in order to explore the ways in which the company conceived the role of the writer and the text in collaboration with the preoccupations and goals of both the director and the performers, ultimately attempting to come to an understanding about the problematic nature of authorship in collaboration.

Working with writers

Chaikin focused the energies of the company on combining the creative agency of the writers and performers through experiments with structured, collaborative devising in the rehearsal room. The Open Theater was primarily concerned with capturing what they saw as the personal, immediate creative impulses of the performer, exploring the incongruity within the inner private life and the public façade of the individual through improvisation, working with a writer in order to record, interpret and structure the material. Chaikin was searching for new forms of expression produced through the relationship between the writer and the performer, communicating in live performance what might otherwise be incommunicable in everyday life through a non-naturalistic style of rhythm, gesture and song to accompany dialogue. Chaikin and the company chose to characterize the outer as being represented by dialogue and recognizable, everyday gestures, while the inner was represented by expressionistic movement, non-lingual vocalization or song. As Robert Baker-White notes,

The Open Theater ... explored the possibilities of both actorly improvisation and textual creation in the process of their workshop exercises. Thus, more than any other prominent experimental group of that period, Chaikin's collaboration achieved a balance of exact language and improvised action in performance.... Chaikin himself characterizes the place of dramatic language in the collective process in terms of structure: 'the text gives a structure for the playing out of the story, and includes places for the company to improvise'.[42]

This particular approach to working was appealing to the company because it addressed the issue of how to facilitate the writer's process through collaboration with that of the performer's problem of expressing both the interior and exterior self in performance. Improvisation proved useful for the exploration of human experience for performers and writers, and writing proved useful in terms of the mediation of these explorations, making the two complementary parts of a whole collaborative practice.

Before the later, more problematic era of the early 1970s, the writers involved with The Open Theater found that working with the performers and Chaikin fruitful because it allowed them to have access to an immediate source of inspiration in the form of instinctive but structured devised material that could be adjusted according to the writer's needs. Terry in particular saw working as a writer with a devising company as a more progressive, interesting way of working than writing alone. In a 1981 interview with Dinah Leavitt, she reflected that 'With the playwriting techniques we discovered or rediscovered in the sixties you can explore interior states. You can dramatize the interior state of being. Once inside one's head, body or soul, it's vast'.[43] What Terry found interesting was the struggle for reconciliation between the interior and the exterior and how the dialogic and physical representations of this struggle could be developed through improvisation in workshops, and later depicted in performance. By working with the same group of performers on a regular basis, through observation (mediated either by their own interjections or Chaikin's directions), writers like Terry developed a way of channelling the physical, emotional and intellectual responses to various games and imagined scenarios.[44]

Viet Rock and the writer-driven devising process

Viet Rock (1966), the first significant production by The Open Theater in which the material was created through improvisation but was recorded, shaped and scripted by a writer; it forged the way for future productions and established the company's trademark style of combining strong physical images with improvised dialogue. In contrast to the process that Littlewood used while making *Oh! What a Lovely War*, the production was structured by Terry (rather than Chaikin) around a series of improvisations on the theme of violence and the Vietnam War, devised by the company and often overseen by Chaikin.[45] *Viet Rock* was produced at Café La MaMa in New York as part of a six-month-long residency in which The Open Theater made the transition from making work solely as part of workshop explorations to making productions to be performed in front of an audience. La MaMa Artistic Director Ellen Stewart had to talk Chaikin into making what he believed was a great and uncertain leap for the company.[46] Terry ran the workshops to devise work for the project, using Chaikin's exercises developed with the company in order to devise material. When interviewed by Robert Pasolli, Terry said, 'The playwright experiments with the actors on movement and visual images, but then he goes home and writes the play, including the words'.[47] Pasolli adds that Terry's description was a simplification and that 'in the case of a workshop-created play it is really not possible objectively to separate the writer's contributions from those of the actors. Most of the *Viet Rock* cast considered themselves authors also.'[48] Much like *Oh! What a Lovely War*, the complex nature of the devising, scripting and authoring of *Viet Rock* is reflected in the existing dramatic text; the script is characterized by detailed stage directions (how and where the actors move their bodies and what each action is meant to represent), lengthy and surreal songs interspersed throughout (often designed to represent the characters' 'inner') and fluid but disorienting scene and character changes.[49] Pasolli notes that the performers were 'especially sensitive to changes of staging or dialogue, to realignment of priorities, to Miss Terry's assumption of total control over the production'.[50] The issue of authorship, which was not considered to be important in the early days of the then-unknown The Open Theater, became a source of conflict and debate as the company began to produce work publicly and become known in New York and beyond. The issue of the writer having ultimate control of what was printed in the performance text became an important one, since the company used a fixed script for performances, as opposed to improvising a different version of the play within a structure for every performance. Ultimately, Terry faced the problematic issue of authorship and control over the piece, not only with the cast but also with Chaikin, who had begun to differ with her regarding the tone and message of the play.[51] After Terry refused Chaikin's requested changes, when the play transferred from La MaMa to the Yale School of Drama, Chaikin was so unhappy with the outcome of this failed authorial negotiation that he asked Terry to take the company's name off the programme for

Viet Rock.[52] Kathryn Mederos and Scott Proudfit explain, 'In the history of collective creation, it is polyphony, not consensus, that is the norm', but in the case of *Viet Rock* and the relationship between Chaikin and Terry, perhaps it could best be described as polyphony that disintegrated into dissonance.[53]

What made the productions of The Open Theater distinctive – the inability to tell what the performers and what the writer created, the fluidity of movement and dialogue – also eventually created discord within the company: the conflict surrounding *Viet Rock* was not an isolated incident. The Open Theater closed in 1973 as a result of ongoing disagreements within the company about the nature of the work; approaches to devising and workshops; and the problems inherent in the writing, authorship and ownership of the material. Chaikin himself stated that he believed he had never found a satisfactory system of working with a writer in collaboration, and perhaps because of this, the importance of the writer decreased with each production.[54] It seems the hierarchy of The Open Theater was never entirely clear; the purported democratic ideals of collective decision making were not always maintained, and Chaikin ultimately believed himself to be the company's foremost leader. Pasolli's observation on Chaikin's role was that 'Chaikin is the leader of the troupe but seems not to be; he controls practically everything while giving the impression of controlling practically nothing.'[55] Pasolli describes the relationship of the writer to the workshopping process as 'elusive', and although the fact that each writer participated in the workshops with Chaikin and the performers before working on the text, the process changed 'from project to project and from writer to writer', 'obscured by the day to day interactions of twenty to thirty people'.[56] The element of the collaborative process that once was so attractive to The Open Theater had become problematic; the practice of allowing a writer access to the director-led devising process complicated the issue of authorship once the resulting production was scripted and staged. The writer in each project had to make certain editorial decisions in order to create a coherent script based on their own judgement and taste; the performers, having created material that went into the script believed that they had ownership over the piece, but sometimes they also felt a sense of betrayal over the decisions relating to the text of what was kept and what was cut. 'When the work is done and ready to be shown publicly, one can look back and say that the writer structured the workshop investigation to make it understandable to outsiders. In doing so, he asserted his own personality and vision, sometimes to the extent of radically altering the actors' private investigation'.[57] The issue of authorial conflict was intensified by the already ambiguous company hierarchy in which Chaikin was ultimately in control, even though he attempted to preserve the illusion that influential decisions were made collectively.

Joint Stock: serving the writer

The Joint Stock Theatre Company (1974–1989) is, arguably, the most influential company in this chapter for contemporary writer–company collaborative practice in the UK in terms of the model of working that it created over a number of years. Joint Stock was established by William Gaskill (artistic director at the Royal Court, 1965–1972), Max Stafford-Clark (artistic director 1979–1993), David Hare and David Aukin, but was run predominantly by Stafford-Clark after the first few years. The company defined and firmly established the notion of 'workshop' within a British context as a means of helping a writer develop a script by drawing from the practice of company-led research and discussion through structured improvisation. Joint Stock adapted The Open Theater method of using director-led, structured improvisation to help the writer create a script through a workshopping process, which we will explore through the case study of the creation of Caryl Churchill's *Cloud Nine* (1979). This section will explore their particular approach to the writer–company collaboration, the significant role of the text and the significance of the writer–director relationship that laid the foundation for future models of working, such as those discussed in Chapter 2 (*Stockholm* and *War and Peace*) and Chapter 6 (*The Odyssey*).

A commitment to writing

The Joint Stock was one of many theatre companies to emerge during the 1970s in the UK that embraced a practice that combined text-based work with devising to explore a highly politicized subject matter, along with others such as Monstrous Regiment, The Women's Theatre Group, Gay Sweatshop (1975–1997) and 7:84, but one of the few that were committed to commissioning work by new writers. Joint Stock worked with a series of writers such as Churchill, David Hare, Howard Brenton and Timberlake Wertenbaker and left as a legacy not only a series of plays that became highly influential additions to the British literary cannon but also an approach to writer–company collaboration that is still visible in collaborative British theatre-making today. Stafford-Clark believed that the role of the writer in the collaborative process was an important one and wanted to combine the more radical method of collaboration through writing and devising that was pioneered by The Open Theater with the more structured approaches to playwriting workshops that Gaskill had been developing with the Royal Court's Writers' Group in the 1950s and '60s. Gaskill's method was rooted in a belief that 'when the writer feels part of the theatrical process ... his work will be better than if he wanders in isolation.'[58] He believed that a writer's work would be enriched if he or she was fully integrated into the collaborative process that directors undergo with actors and designers.[59] Stafford-Clark noted, 'my big influences have been the wild American companies: The Open Theater, the La MaMa and the Living Theatre'.[60] Stafford-Clark did not consider these to be writer-driven companies and believed that 'the writer played quite a small part in that movement', but at the same time, he also thought they had created 'a new language' which was 'electric and interesting'.[61] He valued the impact of the creative agency of the performers on the writer's working process and ability to think three-dimensionally with regard to the text. I believe that here it is important to emphasize that while Joint Stock prioritized the creation of script through writer–company collaboration, like Chaikin's position in The Open Theater or Littlewood's role in Theatre Workshop, Joint Stock was another company that was largely director driven. The decisions made by directors Gaskill and later Stafford-Clark alone strongly influenced the structure of the company, the subject matter of the research, the types of exercises used in improvisations and the style of the productions.

Cloud Nine and the writer's workshop

The Joint Stock developed a distinctive approach to collaborating with writers wherein a workshopping, devising and research process involving performers and co-directors Gaskill and Stafford-Clark was designed to aid the writer in creating a text, beginning with David Hare's *Fanshen*

(1979). This process was then applied to subsequent productions commissioned by the company such as *Cloud Nine*, a play dealing with sexuality in colonial East Africa and postcolonial Britain as a satire of historical and contemporary perceptions and experiences of race and gender. The first half of the play takes place in Victorian colonial Africa, while the second is set in Britain in 1979; the themes of gendered, racial and sexual identity are often represented by casting against age, race and gender, symbolizing the rapidly changing social mores in contemporary British society. The workshop explored the personal lives of the company members – the cast being consciously composed of heterosexual, gay and lesbian couples with varied backgrounds and experiences. The company talked about sexuality and experimented with improvised gender-role stereotyping and role playing with direction from Stafford-Clark, with Churchill observing and also participating.[62] Churchill said, 'For the first time I brought together two preoccupations of mine – people's internal states of being and the external political structures which affect them'.[63] This statement reflects Megan Terry's interest in engaging with workshopping and devising with performers as a writer in order to understand the tension between the individual's inner, hidden self and the peripheral socio-political pressures around them while working with The Open Theater. Churchill's interest in the individual within society intersected with the Joint Stock way of working, which had been greatly influenced not only by the process used to devise *Fanshen* but also the socialist politics of the novel by William Hinton from which it was adapted and subsequently the episodic style in which the play was structured; as a result, *Cloud Nine* retained an imprint of this kind of materialist perspective via the epic approach of using a dramaturgical framework that created parallels between history and contemporary society.[64]

One element that sets Joint Stock apart from the other companies in this chapter is that they allowed the writers with whom they worked to have a great deal of freedom with the devised material, despite (or perhaps because of) the amount of control imposed on the company by the directors. Michael Billington comments that within Joint Stock, 'Directorial taste remained a dominant factor', and collaboration was almost never synonymous with egalitarianism and democracy.[65] Joint Stock performer Simon Callow bitterly recalled his experience, arguing that Joint Stock was a 'directocracy' and that its methods represented 'the tastes of its directors'.[66] Although Stafford-Clark was very much in control of the collaborative process and the kinds of exercises that were used, in contrast to The Open Theater, he indicated that when the workshop period was finished, the writer was free to write whatever they wanted, irrespective of how closely the resulting text would reflect material devised in the workshop. Michael Patterson notes that Churchill in particular had a way of working with the company that drew on 'attitudes and values' of the perform-ers to give them the opportunity to identify with the subject matter around which they researched and improvised during the workshop, seeing the working relationship as a benefit to her writing.[67] Church-ill said, 'If you're working by yourself ... [y]ou don't get forced in quite the same way into seeing how your own inner feelings connect up with larger things that happen to other people'.[68] The position of being a writer on attachment to a collaborating company whose stated object was to support a writer in creating a play text allowed Churchill the freedom to rely predominantly on her own judgement to create a script which drew from material devised by performers in the ten weeks given to her to write independently from the company.

Although the process was productive for Churchill and Stafford-Clark, the case of *Cloud Nine* raises some issues regarding the potentially prob-lematic issues of ownership in devised material as opposed to ownership in written material. The questions which remain are whether Churchill as the writer had a responsibility to the performers to deliver what they would accept as an 'accurate' representation of the devised work that they had produced in the text and also indeed what was the status accorded to the concept of ownership within the Joint Stock process. Stafford-Clark suggests that the matters of creative control and ownership featured prominently at the point of reading Churchill's draft of the play because it dealt with the sensitive personal issues of the company members. In a diary he kept during rehearsals for *Cloud Nine*, the director wrote,

> Clearly the actors had exposed their own lives, and their degree of ownership put great pressure on Caryl. All of us were able to give approval to the high comedy of the first act but found it more dif-ficult to digest and give credence to the reflection of our own experi-ences which Caryl had written for the second half. ... Perhaps we wanted the play to deliver the rounded conclusion to our own lives which we were so signally unable to provide ourselves.[69]

The heightened and stylized satire of the Victorian world in first act of the play was easier for the company to process than the more realistic second half of the play, which reflected (and perhaps altered) the often personal, intimate responses of the performers to the prompts within the workshopping period. As a result, the performers were ultimately uncomfortable with the way in which their personal stories and confessions regarding sexual politics and identity had been appropriated by Churchill; here we are reminded of the difficulty Terry faced after she had drafted *Viet Rock* when faced with the expectations of Chaikin and the performers in The Open Theater, some of which they believed she did not meet. In the case of The Open Theater, with each scripted production, the company increasingly believed that their creative impulses had been manipulated by the writer while working on the script; part of the reason why the company ultimately disintegrated was because Chaikin never developed a way of working with writers which satisfied him or the other members of the company. The benefit of this kind of collaborative process for the writer is that it allows them access to a director and to performers' responses to discussions and subject matter through performance but also the freedom to react to this devised, workshopped material in a period of independent writing. The drawback of the process is that unless expectations are clearly stated and met by the text produced after the writing period (difficult if not impossible within any collaboration), the writer risks an adverse reaction from the company. *Cloud Nine* was a resounding success in London and later transferred to Broadway, making Joint Stock an internationally renowned company and Churchill one of the most significant figures in British dramatic writing. Despite some of the issues related to authorship, Stafford-Clark continued using the writer–company collaborative model, which became known as the Joint Stock Method on subsequent productions and to other writers until the company folded ten years later.

Conclusion

As the practice of writer–company collaboration developed throughout the twentieth century, each writer, director and company reconsidered the role of the text and the writer within the process differently. From the early work of Piscator in the 1920s to the work of Joint Stock in the 1970s, the field of collaborative theatre-making has largely been the domain of the director – the practitioner who, in most cases, sets the terms for the way in which his or her company would create work. Therefore, in discussing the role of the writer within this field, we must also come to an understanding about the role of the director, the writer–director rela-tionship and the director's attitude towards the creation of text. What characterizes each of the historical case studies is that the relationship between the writer and the company was almost always mediated by the director's vision, aesthetics and working practices – all of which were a product of that director's reaction to his or her perception of a particular theatrical tradition and a set of political ideologies. The way in which the roles of writer and director intersected were the guiding influences of the development of writer–company collaborative practices in the twentieth century, as it remains today with contemporary practices.

We can see in each distinct strand of practice that the role of the writer and the role of the text were inextricably linked; the company approached the role of the writer differently, depending on whether or not the director of the company prioritized the development of a dramatic text that would survive the production. If the development of a well-written script was a priority for the director of the company (as it was for Joint Stock), then not only was the role of the writer made to be distinct from the rest of the company, but the writer's process was supported by the company's engagement with research and devising (as it was for Caryl Churchill). If the development of a script was not the foremost priority, then the role of the writer was a less empowered one, as was the case with Megan Terry's role in creating *Viet Rock* for The Open Theater, which shifted focus from the development of new writing to the development of collective creation. However, the third category that has emerged from this study is that of directors who were faced with the problem of not being able to find an appropriate writer whom they believed could write the kind of text that they wanted to produce; as a result, Piscator and Littlewood worked with their compa-nies as writer/directors. Stafford-Clark perceived the writer as a distinct but also vital role to the company's creative process. Directors such as Piscator and Littlewood did not always view the role of the writer as a distinct and creatively autonomous entity within the company, but they recognized the creation of a text as integral to their approaches to theatre-making. Chaikin and The Open Theater understood the writer as a specially skilled role distinct from that of performer or director and necessary to the refinement and organization of material for per-formance, even if they later encountered issues with authorship related to their process of working and the symbiotic relationship between the writing and the devising.

By and large, the company's or director's attitude towards the role of the writer was dependent upon the skills of that company or director with respect to writing: if there was a member of the company who felt confident enough to script, dramaturg or write performance texts, then the role of the writer was absorbed by the company and an external writer was not commissioned; if the company did not believe that they could write the text themselves, the role of the writer as an autonomous creative agent within the process was more likely to be valued. As John McGrath of 7:84 (a writer/director himself) noted, 'Writing a play can never be a totally democratic process. They are skills which need aptitude, long experience, self-discipline and a certain mental discipline.'[70] Gillian Hanna of Monstrous Regiment believed that playwriting was a particular skill, and one which the company 'wanted to acknowledge', but instead she chose to commission writers external to the company, as no one within the permanent company believed that they were able to write a text themselves.[71] Although both Hanna and McGrath believed playwriting to be a particular skill, historically, the writer or writer/director within the context of writing in collaboration was not only someone with a particular skill set but more significantly someone who was, to put it simply, in charge of the scripting or writing process and thus who was primarily in charge of the development of the text over any other company member. For some, such as Churchill and Terry, these writing, scripting and dramaturgical skills were in place before the process began, while for others, such as Piscator and Littlewood, those skills were acquired along the way and developed according to the needs of the production.

Section 2
Collaboration, Text and …

2   Writer as Co-creator

I now turn to the first contemporary model of writing in collaboration: the writer as co-creator. This model is intended to demonstrate a way of working wherein the writer is an equal co-creator with the company, exploring and developing the project alongside the director, performer and designers from its inception. In this chapter, I will present two variations of this method of working: first, the concept of the in-house writer, exemplified by Helen Edmundson writing for Shared Experience, and second, the concept of the commissioned writer, exemplified by Bryony Lavery writing for Frantic Assembly. Both writers are commissioned by the companies with whom they collaborate, but I will use the term 'in-house' to distinguish Edmundson as a writer who has worked with Shared Experience on a number of productions. Chapter 2 will look at the ways in which the role of the writer is constituted within this model of writer as co-creator, how the text is created and how this particular model of writer–company collaboration can be altered, depending on whether the writer is a long-standing collaborator with the company (Edmundson) or the working relationship is new (Lavery). To demonstrate the two stands of this model, I will deconstruct the process that went into creating *War and Peace* (1996, 2008), on which Edmundson collaborated with Shared Experience, and also *Stockholm* (2007), on which Lavery collaborated with Frantic Assembly. Towards the end of the chapter, I will propose a number of practical strategies inspired by these collaborative processes intended to be used by the reader in order to develop their own approach to the writer-as-co-creator model.

Part I   The in-house writer: Helen Edmundson for Shared Experience

Currently run by Artistic Director Polly Teale, Shared Experience was originally established in 1975 by director Mike Alfreds as a touring company based in the Crucible Theatre in Sheffield. It then became a

London-based company that had been run by Artistic Director Nancy Meckler from 1988 and then run by Meckler and Teale together from 1993 to 2012. (Teale joined the company initially as an artistic associate under Meckler's directorship, when she co-directed Edmundson's adaptation of *Mill on the Floss* with Meckler.) Shared Experience is largely concerned with the creation of what Arts Council England describes as 'highly physical interpretations', or adaptations, of classic novels.[1] Describing the company's work, Kristen Crouch says, 'Through the interweaving of text, gesture, movement, and inventive stage design, Shared Experience reaffirms the stage as a place for rediscovery, exploring, and reconstructing the novel anew'.[2] There is a marked difference between its early phase under Alfreds' directorship, where the company focused on physicalized, performer-centred interpretations of adapted novels without the presence of a writer, and the period under Meckler and Teale's co-directorship, which focused on physical interpretations of extant source texts through collaborations with writers and writer/ directors.

When *War and Peace* was initially staged in 1996 and then remounted in 2008, apart from their directorial collaboration on *Mill on the Floss* (2001), the nature of Meckler and Teale's collaboration was such that they made artistic and managerial decisions for the company but largely directed their own productions independently of one other. Theo Herdman, who performed in the 2008 production of *War and Peace*, said Meckler and Teale 'have their own projects and they have various degrees of shared authority and responsibility on a project-by-project basis'.[3] Teale sometimes adapted her own work and sometimes worked with writers external to the company, such as Edmundson. Meckler either commissioned Teale or external writers such as Edmundson to write the play texts for her. This philosophy towards collaboration extended also to the writers whom they commissioned; Meckler and Teale believed each writer's process to be unique, and while they commissioned those who embraced some aspect of Shared Experience's particular aesthetic and approach to working, each writer was given a certain amount of artistic autonomy.

Meckler and Teale's approach to adaptation relies on the interpretation of the co-creator writer to produce physicalized, imaginative adaptations reflective of the company's ethos of investigating classic stories to discover the ways in which they resonate with contemporary audiences. Shared Experience's work is text based in the sense that

Meckler and Teale always work with a script, but much of the adaptation is contingent on physical sequences devised with performers and a movement director. Meckler explains, 'We're still very interested in this idea that you can stimulate the imagination by suggesting things, rather than creating something that tends to replicate reality. ... I think we're always asking how we can distil something and get the essence of it', particularly through the scripting of the play text.[4] In addition to *War and Peace*, Edmundson collaborated with Shared Experience on *Anna Karenina* (1992, 1998), *Mill on the Floss* (1994, 1995), *The Clearing* (2002), *Orestes* (2006), *Gone to Earth* (2006) and *Mary Shelley* (2012), largely adaptations of canonical texts, focusing on depicting the juxtaposition of the main characters' internal fears and desires and their external societal pressures. Shared Experience's approach to collaboration recalls what Megan Terry referred to as dramatizing 'interior states of being'[5] and what Caryl Churchill described as bringing together 'people's internal states of being' and 'the external political structures which affect them',[6] suggesting an ongoing tradition of combining devised work with written text in order to perform ephemeral concepts such as a character's subtext or subconscious. Although it varied to some degree from production to production, Meckler largely derived her approach to making new work from a kind of blueprint of the model of working she developed with Edmundson while working on *Anna Karenina* (the first writer with whom she collaborated on an adaptation), setting a precedent both in terms of content and process for later plays. Meckler explained that she found it easier to commission Edmundson, a writer with whom she could collaborate intimately, rather than devise scenes straight from the source text in the kind of long, labour-intensive process that Alfreds had used.[7] The process of adapting Leo Tolstoy's *Anna Karenina* gave Meckler and Edmundson the opportunity to experiment with techniques in writing and staging in order to subvert audience expectations of a canonical text.[8] It also allowed Meckler to work efficiently, having the advantage of a nearly finished draft of a text with which to work at the beginning of the rehearsal process.

For each production, the company conducted a development workshop at an early stage of the development in order to discover possibilities for staging and movement, as well as the ways in which this visual dimension could interact with the text. The movement director (in the case of *War and Peace*, Liz Ranken) devised a physical language for the adaptation with the performers, experimenting with different ways of creating images with the performers' bodies. The play text inspired physical motifs, scenes and gestures, intended to illuminate the narrative's subtext and the characters' inner thoughts. The company's relationship with collaborators like Ranken allowed them to create a balance between physical and textual language in their work, endowing Ranken with an authorial voice for productions related to the visual and the physical. She has worked on the majority of Shared Experience productions, having worked with Meckler and Teale for over 20 years and explained that she appreciates their 'commitment to an evolution' of the relationship of text and movement on stage – to which Ranken referred as the 'metaphysics' of the novel's subtext.[9] She was free to contribute ideas to each project, not only in terms of the choreography but also in terms of the overall themes of the piece, which she sees in the source text and ways she believes the production can be staged.[10] Ranken focused on movement as the emotional, physical and psychological subtext of the dialogue, or what she referred to as 'body states', the physical language of characters that changes in relation to the character's thoughts and relationship with their environment.[11] Here we can see the parallel between Shared Experience's approach to writing and collaboration and The Open Theater's investigation of the tension between the inner and the outer, the social and the personal; however, whereas Chaikin and Terry foregrounded the physical devising as a way of developing narrative and characters, Meckler, Teale and Ranken employ it in order to excavate the hidden layers of the novels that they adapt and find a way into the developing play text with the writer.

Helen Edmundson and *War and Peace*

Edmundson adapted *War and Peace* for the company in 1996 for a production at the National Theatre and revived it in 2008 for a national tour, co-directed both times by Meckler and Teale.[12] Shared Experience and Edmundson approached the process of adaptation by balancing the prosaic and dialogic with the physical and the visual, using the play text as a framework within which the movement score of the production was developed. Within the basic parameters of the narrative and characters of the non-dramatic source text, Meckler, Teale and Edmundson used performance in order to reinvent and comment on this text by exploring the hidden or underdeveloped aspects of the story which interested them and which they believed would engage contemporary audiences. Edmundson explained that the company's 'mixture of text and physicality' was ultimately rooted in the written and spoken word but used movement to express the emotional subtext of a scene, often replacing 'reams and reams and pages about what somebody's thinking or feeling' with visual motifs.[13] (Edmundson uses the collective 'we' to acknowledge the fact that this approach to adaptation was developed collaboratively with her, Meckler, Teale and Ranken.)

Research and development

In this model of collaboration wherein the writer operates as a co-creator with the company, the mediation of the source text necessary for the adaptation not only leads the process but is a communal process. Edmundson said that she, Meckler and Teale held a workshop with some performers with whom the company had worked before and gave them the task of experimenting with different ways of approaching the novel so that Edmundson could start to see possibilities for adaptation – specifically, what motifs and storylines would be best suited to the stage and which might prove problematic.[14] The workshop was run primarily under the direction of Meckler with the assistance of Teale and the movement direction by Ranken while Edmundson observed and, from time to time, conferred with the directors. As a result of the performers' creative input, the writer was able to begin to visualize the novel as a play text, as she says, to 'bring some life to it and help me think of it as actors in a space rather than words on a page', which she explains is 'quite a big kind of shift'.[15] Essentially, these workshops consisted of Edmundson's requesting certain episodes to be taken straight from Tolstoy's novel and of Meckler, Teale and the performers' devising versions of them, with the help of Ranken to design physical tasks to facilitate the process.[16] As Edmundson said, 'we just kind of [took] the book cold and [said], let's try this bit. What happens when we put this bit on its feet? ... Let's just try it out and split into groups and try different ways of approaching it'.[17] Edmundson, Meckler and Teale asked the performers to find ways of dramatizing parts of the novel in groups, experimenting with improvising different methods of conveying character, setting and narrative shifts so that they could see what was most interesting to watch and what was problematic to drama-tize. This process was facilitated by the three, as well as Ranken, who guided the process of devising movement with the performers in order to make inroads into physicalizing the novel. The writer and the direc-tors then began to collaborate on their vision for the adaptation of *War and Peace*, giving each other a forum to express their opinions of the physical world of the adaptation as well as to gain input from trusted performers who had worked with the company before and understood the way they worked. Shared Experience relied on this balance between the autonomy of individual collaborators with different skill sets and the synthesis of their ideas in order to maintain cohesion within the project.

Along with discussions and workshops, the research process pro-vided a common ground upon which the collaboration could be based and the relationship between Edmundson and the company could deepen, especially before she wrote the text. After the work-shopping process, Edmundson, Meckler and designer Bunny Christie went to Russia together on a research trip in order to research Russian culture at the beginning of the nineteenth century, Russian involve-ment in the Napoleonic War, the life of Tolstoy and other cultural and historic elements pertaining to the novel.[18] Edmundson and the directors also read books about Russian history and culture, such as *Natasha's Dance* by Orlando Figes, in order to enrich their understand-ing of the world of the book.[19] Being able to travel together and be exposed to the same books, films, music, art and other research mate-rial helped create a common framework of inspiration and references for all involved, especially between the writer and the directors. The act of a highly detailed research process with a particular focus on his-torical accuracy and culturally specific behaviour measurably shaped the text, design, musical composition, direction and performances within the production and complemented the early workshops that Edmundson held with Ranken, Teale, Meckler and the performers. Edmundson's next step when she came back from Russia was to 'work out an approach' to adapting the book, to 'choose a through-line' before she began writing, and then to approach the directors with an outline for the play text before she began writing.[20] Going through an extensive research, development and workshopping process with the directors helped Edmundson build a shared understanding of the kind of adaptation she and the company would create.

Shared Experience's *War and Peace*, 2008 © Robert Day

At this stage of the process, Edmundson had the most control over the production since it was chiefly text driven – informed both by Tolstoy's novel and also by her own developing dramatic adaptation. Directors, designers, movement directors and performers looked to Edmundson to provide a main concept, a focused and structured interpretation of Tolstoy's novel with which to work. Edmundson was the primary mediator between the novel and its realization as a stage production from whom all other elements (direction, design and performance) arose.

Relationship between play text and source text

Tolstoy's *War and Peace* (1869) spans four volumes, nearly 30 characters and over a thousand pages, chronicling the lives of Russian aristocrats from the beginning of Russia's involvement in the Napoleonic Wars to Napoleon's invasion of Moscow. The book paints an expansive portrait of Russian society and sketches a philosophical doctrine, 'dismissing free will as an illusion and the exercise of will as futile and dangerous' and proclaiming 'that real freedom lies in relinquishing the will and reconciling ourselves to whatever life brings'.[21] Edmundson found a way to adapt Tolstoy's novel by making bold dramaturgical choices regarding the structure of the play text, focusing on particular characters, themes and narrative strands. The writer explained that the greatest challenge was condensing hundreds of pages of prose into a few hours of stage time,[22] but the advantage of writing an adaptation was that it gave her the confidence to write about subjects and events which she had thought previously to not be 'particularly achievable onstage', such as, 'people drowning in floods' and 'people … throwing themselves under trains', and that this kind of writing process encouraged her to 'expand the boundaries' of her practice.[23] Edmundson had plenty of opportunity to experiment with possibilities for dynamic stage directions, as *War and Peace* revolves around a series of expansive, greatly differing and constantly changing locations. Edmundson's tendency in writing adaptations was to focus on the elements of the source text that were likely to lend themselves to what Meckler referred as an 'expressionistic' style of performance; in other words, she adapted the novel by focusing on aspects of the text that could be interpreted visually and physically, rather than writing dialogue-heavy pieces within a more realistic context. This allowed Edmundson not only to devise a way for the directors to have a certain amount of creative influence over the adaptation once the text was written but also to create shortcuts, truncating the novel's lengthy passages of prosaic description. Edmundson's objective to 'expand the boundaries' of her writing by outlining physical interpretations of narrative developments complements the directors' desire to create a production where, as Meckler said, the performer 'creates the atmosphere' through strong visual motifs and physical work.[24]

Due to the constraint of a three-hour time limit on the length of the play imposed by the National Theatre (which she later expanded for the tour in 2008), Edmundson had to strip away a good deal of Tolstoy's narrative and many of his characters, focusing particularly on Natasha, Pierre and Andrei and their changing world view as the Battle of Borodino approaches. In these three characters, we are shown the way in which the decadent, leisurely lifestyle of the Russian aristocracy was altered by a war, previously considered to be a faraway 'European' struggle, on their own soil. The play text still reflected the structure of the original novel, but in an abridged version; Edmundson condensed *War and Peace* into episodes that lend themselves to dramatically interesting, imagistic moments, representing the original narrative physically and reducing the need for lengthy exposition. This episodic approach allows the adaptation to make the themes of the original source text and the experiences of its characters universal and thus accessible to contemporary audiences, underscoring the struggle for individual thought and freedom in the face of overwhelming pressure from society to conform in order to combat increasing chaos in wartime. Edmundson's text provides a framework for the visual aspect of the production, in terms of both the design and the physical sequences. For example, at the beginning of the play, Pierre, the illegitimate son of a nobleman, returns to Russia from Paris where he has been studying, enamoured with Napoleon's mission to unite Europe under his rule as one whole republic; by the end of the play, having seen the ruin and destruction Napoleon has caused throughout Russia in his quest for power (and after having been taken prisoner by the French army), Pierre realizes that his campaign threatens Russia's existence, limiting national determinism as well as personal freedom. In the novel, while Moscow is being evacuated, Pierre decides to stay to assassinate Napoleon:

> convinced that Moscow would not be defended, he suddenly felt that what had only occurred to him before as a possibility had now become something necessary and inevitable. He must remain in Moscow, concealing his name, must meet Napoleon, and kill him, so as either perish or to put an end to the misery of all Europe, which was in Pierre's opinion entirely due to Napoleon alone.[25]

Here, Tolstoy gives the reader an example of an individual, emotional and absurd response to the horrors and the chaos of the French invasion through Pierre's decision to assassinate Napoleon. Edmundson translated and physicalized this theme for the stage by turning Napoleon into a manifestation of Pierre's imagination. In Pierre's fantasy encounter with Napoleon during the Battle of Borodino in Edmundson's text, Napoleon tells him, 'I am fighting this war for the stability of the world,' and Pierre responds, 'No. You are fighting it so that your power will never again be threatened or your will defied'.[26] This stylized, fantastical conceptualization of the novel reflects an impulse to depict larger political issues within the context of the way that they are embodied in the individual, as well as physicalizing more abstract concepts for the audience. Edmundson reconciles the problem of such overwhelming concepts as the Napoleonic Wars and Russian nationalism by focusing on one man's philosophical, political and emotional journey and his changing perception of Napoleon.

Edmundson's text reflects her role as a co-creator in that she incorporated Meckler, Teale and Ranken's ideas concerning the physical life of the production into the play text by writing highly imagistic, symbolic stage directions that created space for physical sequences devised by the performers. The stage directions which indicates breaks for the physical scenes invites the audience into a surreal corporeal sequence in order to emphasize the juxtaposition of the historical world of the play with the contemporary world of the audience. Edmundson's challenge was to find a way of translating this long novel – heavy with philosophical and descriptive passages – for the stage, for a company which had become accustomed to staging the complex, inner lives of fictional characters. For example, in order to foreshadow the coming Battle of Borodino and the impact of the nature of war on society, she writes the following sequence in the form of a stage direction:

> *All around PIERRE, the injured of the play have gathered – MARIA, ANDREI, PRINCE BOLKONSKY, NIKOLAI, the COUNTESS – everyone in fact. They walk forward and then collapse down as though they have been shot, then pull themselves up and walk forward again.*[27]

Edmundson not only conveys a sense of the universal nature of war but also replaced hundreds of pages of description and philosophical prose with a single image representing the collective sacrifice that the characters make during the Battle of Borodino and Napoleon's invasion of Moscow.

In the 2008 production, Edmundson continued to use the technique of blending one scene into another, allowing different characters' worlds to coexist, but she also included additional short scenes, exploring moments in the lives of the characters; in this way, the audience was able to delve deeper into the world of the play than they could in the 1996 production – juxtaposing, for example, the cosseted adolescence of Natasha, surrounded by her loving family, with the lonely spinsterhood of Maria, who is forced to take care of her demanding, callous father. Not only was this tendency to expand on the number of short, private scenes in the play a result of Edmundson's dramaturgical process, but it also reflected Teale and Meckler's goals. In the education pack provided by Shared Experience, Teale is quoted as saying,

> Tolstoy is brilliant at dipping inside a person's consciousness and describing the inner sensation of the moment. Often this is at total odds with what the character allows other people to see. It is this conflict between the outer and the inner self which fascinates us and is crucial to the physical life of the work.[28]

Edmundson's artistic choices in her mediation of the novel can be seen as a product of the co-creator–writer model of collaboration; she

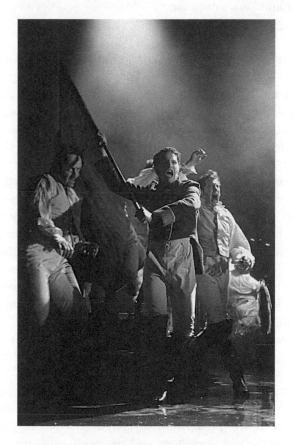

Shared Experience's *War and Peace*, 2008
© Robert Day

aligned her objectives in adapting the novel with the directors' vision for the production. Edmundson commented on Tolstoy's narrative in a way that would engage contemporary audiences while retaining the essence of the time period in which the novel was written; she investigated the emotional and psychological motivations of the characters and demonstrated them through what Ranken called the 'metaphysics' of the physical language of the productions.[29] The audience was not only given a window into the world of the novel but also allowed to look through the lens of a contemporary perspective, trying to imagine parallels between the characters' world and their own. Edmundson did this while also truncating the original narrative in order to highlight the most dramatically significant points that would come across clearly in Meckler and Teale's direction.

Edmundson's dynamic within the company

As a co-creator writer, Edmundson situated the adapted play text at the centre of the project; this particular approach to collaboration was achievable because of the pre-existing relationship between Edmundson, Meckler and Teale, their shared aesthetic values, the group's perspective on Tolstoy's novel and mutual respect for each other's artistic boundaries. Edmundson stated that once they had held the preliminary workshops, she was free to write a draft of the play text, which was then given a dramaturgical examination by the directors; after taking in their feedback, she would write another draft, which would be used in rehearsals.[30] As to her involvement within the rehearsal room, Edmundson said, 'it's more a question of cutting and sometimes slight editing things and putting things together in a slightly different way' than using the time with the performers and directors to make major changes or additions to the text, as she had done during rehearsals for *Anna Karenina*.[31] This particular approach to working embraces a high level of autonomy for the writer and director(s) alike.

The way in which Edmundson interpreted the novel and, subsequently, constructed the text guided the production and allowed the text to serve as a framework for the physical sequences. The movement was devised in workshops and rehearsals with the performers and Ranken in response to the text Edmundson created. In the case

of *War and Peace*, the role of the text and of the writer was to create structure for the staging created by the directors and the movement devised by the movement director and performers. Meckler
believed that, ultimately, a director needed to make final decisions for
the group, which she defined as 'The person with the strongest personality, the strongest desire to get everyone to do what they think,'
that she did not know 'if you could really ever put together a piece
and have it be what everybody wants'.[32] Meckler's statement reflects
Edmundson's: the process in which she engages with Shared Experience is reliant on trusting relationships, the specific demarcation of
tasks and the specialized skills of each practitioner. Each member of
Shared Experience's pool of collaborators was carefully hand-picked
by Meckler or Teale on the basis of their expertise and shared aesthetic; therefore, the directors work with their collaborators again and
again, rather than bringing new practitioners onto each project, in
order to have a stable working environment governed by those with
separate but equal skill sets.

It is significant to note that this process relied on the fact that
Edmundson was an experienced, self-sufficient writer, able to work
independently. Meckler explains that Edmundson's adaptations are
'very unusual ... because they're almost complete when we go into
rehearsal' and that Edmundson is 'rare in the sense that she can
picture the action, and she has a lot of very strong visual ideas, but
also she will write something knowing we'll be able to find a way
to abstract it physically'.[33] Since the writer had already worked on
other productions with the company, she was familiar with their
aesthetic, as well as the directors' desire to have highly demarcated
roles – independent but supported by collaboration. Additionally,
movement director Ranken worked with the performers alongside
Meckler and Teale during rehearsals to improvise the movement
sequences, which served not only as an expression of what Teale
refers to as the 'inner' selves of the characters but also as a visual
shorthand to blur the lines between different settings (such as a ball-
room and a battlefield) and developing the narrative, all of which
Edmundson has loosely indicated in the stage directions of the play
text. Herdman noted that during rehearsals, Ranken would lead the
movement sessions and Meckler would watch, 'often trying to bring
out links and connections between the exercises and the ... world
of the play'.[34] Ranken served as another interpreter of the text for

Meckler and Teale, bringing an ability to develop the physical language of the play without conflicting with or infringing upon the directors' authorial and artistic territory. Not all writers and companies attempting this approach to working will necessarily have this level of experience, but the process of creating *War and Peace* is instructive in that it can be seen as an example of a combination of artistic autonomy and collaborative decision making.

Part II   The commissioned writer: Bryony Lavery for Frantic Assembly

Now I will turn to the model of the writer as the commissioned co-creator and the collaboration between writer Bryony Lavery and Frantic Assembly on *Stockholm*. Founded by artistic co-directors Scott Graham and Steven Hoggett in 1994 (and run by Graham alone since 2013), Frantic Assembly devises physical language with performers to complement the textual language created by the commissioned writer. Graham summarizes the way he and Hoggett work with writers:

> It is different for each production. … Each writer still finds the act of writing a very private process and we respect that. … We include the writer at very early stages of development. We have the initial idea ourselves and then approach a writer with a proposal to join us on this project. We don't tell them what to write. We try to explore a world together and arm them with a physical and visual vocabulary that they use to write the first draft.[35]

The company is best known for work such as Chris O'Connell's *Hymns* (1999), Michael Wynne's *Dirty Wonderland* (2005), Mark Ravenhill's *pool (no water)* (2006) and *Stockholm* (2007), among others. Beginning with a physical theatre adaptation of John Osborne's *Look Back in Anger* for the Edinburgh Fringe Festival in 1994 with the help of writer/dramaturg Spenser Hazel, the company's remit came to be to use choreographic dramaturgy to create a different kind of theatrical language which simultaneously subverted and complemented the textual dialogue. They adapted Osborne's play into what Hoggett referred to as a 'pared-back' version to accommodate the movement score that he and Graham devised and performed under the guidance of choreographer Juan Carrascoso.[36] Graham explained that his and Hoggett's goal was to enable their audiences to understand the 'mechanics' of performance and enable them to believe that it was relevant and interesting by emphasizing the way in which performers' bodies were affected by physical and emotional forces within the play.[37] Hazel wrote the texts, with dramaturgical assistance from the directors, and performed in the productions – and all company members discussed the development of each production collectively. The directors then commissioned Hazel to write a trilogy: *Klub* (1995), *Flesh* (1996) and *Zero* (1997); the process which Frantic Assembly used with Hazel on the three productions was constantly changing so that they could find the most pragmatic approach to creating text and movement together. Graham explained that some scenes were unscripted because they originated as 'physical ideas' rather than textual ones, and Hazel would take notes during group discussions and script other scenes: 'sometimes the need for more script came about through the failure of a physical idea'.[38] Hazel employed the performers involved 'as a device, as a conduit for a theme or idea', writing scenes and monologues through which to work in the rehearsal room on the basis of various conversations.[39] The productions Frantic Assembly made in its early years were the products of an intensely collaborative, company-driven working process where company members' roles often overlapped, but the two directors came to prioritize working with a specifically designated writer on a new text for each project so that the text and the physical score could be created simultaneously.[40]

Frantic Assembly became structured in the form of a small, permanent base co-directed by Graham and Hoggett together, working with a variety of freelance writers external to the permanent artistic directorship. The commissioned co-creator–writer model developed as the need to work with different writers with distinct authorial voices and approaches to collaboration became more pronounced; the two directors wanted to create what Hoggett referred to as a 'different physical pallet' and a unique aesthetic style to suit the subject matter of each play.[41] By 1998 when they worked with their second commissioned writer Wynne, on *Sell Out*, the directors found that their increasingly sophisticated choreography demanded a commissioned writer who could script a narrative and characters that would facilitate the emergence of a devised movement score. Hoggett explained, 'I think we're much happier looking at text as a starting point for physicality, rather than the other way around'.[42] While Hazel's scripting process was integrated within the rehearsal and physical devising processes, Wynne's was separated, affording him more time to write independently and 'concentrate on the integrity of the text'; a more substantial piece of writing would give the directors a better starting point from which to devise movement sequences.[43] After a research-and-development period and then a long period of independent writing, Wynne gave the company a draft of the text with which to work and develop in rehearsal, making rewrites and changes himself along the way in response to the company's amendments, additions and suggestions.[44] This process led to the two-year-long time frame the company currently uses for a period of development of any given project, which roughly entails two developmental periods ranging from one week to two weeks for research and development that involves the writer, directors and performers over the course of two months; between six and twelve months for the writer to write the text alone; six months of dramaturgical meetings between the writer and the directors to edit and develop the text into a working draft; and finally a four-to-five week rehearsal period.[45] Although each production would vary in terms of the nature of the project's style, subject matter, number of performers and commissioned

Steven Hoggett and Scott Graham in rehearsal, 2007 © David Sibley

writer's process, Graham and Hoggett found they were able to form a relatively constant working method through a process of negotiation and discussion with the commissioned co-creator writer to facilitate the development of the text and the production.

Bryony Lavery and *Stockholm*

After Lavery heard from John Tiffany and Vicky Featherstone at Paines Plough about a project revolving around the Stockholm syndrome and domestic violence that Frantic Assembly was planning, she spoke to the two directors about working on it as a commissioned writer, and they invited her to join the project.[46] Lavery says, 'It has been so far charmed in that, I think that they were looking for someone like me and I was looking for someone like them.'[47] Although she did not know the company's work previously, Lavery found she got along well with Graham and Hoggett from the beginning, and both parties believed that there was a natural sense of ease about the collaboration. Regarding Lavery, Hoggett said, 'She's happy to explore. ... She thinks about more than just the words and she responds brilliantly to movement, physicality, to choreography, music'.[48] Hoggett attributed Lavery's bold approach to writing to the fact that she had worked in the industry long enough to be able to try different forms of composition that involved different sonic, spatial and visual elements of performance. Ultimately, Lavery fulfilled the company's need for a commissioned writer who would treat the text as a kind of blueprint for movement as well as a piece of work with its own inherent dialogic integrity.

Research and development

The research-and-development process within this model of working functioned not only as a chance for the writer and the company to explore the material (as was the case with *War and Peace*) but also as a way to get to know each other's process, aesthetic and vision for the production. Lavery and the company entered into the research-and-development process with a number of elements crucial to this model of collaborative practice (and also unusual for a new partnership):

a sense of trust, confidence that sprang from years of experience, a willingness to experiment and a firm structure within which to do it. In order to facilitate the physical devising process in the workshop, the company and Lavery discussed any books, films, stories or personal experiences to do with the Stockholm syndrome; when they had narrowed the project to the idea of personal relationships, then the realm of the domestic sphere and concepts such as kitchen spaces and recipes were used as starting points.[49] For two weeks, Graham and Hoggett worked with performers to devise movement inspired by research and discussions while Lavery watched, took notes and made sketches. The writer had a relaxed but receptive approach to working with the company during the research-and-development period, knowing that it would be to her benefit to understand the company's style of and approach to devising movement, explaining that 'the narrative unfolded in a very different way' than if the text had led the development process.[50] In addition to the first two weeks of workshopping, the company also held a week-long workshop after Lavery had produced the text, in order to explore ways in which the movement and dialogue could be combined, which allowed her to make adjustments to the structure and content of the piece before rehearsals began so that the text could best serve as a basis from which the movement could be created.[51] Lavery had the support of the company in investigating the themes and the potential physical life of the project but was free to use what she had witnessed within the creation of the text in the way that she saw fit, an element of the process which is essential to the writer-as-co-creator model of working. Graham and Hoggett were pleasantly surprised when they read the first draft of *Stockholm* and found that Lavery had incorporated much of the research and ideas that were discussed in development, as well as the initial physical work that was devised.[52] Whether it was the fact that all those involved in the devising process were particularly inspired by the material, sheer luck or a combination of both, Hoggett said that they were able to make 'quite precise material from very vague ideas', in a process which the company found successful.[53] Graham believed that working with the physicality at the forefront of the project encouraged Hoggett and himself to be more 'confident about creating physical work and understanding where it might sit' within the overall production.[54] One of the main distinctions between Shared Experience and Helen Edmundson's model of the in-house writer as co-creator and Frantic Assembly and Lavery's model of the commissioned writer as co-creator is that while Edmundson helped shape the model that Shared Experience used for working with writers because she came to the company towards the beginning of Meckler's tenure as artistic director, Lavery came to Frantic Assembly's process after the company had already been working for many years with other writers and contributed to a shift in that process.

The movement sequences in Frantic Assembly's productions articulate the subtext of the dialogue, emphasizing characters' complexities and contradictions by creating a counterpoint to and a subversion of the text.[55] The physical score of each production runs alongside the textual score, complementing the text but also articulating the subtext of the scene and conveying another layer of complexity of concept, characterization and narrative. 'It is very important to aim to express what is not said verbally. If you are enforcing what has been said verbally, then you are just saying things twice'.[56] The process of starting with a draft of a commissioned text demanded that Graham and Hoggett devised a kind of movement score with the performers that was both complementary to the written dialogue and also subversive in the kind of second narrative it tells through the characters' bodies,[57] making sense of the character's journey and the themes within the play.[58] Lavery's text was composed with the potential visual and spatial elements of the production in mind and thus influenced the way in which the movement was devised by the performers.

This model of collaboration with a commissioned co-creator writer evolved to allow a kind of reciprocity in terms of communication among the writer, directors and performers, using the text as a blueprint for the devising. Graham and Hoggett separated their collaborators (writer, designers, performers) into units so that they could maintain a dramaturgical oversight over the written and the physical work created in order to afford the writer and performers a certain amount of artistic agency but also to adhere to the principle that the text and movement should not articulate the same idea. In terms of the working relationship between the two directors, both have stated that they did not always agree, but they made sure to discuss all the decisions that were made together.[59] *Stockholm* performer Samuel James explained the synchronicity of the directors' relationship, that they discussed rehearsal room issues between themselves and resolved any disagreements before returning to the discussion or activity with the performers, in order to keep rehearsals running smoothly and efficiently.[60] All devised physical work was recorded so that at the end of each rehearsal day, Graham and Hoggett could watch the sequences again, in order to decide which ones should be kept and which should be cut – making decisions that affected the physical dramaturgy of the production in a similar way to which a script is edited. Having a visual record of the movement helped the performers recall what they had done before, in order to be able to replicate it and create new sequences, either incorporating established physical tropes or avoiding such repetition and creating new ones. As Lavery composed with written text, the performers composed work physically, writing through the body. James explains that Graham and Hoggett did not choreograph, in the sense that they directed the actions and movements of the performers. He says, instead, that 'They give you an idea or a particular story to tell and you come up with something', that he and co-star Georgina Lamb, 'had to go off on our own and we had to come up with a sequence and when we came back together, they said, that's the sequence'.[61] James added that all inspiration for the movement came directly from Lavery's text for *Stockholm*, and he, Lamb and the directors worked to observe the dictates and constraints of the text.

As a result of this kind of process of development that sprang from a strong writer–company collaboration, the kinds of texts that Graham and Hoggett have commissioned from writers bear the imprint of the exercises, games and patterns of movement they have designed to devise physical sequences with the performers. The directors supervised as the performers devised sequences of movement in pairs or groups in response to scenes from the text, using a physical improvisation technique called 'contact improvisation'. Graham and Hoggett approached the composition of the movement applied to each written scene in an open, flexible fashion in order to make any necessary changes and additions.[62] Although the performers were responding to the text and created physical scenes in response to what the writer had written, the remit that Graham and Hoggett would give was to concentrate on a particular theme or concept that reflected the play, rather than on individual scenes.[63] This technique allowed the performers to devise within thematic parameters dictated by the text, but it also allowed them to avoid falling into the trap of devising movement that simply reinforced or mimicked the dialogue in a particular scene. Contact improvisation allowed the performers a certain amount of creative license within a tightly framed rehearsal structure, breaking each physically devised scene into what the directors call 'tasks', lasting only short periods of time, in order to prevent the performers from becoming overwhelmed with the pressure of having to think about the text or the production in its entirety.[64] In an interview with Nina Steiger in 2006, Graham explained that he credits the success of their approach to devising with the fact that he and Hoggett set 'strict parameters' on the length of each devising session, setting the performers the task of devising for no more than 'three or four minutes' at a time, usually to the track of a piece of music, finishing when the music stops.[65] Contact improvisation relies on the interaction between (often two) performers who take recognizable, everyday movements and extend or exaggerate them in a call-and-response fashion of gesture, which Graham and Hoggett often use in order to illuminate the characters' interior states (an intention which mirrors Meckler, Teale and Ranken's approach to physical devising). Graham and Hoggett found that they were able to create a research-and-development process that involved a commissioned writer as an equal collaborator by allowing the writer a certain amount of artistic freedom within a process that was informed by a number of dramaturgical and conceptual parameters. As a result, the movement devised by the performers under the directors' guidance responded to the parameters set by the text, endowing the collaboration with a kind of mutual reciprocity.

The relationship between text and movement

It was crucial that the writer functioned as an equal creative collaborator with Graham and Hoggett because the text had to function in tandem with the physical language of the production. 'One of our main requirements when commissioning a writer is to consider space. By that we mean the unsaid. ... By remaining unsaid they offer rich pickings for choreographed physicality'.[66] Graham and Hoggett required a writer to be able to provide them with a text that was open enough to inspire the physical devising process for the directors and the performers, but also one which was structured enough to have what Hoggett referred to as 'integrity'.[67] Hoggett and Graham viewed the text by itself 'as a piece of literature', considering the integrity of the script as something that, 'stands up as a piece of writing first and foremost', rather than simply a basic framework incomplete without the corresponding movement.[68] In the case of *Stockholm*, the text created possibilities for and even necessitated the intervention of movement sequences. *Stockholm* is the story of Kali and Todd, a couple living a seemingly perfect existence from the outside, secretly locked in an abusive relationship. The entire play takes place over the course of an evening in Kali and Todd's home, as Todd cooks dinner for the couple and Kali becomes embroiled in her own fears and jealousies about the relationship which manifest themselves in outbursts of anger:

KALI

Why does he pretend to forget the fennel?
So he can sneak out to pretend he's buying fucking fennel?

How remedial does he think she is?[69]

We slowly discover Kali is emotionally and physically abusive to Todd, who, being unable to leave her, is the play's embodiment of a victim of Stockholm syndrome, someone who has identified with his captor. Graham and Hoggett explain:

The tension built up to a brutal and shocking fight between a couple who had charmed us and sold us a vision of their perfect life together. All their defenses drop as they shatter in front of us. The intention was that these people would feel like our friends and while we are shocked and appalled by the nature of their destruction, there is still a part of us that understands why they will forever crawl back to each other.[70]

After the explosive fight, the last scene depicts Kali and Todd lying together on a precariously tilted bed high above the stage, reconciled, but it also foreshadows a sinister end that suggests children, darkness and death. Lavery expresses their relationship in an abstract, distanced style by making use of pronouns such as 'we' and 'I' to suggest when there could be contact between the performers and the audience, when there could be contact between the two performers and when this contact has potentially been shut off. (The use of the conditional is appropriate here, as little in the stage directions that indicates how the lines are delivered, other than poetic and opaque statements open to interpretation.) The use of 'we' is sometimes expressed by Kali and Todd in earnest – demonstrating the happy moments in the relationship – and is sometimes subverted by the physical action, gestures or tone of voice of the performers, indicating the underlying strain and mistrust between the two and demonstrating the extremities of their co-dependency.

Lavery embedded a need for physicality within the text by creating a continuous contradiction between what Kali and Todd say and what they do; the act of movement is needed to tell the whole story of the relationship, to convey the disturbing aspect of how quickly their interactions switch from romantic to destructive, as well as how the characters feel about each other moment to moment and what they actually admit to feeling. Her stage directions are written in a loose, poetic style, suggesting physical acts, but not dictating exactly what should take place. For example, in the turning point of the play, Kali starts a physical fight with Todd, enraged by the suspicion that Todd is having an affair. It reads,

KALI
Let's remove that smug fucking expression …

And now, a terrible beautiful fight.

Let's kill him for this betrayal

She, trying for his absolute annihilation.
He, trying to hold her, contain her until the fury passes.
But it's probably a beautiful wild dance …

TODD
This
With improvisations on a theme
Is how it goes
She leaps for him

KALI
You fucker!!!!

TODD
He tries to contain her
Tries to anticipate her
Parry her
Until all her stuff's out[71]

Lavery dictates that there will be a fight but imbeds a layer of ambiguity and complexity by describing it in the stage directions as 'beautiful'. The nature of the relationship between Kali and Todd is exemplified in this moment where Kali lashes out irrationally at Todd, but Todd not only expects her outburst but knows what to do to stop, or at least endure, her attacks. We are caught off-guard by Todd's measured, aware reaction, which subverts the violent language of the stage directions. What Lavery did here was unusual for Frantic Assembly; instead of the characters' physicality representing the internal and the dialogue representing the external, here, we see the indications of movement representing the external and the dialogue narrating the internal world of the characters, more so than acting as communication between them. For the most part, Kali's and Todd's lines are directed out (suggested by

Frantic Assembly's *Stockholm*, 2007
© Manuel Harlan

Lavery's use of third person), making the audience complicit in their poisonous relationship. The stage directions are inserted in the middle of the characters' speeches to indicate a shift in tone and/or action. In the production, James and Lamb not only conveyed a sense of violence and destruction, but also, reflecting the complexity and ambiguity that Lavery indicates in the script, recalled the more affectionate scenes from earlier in the play, specifically the scene in the kitchen where Kali and Todd dance together as Todd tries to cook dinner. This movement sequence is both a fight and a dance, coordinated in a way that suggests that they have fought physically before. The tone is layered and the sequence is designed not only to distance the audience but also to remind them of the obsessive desire bound up in the cruelty and destruction of the relationship.

While rehearsing *Stockholm*, the challenge for the directors and performers was discovering the amount and placement of movement to complement the text. Hoggett noted that the physicality, 'had been placed by [Lavery] in the text already'.[72] Graham, Hoggett, Lamb and James found the text so open to physical intervention that one of the main problems became which movement sequences were necessary for the telling of the story. Lavery performed the function of dramaturg at this stage, coming in occasionally to lend an outside, critical eye while Graham and Hoggett recorded all the physical pieces that James and Lamb devised in order to go back and decide which material would be kept and refined and which would be cut. At the Frantic Assembly devising workshop in November 2007, Hoggett commented that *Stockholm*'s physical sequences were devised around pair work with Lamb and James, concentrating on the principle of a start-stop motion where one person starts a movement and the other stops it from following through; this approach allowed the performers to convey the element of surprise and unpredictability while avoiding clichéd, easily recognized movements. In an article in 2004, Helen Freshwater described Frantic Assembly's ethos:

> They identify accessibility as a core value of their work, and are preoccupied with the way our personal relationships function. They explore the ordinary, the everyday, and the contemporary, whilst their performances trade upon emotional involvement, common experience and a sense of proximity between the performers and their audience, and the performers and the characters they present.[73]

The stop-start, or push-pull, motion is symbolic of the ambivalent, volatile nature of Kali and Todd's relationship; the tone of the production changes from intimate to claustrophobic, alternately pulling the audience into the world of the play and pushing them back out again – simultaneously exploring the ordinary and everyday as well as the dramatic.

The structure and style of the writing allowed for the freedom of physical interpretation of the directors and performers; Graham and Hoggett were given space to devise movement within the script and the performers were given space to develop their characters, depending on how they interpret the unusual punctuation of the dialogue and the lyrical stage directions. James (playing Todd) explained that this fluid use of pronouns in the text allowed Lamb and him to experiment with the characters' relationship to each other as well as to the audience – what they wanted the outside world to see of their relationship and what they wanted to shield from the audience. James explained that there

> was extensive discussion and experimentation with how much of it we played to each other and how much of it we took out. ... You invite this audience in and you say to them, look at us, isn't it great to be us, and share our joy, and then, at a designated point you tell them to fuck off again and that it's none of their business.[74]

James said that this particular device in the script allowed Lamb and him not only to explore the character's relationship but also to find a way of exposing the dysfunction, by shutting the audience out with their physical and verbal language. This aspect of Lavery's dialogue can be connected to Graham and Hoggett's decision to base the devising process on the push-pull/stop-start principle; the nature of the subject matter agreed upon by the company at the start of the process informed the workshops during research and development, which then informed the style and content of Lavery's script, which subsequently informed the nature of the exercises and concepts used to guide the physical devising.

Lavery's dynamic within the company

Through the years leading up to the production of *Stockholm*, Graham and Hoggett realized that the relationship between the written text and the physical score must be reciprocal from the start of

the development of a project to the end in order to produce a dialogue between the two. When the directors worked with Hazel on
the *Generation Trilogy*, they did not wholly rely on Hazel's text to
generate material for their productions; rather, they devised movement and worked from Hazel's texts alternately, moving back and
forth between physical and textual composition, creating a natural
balance between the two. As the company began working with writers external to the permanent artistic directorship, Graham and Hoggett increasingly relied on writers to provide the text from which
they would then use as a springboard for devising movement, which
destabilized the balance between the text and physicality. Graham
and Hoggett wrote,

> For a long time we maintained that the words always came first
> in our devising process. That rule is not so hard and fast now that
> we feel more confident about working from images and through
> physicality. Our experiences on *Stockholm* and *It Snows*, both
> with Bryony Lavery, have shown us that the physicality can be
> just as inspiring to the words as the words have proven for the
> physicality.[75]

When the directors worked with Lavery, they created a development
process wherein the directors were able to explore the subject of the
piece physically before a script was produced, and the writer was enabled
to understand the company's style and devising process as thoroughly
as possible. As a result, Graham and Hoggett came to understand that
just as physicality could result from the text as a starting point, the text
could also result from the physicality. Lavery was able to create a script
that provided a balance between structure and openness, allowing space
for the intervention of physical composition. The *Stockholm* text was a
response to conversations that Lavery had with the directors regarding the subject matter of the play during the research-and-development
period, as well as the initial two-week devising workshop that the writer
witnessed. In order to do this, the directors had to be active dramaturgs throughout the production, from the beginning of the research-
and-development period to the opening night, layering their editorial
adjustments within the textual and physical compositional process to
achieve thematic and stylistic continuity. The two directors also functioned as dramaturgs, for the text and movement alike. Although Graham and Hoggett maintain that they had 'no commitment to any one

process', they did, in fact, establish a rough model of working designed to create productions which combine textual and physical composition.[76] They found they had to adjust this process to compensate for the particular needs and attitudes of the continually changing group of freelance writers, performers and designers hired to work on each production.

The company's attitude towards working with writers was a product of many years of writer–company collaboration under various conditions, and as such, Graham and Hoggett recognized that every writer's process and attitude to the material would be different, so the lines of communication must be clear and the needs of each party must be considered and negotiated:

> Your practical relationship with writers is as idiosyncratic as the writers themselves and the project you are working on. ... This is the most important relationship to have clear and understood from the start. You must both know what you expect from each other. ... You need to know whether the writer is expected/willing/able to write in the rehearsal room. You need to know if your writer is going to take inspiration from the devising processes or whether they need the privacy to follow their own clear line of creativity and then pass that on to you/the devising company.[77]

Their use of the conditional 'if' in this statement demonstrates that despite the fact that they learned that an initial research-and-development process integrated the writer into their physical devising process, they realized that some writers would not find this useful to their process, which is something Graham and Hoggett were prepared to respect. They explained in an interview with Alex Sierz in 2005 that they wanted to bridge the gap between physical theatre and text-based performance, 'to invent a physical language'.[78] The directors moved towards a more holistic text-movement hybridity in order to create productions which consider not only the text but also spatial and physical considerations integral to theatre-making; as such, their relationship with writers was also informed by a desire to create possibilities for collaboration with other practitioners, such as performers and designers. Lavery referred to the role of text in Frantic Assembly's work as 'a kind of stepladder' to 'the release of the body into the movement', indicating that text and movement were intertwined in the company's work and that one facilitated the other.[79] Graham stated, 'Devising is not to the exclusion of working with a writer. And that writer has to be allowed the freedom to develop a text and not just be expected to be inspired by what is created in the rehearsal room'.[80] Graham and Hoggett created a working environment wherein writing and devising were two complementary practices of making work, but also one in which writing could be practised separately, outside the rehearsal room, giving the writer as much support as possible but enough artistic autonomy to be able to express their voice.

Part III   Practical strategies

Adaptation through collaboration

Taking the Shared Experience process as framed by the writer-as-co-creator model of working as inspiration, the following three strategies are designed to serve as a basis for exploring the process of adapting a non-dramatic text for the stage collaboratively with a writer present. Although they do not necessarily place the writer at the centre of the collaboration, they are designed to serve the writer's efforts in scripting the adaptation, as well as enable the writer to develop an understanding about the source text with their collaborators. I have broken the process of collaborative adaptation into three elements that pertain to the source text: research, narrative/plot and character. These three strategies are by no means exhaustive with respect to collaborative adaptation but rather are designed to serve as a kind of foundation for a more extended process of creating a script with a writer collaboratively. It is my hope that they can assist a writer and a company in finding a kind of thematic foothold in the source text.

1) Research/exploration

When I have engaged in collaborative adaptation as a writer myself, I have found it useful to explore the world of the source text alongside my collaborators. In adapting a text for performance, I enjoy coming to a deeper, more thorough understanding of the world from which the text emerged and also the one that it reflects. It is fruitful to engage in the research process as a group so that all involved in the production can share this knowledge and reflect back on it later in meetings, workshops and rehearsals. This approach not only helps to cement relationships between company members but also relieves the writer from having to shoulder the burden of doing the research alone (and then, inevitably, having to recount some of that research later on). In addition to being a collaborative research method I like to use and one that I've loosely extrapolated from the process used by Shared Experience and Helen Edmundson during the development of *War and Peace*, it is also inspired by the approach to research taken by Joint Stock, as discussed in Chapter 1.

- After everyone has read the source text, as a group (involving the entire company, such as the writer, director, performers, designers, dramaturg and movement director), come up with additional material that might be useful to mine as research, such as works of art, photographs, books, poems, articles, TV shows, films, documentaries, museum exhibitions, diaries, interviews and music that either relates directly or tangentially to the source text. I would suggest compiling a document as a group that can be accessed and expanded collectively, such as an online sharing platform.
- The group can then make a list of topics and themes central to the source text or relating to the history and sociocultural context surrounding it. Each member of the company can then choose or be assigned a topic to research. This can be done in terms of relating the person's role within the company to the material; for example, you can assign the composer or sound designer the task of investigating the sounds and music of the world of the source text. Alternatively, each person in the company can be randomly assigned a subject to research, if that feels more appropriate to the process and makeup of the company.
- Each person then researches that topic, drawing from the collective list of sources compiled by the company as a starting point, adding their own as they go along.
- After a mutually agreed-upon amount of time, the group can then reconvene to share their research. This is not to say that everyone needs to share everything they have discovered, but rather anything they believe might be interesting to the group and useful for the production. Ideally, this discussion will serve as a starting point for further discussions about research around the source text and can enrich the writing, workshopping and rehearsal processes, opening the source text to deeper, more expansive interpretations.

2) Performing the source text

Although there are a number of ways to find a path through the source text and plot the stage adaptation (especially if it is long, like *War and Peace*), this strategy is designed to help the writer and the company develop an understanding of the theatrical possibilities in a collaborative fashion. The writer can choose to partake or watch and take notes instead. (If the writer chooses to take part, it might be useful to record this process so that the writer can watch it later.)

- The source text is broken down into significant moments or episodes. This can be done by the writer, director, writer and director together or, if preferred, the company as a whole (though this is likely to be the slowest option).
- Performers and non-performing members of the company can then form small groups and be assigned an episode. Each group is then given the task of finding a way of staging their given episode.
- Each group then performs these scenes for each other, in accordance with the order in which they occur in the source text.

3) Character journeys

A third foundational strategy for the collaborative adaptation process engages primarily with the characters of the course text. It is designed to aid the writer in exploring the source material through the lens of different characters.

- The writer, director, writer and director together or the company as a whole decides on several characters from the source text on which to focus.
- Depending on the size of the company and number of participants in this activity, either individuals or small groups can each take a character to explore.
- The following are some questions to consider:
  - Who is this person?
  - How do they see the world?
  - What are their distinguishing characteristics?
  - What do they want?
  - How do they change?
  - What is their journey?
  - What is their relationship to the other characters?
- Each individual or group can then present their characters to the rest of the group somehow, either through a devised scene, a piece of writing, a drawing or a storyboard.

Physicality and text

Using the Frantic Assembly process as framed by the writer-as-co-creator model of working as inspiration, the following three practical strategies are intended for a process involving the creation of text and movement, involving a combination of a writer, director and movement director or choreographer. They are designed to enable a reciprocal relationship between text and movement as they are developed by the writer and director(s). These approaches are designed to be used to develop a new play from its earliest stages (when the writer may only be starting with notes and ideas), gradually moving towards negotiating a process based on a more substantial performance text, developing movement alongside that text.

1) Dramatic themes and physical tasks

The following approach is designed to facilitate an understanding of the play in development from its nascent phase. It can be attempted at any point in the development of the play text – at the beginning, when the writer has only sketched an outline and some characters, or further along, when there is a more substantial text in existence. It may, however, be a useful strategy to explore when the movement score is in an early stage of development so that a physical vocabulary can be constructed.

- The company discusses the themes and possible themes (depending on the stage of development of the text) of the play.
- The group can then brainstorm a list of physical tasks (however concrete or abstract) that can relate to or represent in some way the themes of the play. Alternatively, the performers can discover tasks individually, in partners or in small groups, with the direction of the choreographer.
- The writer can either be involved in the development of the tasks or can simply watch the devising process and take notes. As with the other approaches, recording the process may prove to be helpful later on.
- Whatever their involvement, the writer should be allowed time to ask questions of the performers once one cycle of physical tasks has been devised and performed. After one cycle of tasks, additional material written by the writer and/or prompts or provocations can be offered by the writer and/or director, either through the choreographer or to the performers directly.
- The performers can take time to allow these offerings to sink in and then devise another cycle of tasks, in collaboration with the choreographer or independently (depending on the preferences of the company). This process can be repeated as many times as desired by the group.

2) Silent film

This strategy is intended to assist the writer in finding what can be physicalized within a text that is in a draft form. This may prove useful for a writer who is trying to find ways of making space within a text in development for movement sequences, whether standing alone apart from or woven into the spoken dialogue.

- The writer sketches a kind of 'silent film' version of the play, the plot described only in stage directions, without dialogue. The descriptions can be as concrete or abstract as desired. (Or perhaps they will be concrete in some scenes and abstract in others. This may be an interesting moment for the writer to experiment with writing more surreal, fantastical scenes than they would normally attempt.) The descriptions don't have to be long, just long enough to encompass the central points and actions of each scene.
- When finished, the writer then gives these scenes to the director or choreographer. They can discuss these scenes together, taking out anything that might not lend itself (or be interesting or indeed useful) to an interpretation through movement. This might also provide an opportunity for the director(s) to suggest new scenes that could be more movement driven. Alternatively, the writer can work directly with the performers, exchanging ideas for physicalizing the different scenes.
- The performers can then work through the scenes, devising movement independently, experimenting with working singly, in pairs or groups, depending on the needs of each scene. The style of and approach to the physicality is entirely dependent on the experience and preferences of the performers and director(s), as well as the nature of the play in development.

3) Gesture

As in the previous approach, this strategy is designed to facilitate the development of a script that is in draft form through the physical intervention of performers and director(s). It is also intended to develop the nature of the relationship between the spoken and written dialogue and the gestural, physical life of the play. It would be ideal for a company to attempt this approach to working when the play has been cast and the script has a significant amount of dialogue, even if it is still unfinished.

- After a read-through of the script, each performer is given time to pick out what they believe their character's most significant lines or phrases are throughout the play. (I would recommend three lines maximum.)
- Each performer then decides what concept or truth lies at the root of each line. The following are some questions to consider:
  - Why is that line significant?
  - What is driving the character in that moment?
  - What does the line say about that character?
  - What does it say about the physical nature of the character?
  - What movements or gestures does it conjure?

- Each performer can then develop a different gesture to symbolize the essence of each of the three lines. They can do this alone, with the group or in collaboration with the director(s).
- The performers can then experiment with playing the scenes from which they extrapolated these lines of dialogue, incorporating the found gestures where the impulse is strong, modifying them as the scene is repeated. Again, this can be done in collaboration with the directors(s), writer or other performers or done singly, as desired.
- The writer can then watch the development of these scenes with the newfound gestures. It might useful for the writer to be able to discuss these decisions in order to allow the devised gestures and movement to influence the script and also to allow the script as it develops to impact the movement.

3   The Writer as Company Scribe

Chapter 3 will present a second model of writing in collaboration: the writer as company scribe. This model is designed to consider a way of working wherein a company has developed a process of writer–company collaboration through the search for a balance between writing and devising. In this chapter, I will analyse the relationship between several commissioned scripting writers – Dawn King and Ollie Wilkinson and, later, Stephen Brown – and a company, Filter Theatre, by examining their production *Faster*. In breaking down the three phases in which *Faster* was developed, I will draw some conclusions about the process that was used, the role of the text and the ways in which the company hierarchy was adjusted to suit the project. The model of the writer as company scribe is an exploration of a young company's experiments in combining writing and devising, finding equilibrium between the authorship of the commissioning company and the commissioned writers; although this case study does not reflect an established practice such as those in Chapter 2, taken from Shared Experience and Frantic Assembly, I believe that the process that emerged makes a significant contribution to the possibilities for writer–company collaborative practice. As in Chapter 2, towards the end of this chapter, I will present a number of practical strategies inspired by this model of working intended for the use of the reader in developing their own approach to the writer as company scribe model.

Part I   Stephen Brown, Dawn King and Ollie Wilkinson for Filter

Filter Theatre was established in 2001 in London by Oliver Dimsdale, Ferdy Roberts and Tim Phillips, and it has since produced original productions *Faster* (2003), *Water* (2007) and *Silence* (2011), as well as adaptations of *The Caucasian Chalk Circle* (2007), *Twelfth Night* (2007–2008) and *Three Sisters* (2010). Filter's method of devising new work has been structured in such a way that the creative agency of the commissioned writer or writer/director and the work that they have produced have been informed by the company's politics of authorship. The mission statement for the company's profile on the arts division of the British Council's 2009 website read,

> Filter Theatre brings together actors, musicians, technicians, designers, writers, and directors to create both new works of original theatre and thrilling incarnations of existing texts. Filter's shows create an on-stage fusion of live and recorded music and sound, naturalistic and stylised physical movement, and video images. The live chemistry between these elements is a vital aspect of the company's work.[1]

The principles behind Filter's collaborative practice stem from the artistic directors' desire to make theatre that reflects their personal tastes as audience members and knowledge of working methods as practitioners, allowing them to have the kind of creative control over their productions which they would not have had otherwise as freelance performers. Dimsdale, Phillips and Roberts met when they were students at the Guildhall School of Music and Drama – Dimsdale and Roberts studying drama and Phillips studying music. Roberts explained that they began working together in order to fulfil a personal need to express themselves as creators and find their creative voice in response to the techniques they were learning:

> We found that the music discipline and the acting-training side of things didn't really cross at all, so therefore, we would meet ... and talk through ideas and discuss the possibilities of the ways in which the music can interact as organically as possible with the acting and the movement and the textual training we had been given.[2]

Roberts emphasizes that the particular frustration that encouraged the group to make their own work was the shared feeling that they were being 'taught to be directed', but not to be creators themselves, to make their own productions.[3] The trio's main goal was to apply actor- and musician-training techniques to a method of collaboration that combined musical with theatrical modes of generating material for performance to allow them to collaborate and devise productions in the rehearsal room. Filter's interest in a theatre-sound crossover led to a student production called *Four Horsemen of the Apocalypse* (2000); the idea behind it was to devise a performance through the close collaboration between actors and musicians, with the contribution of each side being integral to the production. Filter continued to create a similar production every year, and when Dimsdale, Roberts and Phillips graduated, they applied for and won the 2001 Deutsche Bank Award, which gave them the money to establish Filter Theatre as a company. Unlike Shared Experience or Frantic Assembly, when Filter was established, the roles of the writer and the text were not the primary considerations for the company but rather aspects of their working process that they began to take into consideration only as they became practical issues for the company while making *Faster*.

Although it was a difficult process typical of a new company developing a method of making work, *Faster* provides a possibility for writer–company collaborative practice that is different from the writer-as-co-creator model: the writer as company scribe. In this model, the writer is not at the forefront of the process but rather collaborates in response to concepts and material generated by writers and performers taking the creative lead. We can trace the creation of *Faster* through the way in which each draft of the text for performance was created because it represents a tangible record of the changes to which the entire project was subjected, as well as being a representation of the way in which the company viewed the writer's (or writers') role within the developing project. This case study also provides a useful example of an adaptation process distinct from *War and Peace* – that of working with the particular challenges of a nonfiction source text. *Faster* was adapted from the nonfictional book *Faster: The Acceleration of Just About Everything* (Abacus, 1999) by James Gleick. The book is rich in information, philosophy and sociological theory, but it does not lend itself easily to dramatization, as there are no characters or narrative per se. It appealed to Dimsdale, Roberts and Phillips because they believe that it accurately described the fast-paced, increasingly mediatized culture in which they lived and that it was rich material to stage by incorporating technology into a devised performance. Each chapter of *Faster* is an essay dedicated to different time-saving devices and the way in which human psychology and behaviour have been altered in response to their proliferation in late twentieth-century America; in doing so, he looks backwards in time, at different scientific and industrial revolutions around the world that brought society to this particular point of technological development. Gleick argues that while modern technology has allowed people to do more things, see more places and communicate with more people than at any other time in history, our quality of life has suffered, using interviews, statistics, scientific data, novels, poetry, academic essays and magazine articles to support his argument. The process of adaptation involved several stages of work and layers of influence from different people over the course of 18 months. (As a result, those who were involved said they found it difficult to describe what exactly happened on a day-to-day basis and sometimes who was responsible for a particular stage of the development of the project.) To clarify this process and the role of the text and the writer within it and demonstrate how the writer-as-company-scribe model developed, I will separate it into three stages: the first stage involves the production team without writers; the second stage involves the production team with writers Ollie Wilkinson and Dawn King; and the third stage involves writer Stephen Brown.

Faster

The process used to create *Faster* was overseen by Dimsdale, Phillips and Roberts, all of whom wanted to establish as much of the style and the content of the piece as possible before inviting artists external to the company to join the devising process. They first brought their idea to adapt Gleick's book in the fall of 2001 to the Battersea Arts Centre, where they were able to gain artistic support and rehearsal space to develop the project. Dimsdale, Roberts and Phillips went through the process of a research-and-development week dissecting *Faster*, trying to conceive a provisional storyline, characters and dramatic conventions stemming from themes and ideas revolving around speed and technology. Filter then invited other performers to join the project, as well as director Guy Retallack, who was hired to oversee the devising process, with the aim of creating enough material for a scratch performance for funding bodies and other potential collaborators. Dimsdale described the company's approach to control as a system of checks and balances designed to situate all outside artists 'inside the collaborative mix as democratically as possible', while at the same time admitting that the process was 'about retaining as much artistic control' as possible for themselves.[4] The decision to work with a writer for Filter contrasts with that of Shared Experience and Frantic Assembly, two companies who sought out writers as collaborative partners from the beginning, perhaps even reflecting the kind of ambivalence towards working with a writer that was expressed by a number of historical practitioners discussed in Chapter 1. When Filter realized that they needed a designated writer to help shape the written and devised material into a cohesive whole, they first employed Dawn King and Ollie Wilkinson (whom they met through the Soho Theatre Young Writers' Programme) to script the text. Although they produced two drafts of the script, the writers were ultimately too unfamiliar with Filter's needs, tastes and process of working to give the company what they wanted, which was complicated by fact that the company itself was not entirely sure of its vision for the final production. After working with King and Wilkinson, Filter commissioned writer Stephen Brown, an older and more experienced writer who had the advantage of already knowing members of the company and also being able to see the process that had played out before his involvement through recordings of scratch performances, drafts of previous versions of the script and discussions with Retallack and the company. By the end of the process, however, as a result of the complexity of the collaboration and the number of voices that influenced the text and the production, the authorship of *Faster* was shared between Filter, the performers they engaged in the devising process, Retallack, King, Wilkinson and Brown.

Stage one: Filter, James Gleick and Guy Retallack

When Filter began developing *Faster*, the possibility of working with a writer as a scribe within the devising process had not yet emerged and the team was as-yet without a writer. At the beginning of stage one, Filter's initial approach to collaborating on *Faster* was developed to give Phillips, Roberts and Dimsdale a maximum amount of authority over the content and process, while also benefiting from the creative input of practitioners external to the company's artistic directorship. Filter came to rely on director Retallack and producer/dramaturg Kate McGrath in order to maintain a structure for the emerging text without the participation of a writer. The performers worked to develop a series of structured improvisations around a theme and a set of characters under Retallack's guidance and direction, with the aim of creating a

rough draft of a text for the scratch performance, which Phillips ultimately put together. The company tried to work together through
Gleick's book and find what Retallack called the 'obvious scenes', but
this process proved difficult because *Faster* is nonfiction, so the adaptation necessitated a transformation of genre as well as medium;[5] the
company realized that they would have to find a way of appropriating
the source text as a springboard for creating a narrative and characters to dramatize Gleick's concepts. Since Phillips became increasingly
involved with the sound design for the project, McGrath became the
dramaturg, playing a more important role in the making of the text
than Filter had anticipated in the beginning. Cathy Turner and Synne
K. Behrndt explain what happened:

> During the public seminar, 'Structures in Devising' (2003) ... Retal-
> lack commented that [McGrath's] input and dramaturgical structural
> overview was invaluable when it came to pulling together the differ-
> ent strands and elements. Retallack pointed out that it was immensely
> useful to have someone who could come in with fresh eyes to make
> observations on structure, dynamics and communication.[6]

Since there was no scripting writer in the beginning to watch, record
and organize the material produced through the devising sessions, Filter relied on McGrath for her dramaturgical judgement in coordinating
all the elements of the creative material that contributed to the production, such as the staging and design concepts, discussions, ideas and
devised material. However, having more control over the shape and
direction of the project, Retallack was performing the task of a kind of
second dramaturg in addition to McGrath. Turner and Behrndt explain
that 'ideas of bridging, translating, framing and contextualizing run
through most of the dramaturg's work', which is how Retallack's role
could be described, in addition to his directing work in guiding the
devising process.[7]

Filter initially aimed to devise the project for as long as possible without a writer, which was partly due to Phillips, Dimsdale and Roberts'
preconceptions about collaboration and devising and partly due to
some apprehensions about text and writer-driven processes. Initially,
Dimsdale, Roberts and Phillips had believed that a piece written by
a commissioned writer would inevitably be too reflective of a single
perspective to create a text for a production significantly informed by

music and sound design. Roberts said, 'More often when you go and see plays, you just hear the writer's voice ... and no matter what they write, however brilliant, there's always going to be an element of them in ... every character'.[8] Not having worked with a writer before, the company was concerned that the single voice of the writer would take the artistic and authorial lead, eclipsing the intended collaborative, multimedia nature of their work. The three directors acknowledged the conundrum that they did not have the skills to script a production themselves but that, at the same time, they wanted to retain as much control as possible over the development of the script. They also acknowledged the need for a central dramaturgical influence on their work – apart from Retallack and McGrath, who were already occupied with their roles as director and producer.

In order to understand the way in which the writers and dramaturgs who participated in the project were incorporated into the process (which evolved into the writer-as-company-scribe model), it is important to consider how Filter developed as a company throughout the three stages of the creation of *Faster*. Filter was both centralized because Dimsdale, Roberts and Phillips acted as the company's leaders but also decentralized internally when they were collaborating within the rehearsal room, taking ideas and suggestions from visiting outside artists, such as Retallack, hired for that particular production. At the time of the first stage of creating *Faster*, Filter was a semi-decentralized company trying to balance the decentralized aspect of collaboration with outside artists with the centralization of a top-down power structure, and Retallack functioned as a leading facilitator in order to get the other members of the group to work together within a relatively structured fashion without imposing too much control. It was his job as the director to facilitate the improvisations and the relationships between the performers, writers, musicians, designers and technicians, alternatively stepping away from the work from time to time to allow the company to generate material and then stepping back in to check the progress of the production and the direction in which it was going. Although Retallack was frustrated by the often disorderly nature of the rehearsals, he also brought a certain amount of disorder to the project himself because of the ambiguous nature of his role, of the project and of the process of devising without a writer.

In the first draft of the *Faster* text for the first scratch performance, the company was devising not only the dialogue but also approaches to staging in order to facilitate the narrative through uses of sound, move-ment and design, under the dramaturgical guidance of Retallack and McGrath, in lieu of a writer. The first draft (devised by the company, recorded by McGrath and edited by Phillips) was irregular in its style, giving a sense that it was a product of many voices and much explora-tion. It roughly outlined the ways in which the lives of four characters – Ollie, Ben, Victoria and Rachel – were affected by the speed of modern technology, in order to dramatize Gleick's *Faster* and his perspective on the impact of speed and efficiency on human psychology. The stage directions indicate that Filter was developing a particular style of stag-ing reliant on lighting and sonic cues to indicate quick changes and place, time and atmosphere, and the style of the language is exempli-fied by the cutting and changing of characters' lines, switching back and forth between stories.

In lieu of a collaborative model involving a writer, Retallack wanted to find a way of allowing the performers to develop the storyline with a certain amount of structure without taking too much control from Dimsdale, Roberts and Phillips. Retallack said that without the involve-ment of a writer, rehearsals were often difficult in terms of finding a systematic way of producing material.[9] This is not surprising consider-ing the fact that *Faster* was Filter's first production, the company hier-archy was not entirely clear at this stage in the process and the nature of devising with performers in a rehearsal room can often be chaotic, confused or disorganized even under the best of circumstances for any company:

> A devising process might ... require, on the one hand, a search for structure, while on the other hand, the facilitation of possibilities. The need to keep the process open can make it seem chaotic because one idea might lead to an exploration of parallel stories or ideas which in turn lead to other ideas and before long the process is going down different, perhaps disparate avenues and paths. It is easy to get lost in the creative turmoil of devising ... Paradoxically, this seem-ingly free and open-ended process might require an even stronger sense of structural organization and overview than a production of a conventional play would demand.[10]

When devising *Faster* in the first stage, both Filter and Retallack wanted to create as much material with the performers around the theme of speed as possible, but in order for that to happen, they had to allow for a certain amount of disorder within the process. Retallack described the project as 'something that was evolving and constantly shifting and subject to instant change', and he said that his role was to 'be constructive' while encouraging the actors.[11] Retallack continued, 'I used to call it 'punk theatre' – that it was both chaotic and organized simultaneously.... It was always a bit of a struggle to ... find the direction that we were going in'.[12] To compound the lack of clarity regarding roles within the production, the nature of the devising process is often a complex and indirect one: as deviser and artistic director Joan Schirle says, 'Devising generally takes us off the beaten path, where we may encounter ruts, potholes, mysterious cul-de-sacs, and wilderness areas.'[13] The nature of the production kept changing, and Retallack's approach had to change with it in order for the devising to continue to progress in order to create enough material for a scratch performance. In order to develop a narrative structure that that would help create 'a piece with real meaning and depth', Retallack believed the company needed the organizing presence of a writer assigned to script the text.[14] As this point in making *Faster*, Filter reconciled themselves to commissioning a writer to script a text for the production, rather than beginning the project with the expectation that working with a writer would be inevitable and desirable and then commissioning one before beginning the process of making the work, like Shared Experience or Frantic Assembly.

Stage two: Dawn King and Ollie Wilkinson

By stage two, the writer-as-company-scribe model had begun to emerge out of necessity, but the ways in which a writer and a text could function within Filter's process was not yet evident. After the first scratch performance of *Faster*, Filter commissioned King and Wilkinson to help them write the second version of the text for performance. However, neither Wilkinson nor King had ever worked with Filter, and both were professionally inexperienced as writers.[15] At this point, the main conundrum was how these two novice writers, coming into the project after a significant amount of work had already been done without them, could develop a text with a certain amount of creative agency, while also maintaining a line of communication with the company. Filter was, at this point in the process, a semi-decentralized organization whose collaborative practice with respect to working with writers was informed by the way in which the hierarchy of the company operated. After the first scratch performance, Dimsdale, Roberts and Phillips agreed with Retallack's decision that they needed someone who was able to fill the position of a scripting writer working to their specifications with the material given to them and, as Phillips put it, 'Make them better. Make them read like a play'.[16] Filter wanted to have a collaborative and semi-decentralized devising process but also to hire an outside writer (and in this case, writers) who would be in charge of the scripting of the improvised scenes and characters (adding an additional element of centralization on top of Dimsdale, Roberts and Phillips's control over the project). Filter wanted Wilkinson and King to be able to produce a script to their specifications – incorporating the material already developed for the first scratch performance – within the hierarchy of the company. What proved challenging with respect to the emergence of the writer-as-scribe approach within the devising process in this second phase in the development of *Faster* was that Dimsdale, Roberts and Phillips considered themselves and the company the authors of *Faster*, but as writers, Wilkinson and King were placed in a position of control over the script. Although the need to work with writers was clear, what was still unclear to all involved was how they should facilitate the collaboration while maintaining roles and boundaries. Filter expected that the writers would script a text directly from the devising sessions going on in the rehearsal room under Retallack's direction, editing the improvised scenes into a cohesive text, rather than write a script independent of the devising process. The relationship within the working process between the freedom those involved were given to contribute material and the authorial hierarchy that governed the collaboration was never entirely clear, which is a common pitfall of the collaborative process – especially if those involved do not have previous experience working together. Writer Margaret Atwood's description of the experience of being a writer and the expectations surrounding that role is particularly illuminating here:

> *Being a writer* ... seems to be a socially acknowledged role, and one that carries some sort of weight or impressive significance. ... It is not always a particularly blissful or fortunate role to find yourself saddled with, and it comes with a price; though, like many roles, it can lend a certain kind of power to those who assume the costume.[17]

King and Wilkinson worked unsupervised most of the time, faced with the difficult task of co-writing the text side-by-side while unfamiliar with the way that Filter worked and uncertain of the company's expectations. They were both endowed with the authority and significance described by Atwood, but they also came with the price of being responsible for a text over which they were not in complete control, within a process in which they were not fully integrated. In a personal interview, King commented that attempting to co-write a script with another inexperienced writer, under the absented authority of the company, was difficult and entailed series of disagreements, miscommunications and compromises.[18]

In addition to the lack of communication, one of the main impediments to the functioning of this way of working was that Retallack represented one kind of authority within the process, while Wilkinson and King represented another. Retallack (who was more familiar with the project) was in charge of directing the devised scenes in the rehearsal room, while Wilkinson and King were in charge of the written scenes, essentially working alone. In the beginning, King and Wilkinson met several times with Retallack, Dimsdale, Roberts and Phillips to establish their responsibilities within the project. Retallack instructed King and Wilkinson to read Gleick's book and select excerpts that they found interesting and relevant to the project. They were also given access to draft one of the text and also the video of the first scratch performance, material they were expected to incorporate into draft two, to some extent. Occasionally, King and Wilkinson would come to rehearsals to see what the company had produced and try to work from those scenes, but most of the time the writers would bring in scenes they had written for the performers to develop those scenes with Retallack. When King, Wilkinson and Retallack did have contact, it was unclear to the writers as to who was the guiding force within the creative process; the roles of writer and author were in conflict, and the expectations for those roles were not made clear enough to them by Filter. King noted, 'The hierarchy was really fuzzy and that's when we got into trouble'.[19] Dimsdale, Roberts and Phillips grew concerned when they believed the writers had become too separate from the devising process and worried how they would deliver a text that reflected the company's needs and desires for the production. Phillips said, 'We kept sending stuff back to them going, this isn't what we want. We would be in the rehearsal room and they would be next door writing', but he also admitted, 'It was our fault as well. ... [W]e hadn't explained to them how it was going to work in the first place'.[20] Filter had a vague notion of the role that they wanted the scripting writers to perform but were not able to clearly articulate how exactly this approach was to work, and the writers were not experienced enough at the time to discover a way of scripting the text that would suit the company's needs.

The second draft (scripted by King and Wilkinson) was roughly twice as long as the first: It developed the characters and narrative, but it sacrificed most of the references to Gleick's *Faster*.[21] It is difficult to tell whether the changes made were by the writers, were a result of developments during the devising sessions, reflect a decision made by Retallack in rehearsal or were a combination of all three. Draft two depicts a love triangle between Will, his flatmate Ollie and his childhood friend Gemma, whom Will secretly loves and with whom Ollie has a relationship. The style in which the dialogue is written is smoother and more edited than that of the previous draft, a reflection of the fact that the company had spent more time developing the storyline and characters than they had in stage one, but also evidence of the influence of the two writers. King said she and Wilkinson found it difficult to incorporate the original book into the script and that their replacement, Stephen Brown, was more successful with that element of the adaptation.[22] She speculated that besides Gleick's *Faster* being difficult to incorporate into fictional narrative, one of the problems was that she had no previous experience with that kind of specific, commissioned work as a writer.[23] The process of creating *Faster* was a particularly challenging one; not only was the way forward unclear for those involved, but the source text continued to prove difficult to adapt. The team faced the problem of balancing a need for a dramaturgical through-line that would engage audiences but also include material from the nonfiction source.

With the primary challenge of working within an unclear collaborative process and the secondary one of carving a performable narrative out of a nonfiction source text, Wilkinson and King felt the need to resort to drafting their own narrative in order to write a cohesive text for drafts two and three. Draft two ends with Will's monologue, which is implied to be a voice from beyond the grave, after his death in a car accident:

> We are in a race. With each other, with ourselves, and to go slower is an admission of defeat. The world had defeated you. But speeding up takes us further and further away from each other and we don't notice until something sends us hurtling to a sudden stop.[24]

The narrative in draft two is more complete than that in draft one and each character's journey is informed by Gleick's theory that we are, as Will said, in a race that we do not notice until 'something sends us hurtling to a sudden stop'.[25] It is reasonable to assume that if the roles and company hierarchy had been clarified before draft two was finished, there might have been a more harmonious relationship within the text between the composition through writing and the composition through devising of staging and performance. As a result, in draft three there seemed to be an increased tension between the original intention to adapt the book and the new story that was being developed by King and Wilkinson. The third draft continued to develop the storyline, but it relied more heavily on dialogue and exposition than the first two drafts did, which relied on sound cues to facilitate transitions between scenes. Draft three was less clear in terms of the narrative than was draft two and was increasingly reliant on the love triangle between Wole, Gemma and Will to push the story forward.

Stage three: Stephen Brown

By the end of stage two, there were so many people responsible for generating different ideas to be fed into the scripting and devising process and too many variables within the project for an effective method of working to emerge. Marking the beginning of stage three, as well as the clarification of what had become the writer-as-company-scribe approach to working, the company ended up replacing Wilkinson and King with writer Stephen Brown, who was commissioned to be the scripting writer. Brown had the advantage that both Dimsdale and performer Will Adamsdale knew him previously before inviting him to make a preliminary assessment of the material that had gone into *Faster* at that point and also the advantage of having been given access to the videos of improvisations and previous drafts of the script, as well as having seen the scratch performances of versions two and three. Filter encouraged Brown to be a more integral part of the creative process, as they had learned that keeping King and Wilkinson at a distance from the rehearsal room resulted in a script that was incompatible from the devising carried out under Retallack's direction. Roberts notes that Brown was hired to 'collate everything we'd done and to try and write something using all our ideas and our improvisations' – essentially

function as a writer distinct within the team but required to be responsive to the material provided by the company, rather than a co-creator,
like Edmundson and Lavery.[26] Brown estimated that he wrote roughly
a third of the script before rehearsals started and the rest over the next
three weeks, working both by himself as he wrote scenes and in the
rehearsal room as he watched improvisations and discussed decisions
with the company. He struggled to recall the exact process by which
Faster was scripted, but he admitted that he 'played around' with the
material, adding in what he called 'my particular obsessions' to the story,
and then adjusted the rest with the help of the company.[27] Brown, the
company or the two together would come up with an idea for a scene
and then work with it until it came out in a way that suited the rest of
the piece: 'Some of it was fairly rapidly just taken up and put on its feet
and played about with and tweaked a bit'.[28]

Once Brown joined the project, in addition to a scripting writer, *Faster*
in effect had three dramaturgs who functioned not only in accordance
with their primary role within the production but also in relation to
each other, helping Brown integrate into the unusual hierarchical balance within the production team. Even after it became clear that Brown's
job would involve writing additional material to develop the existing
script, his role continued to have a dramaturgical function as he shaped
and edited the material created before his arrival. Retallack – who had
served as a kind of director/dramaturg to the compositional process
through writer-less devising from the first stage – maintained his role as
director/dramaturg, liaising between Brown and the performers in order
to work out issues relating to the script. McGrath also continued to play
the role of dramaturg, in addition to her role as producer; having been
present at all the rehearsals and devising sessions, she liaised between
Retallack and Brown, as well as Brown and the actors, allowing Retallack to spend time working with the actors. Brown noted that during
the three-week rehearsal period, he met with Retallack and McGrath
separately and together several times in order to keep track of how the
drafts of the script were being changed during rehearsal without inter-
fering in the delicate dynamic between the actors and director.[29] Brown
described McGrath as a 'sounding board', that one of her strategies was
that after a group meeting and discussion, she would summarize the
key points of the meeting, 'constantly kind of nudging and pushing'.[30]
As Turner and Behrndt explain, 'the dramaturg represents the audience
within a rehearsal process, able to identify the potential gap between

what is *intended* and what is likely to be *received* and to give the artist a perspective on what they are creating'.[31] McGrath functioned as a member of the production team who was able to watch rehearsals and read drafts of the script with the perspective of the audience in mind. This three-layered approach to the dramaturgical, editorial process of *Faster* allowed Filter to maintain a balance between the organization of both editing and writing and the chaos of devising throughout the third stage more successfully than the previous two.

The fourth and final draft was scripted by Brown, is roughly twice the length of drafts one and two and not only belies a different style of writing than the previous drafts but widens the focus of the production to include more of Gleick's concepts. One of the main differences between the final draft and the previous ones is that the language in draft four is more reflective of the message and themes of the piece. Both the syntax and the length of the sentences portray Will, Ben and Victoria (now the three main characters) as young, impatient people living in a fast-paced urban environment: their sentences are short; they often speak in one-liners or with one-word responses, cutting each other off and preventing each other from finishing their sentences and thoughts. The communication has broken down and, as we can see from the stage directions, the audience has been left with insertions of expressionistic aural cues and signifiers to fill in the blanks regarding the rest of the characters' world and how they feel about each other. In other words, the text was designed to reflect the way in which the characters saw reality in terms of filming techniques.

By draft four, Brown's script reflected a tendency similar to Edmundson's and Lavery's when they were writing *War and Peace* and *Stockholm* (respectively) in that he allowed the concepts that had emerged from the devising period to be reflected in the stage directions. *Faster* had become a piece about the media generation, who seem to experience the world in terms of close-ups, long shots, freezes, flashbacks and flash-forwards, the editing techniques of cutting and splicing. To complement Filter's tendency to use quick transitions and technology to enhance the narrative, Brown added moments in the text where the characters' perceptions of reality are shaped by what Gleick calls 'the acceleration of just about everything' (although, again, as with Wilkinson and King, it is not certain who was responsible). Regarding the process of adaptation, Govan, Nicholson and Normington state that 'The use of fictional material provides theatre-makers with an opportunity to discover a language of multiplicity and excess' and that the process of adaptation 'poses creative problems that often prompt stylistic innovation'.[32] The problems that the original text or what Govan, Nicholson, and Normington call 'artefact' pose to the company dramatizing it are often solved through technical resourcefulness and originality. This was indeed the case with Brown's draft four, which reads somewhat like a television or film script with shorter, tighter scenes than those of previous drafts and less exposition. For example, in the beginning of the story, when Victoria has just met her friend Will's flatmate Ben, Ben drives Victoria home after having had dinner with Will and him, and the stage directions read, *'[Will] hurtles into the background as [Victoria] and [Ben] leap into the car together and are driving along at breakneck speed. [Will] is watching them'*.[33] Not only is the scene expressed in televisual terms, but the characters even articulate a desire that their lives play out like a film. Just before Victoria and Ben kiss, Victoria says in direct address to the audience, 'I always want – that moment just before you kiss somebody for the first time – I want it to stretch out forever', pauses and then finishes this sentiment with, 'I suppose that's impractical', acknowledging the reality of speed, competition and progress which Gleick described in his book and which informed the world of the play.[34] This scene exemplifies Gleick's observation of the (largely negative) effect of speed and technology on human relationships while also demonstrating Filter's own thoughts about the effects of the media on the way people perceive each other and the world around them.

Role of the writer(s)

By the time *Faster* was completed, the process Filter had developed was one in which the authorship of the piece was (to borrow a phrase of Retallack's) 'filtered' through a process involving a group of people with specific roles at different points in the collaborative process, finding a balance between what was for them the chaos of devising and the order of both writing and dramaturgy within a process in which the writer functioned as a scribe for the company. Even though Dimsdale, Roberts and Phillips initially believed that a dynamic, complex production was more likely to be produced by a collaborating company than by a single writer, Retallack believed that once a piece was devised by a company, it could become textured and complex only once a writer was involved.

As the scripting writer, Brown unified by the third stage all the improvisations, ideas and research that had gone into the production, in order to make the text appear less inconsistent and disunited. Retallack noted that while Filter 'did have a lot of imaginative things to say, what it really needed was somebody who was going to record those voices'.[35] Retallack believed that a writer was needed to give a devised, collaborative production a distinctive voice, especially with a piece that had been through as many scratch performances, written drafts and creative contributions as *Faster* had. The director said the company needed someone to 'record' the different voices that were creating material for the production, but what Brown did was not simply record but organize and augment those voices with written material. For reviewers who had seen scratch performances of *Faster* as well as the final version, Brown's contribution to the production was obvious. In her review, Halliburton says, 'An earlier version of the show seemed slightly lost in the swirl of technology and speed-fuelled concepts, but this hugely improved production owes much to a strong script by Stephen Brown, which cleverly balances Faster's emotions with its intellectually fleet-footed observations'.[36]

By the time Filter had reached stage three, they had learned from the mistakes they made with King and Wilkinson and knew how much structure, freedom and trust they had to give Brown as a commissioned writer – that they had to abdicate some control to Brown in order to produce a cohesive script. Filter's method of working with writers stems partly from the artistic directors' prejudices against single-authored work. Brown allowed the company to reach a compromise in experimenting with written and devised composition because his creative aesthetics and his working practices happened to complement Filter's. Brown dealt carefully with his revisions of *Faster*, always referring back to Retallack and McGrath as he worked so that he did not stray too far from the company's intentions for the production. He was also an older, more experienced writer than King and Wilkinson and was better equipped to negotiate the personality conflicts within the project as they arose, as well as navigate the adaptation of the unyielding source text. In the end, the process of composing *Faster* in a collaborative fashion was not necessarily, to borrow Dimsdale's word, 'democratic' in that everyone involved was given the opportunity to vote on each decision made, but democratic in that there were continual discussions among various combinations of people within the company in order to push the project along and develop the script alongside it.

Within this model of working, as a writer closely involved in the collaborative process in order to create a text that satisfied the company, Brown had to develop a strong narrative structure in order to help Filter organize their material but also allow the company leeway to experiment. First, he had to incorporate a significant portion of Gleick's book into a fictional narrative that allowed the company to experiment with the integration of music and sound design. Second, Brown had to edit the dialogue and stage directions in such a way that they allowed for a series of quick, smooth transitions, changing time and place rapidly, all within the running time of 75 minutes. Roberts admitted that 'Without [Brown], we … would have had a very devised script' and that Brown was not only 'important' but 'integral' to the process.[37] Brown said that this task was a challenge but that 'working with Filter made me feel much freer about location and about creating worlds rapidly' and that the involvement of the performers pushed him to 'think through 360 degrees' of the world of the play.[38] (Which is reminiscent of what Edmundson said about the challenges and advantages of adapting work for Shared Experience.) Filter managed to work with Brown in a way that was mutually beneficial for both parties; the company found a writer that could work to their specifications, helping them realize a particular vision for the play, and Brown found a company that could help him find new ways of composing material. What helped Brown in achieving this three-dimensional world within the text was not only the assistance he received from Retallack, the performers and producer/dramaturg McGrath but also the method of working with writers that Filter had developed through trial and error over the first two stages of *Faster*.

Conclusion: authorship and the role of the writer

The authorship of *Faster* can be traced through the layers of creative contributions that were manifest in each of the three stages of the compositional process that led to the development of this model of writer–company collaboration: the scenes and approaches to staging devised by performers under Retallack's guidance, the writers' amendments to these improvisations and new written scenes (Wilkinson, King and Brown), and Dimsdale, Phillips and Roberts's final decisions regarding what would be cut and kept in the final script. Retallack called the process 'an ensemble effort' and attributed the authorship to the entire company but said that Brown 'had authorship of *Faster*'.[39] In this case, Retallack defined 'authorship' as, 'one person ultimately taking everybody else's contributions and shaping them into an organic mould' and that Brown 'took the role of taking and pulling all of that together and giving it a very definite texture and wit'.[40] Brown fulfilled Filter's role of the scripting writer able to make his own contributions while incorporating the scenes the company devised, accepting Filter's final editorial decisions while unifying the work into a tangible, written whole.

Filter's approach to authorship was influenced by the way in which the hierarchy influenced decision making during the compositional process of each production. The authors in the case of *Faster* were the people responsible for the origination of the concept for the project but also those who have the most influence regarding the final editing and structuring of the material. Similarly to the artistic directors of Shared Experience and Frantic Assembly, Dimsdale, Roberts and Phillips established the central theme for each production before the devising process began and approved all the final decisions made to the production and the text. In a sense, they were the authors of each production, but this was complicated by the involvement of directors, designers, performers and writers who all contributed material in both instances.[41] Filter's method was marked by the fact that Dimsdale, Roberts and Phillips were the authors and legal owners of each Filter production, but they did not compose the material that went into each production alone; the final production was a reflection of Filter's vision for that particular piece, but a vision that could be realized only with the help of outside artists. Filter relied on Brown and Retallack as organizing presences in order to help shape, guide and create material for the text for performance, maintaining a balance between the chaos of creation and the order of both writing and dramaturgy integral to their process.

Filter's process was influenced by the intricacies of the channels of communication, involvement of various practitioners and the company's power structure during each project; as a result, it changed to suit the circumstances of each production, so there was not, strictly speaking, any one model to which Filter adhered after *Faster* (especially since some of their work consisted of remounting versions of canonical plays, such as *Three Sisters* and *Twelfth Night*). Filter did not adhere consistently to the writer-as-company-scribe model after *Faster* partly because each project upon which they embarked was so different from the last – in terms of the practitioners involved who were external to the company, in terms of subject matter of the piece and also in terms of the venue and purpose of the project. The main difference between the model of writer as co-creator as exemplified by Shared Experience and Frantic Assembly and Filter's approach is that while the former model affords the in-house and commissioned writers a certain amount of freedom and time to compose a script independently, the latter model is intended for a process wherein the script is created alongside a devising process and as a response to discussions and meetings with the company. Dimsdale, Phillips and Roberts use a framework within which the script was created continuously alongside the work devised in the rehearsal room so that the final product reflected their vision and remained under the company's control. The combination of written text, devised material and ideas during rehearsal which any writer, writer/director or writer/dramaturg was expected to incorporate into a Filter production complicated the authorship of each piece and blurred the boundaries between contributors involved in each production, whether they were part of the company's permanent artistic directorship or not, making the nature of authorship and the writer's role more complex than in Shared Experience and Frantic Assembly productions.

I propose that the 'authors' of *Faster* are not only those responsible for the origination of the material for the project but also those who had the most influence regarding the final editing and structuring of the material. Dimsdale, Roberts and Phillips are the authors and legal owners of each Filter production; the final product is a reflection of the vision of the central artistic directorship, but one which could only have been realized with the help of outside artists. Filter's method of composition is structured in such a way that the artistic autonomy of the writer is limited and their work regulated by the company's semi-decentralized hierarchy. The writer's role in a Filter production is to script a text in collaboration with the directors and performers, structuring the work devised in rehearsal and combining it with text written outside rehearsal. As a result of the collaborative nature of Filter's approach to writing and scripting, the authorship of *Faster* is shared between the director, writers, dramaturg, designer and performers, as both written and non-written applications of creation of material were important to the genesis and structuring of each piece.

Part II   Practical strategies

Scripting and devising

Using Filter's process as framed by the writer-as-company-scribe model, I have designed the following strategies to enable a scripting writer to script a text in collaboration with performers and a director through writing and devising, incorporating the material generated in the rehearsal room into the text. I have broken this process down into two stages, which will facilitate a reciprocity between the written and the devised material. The first approach is intended to be executed when the project is in an early stage; the second is for a later stage, when the writer has gathered together the written and devised material for a draft of the performance text.

1) Call and response I

I have intended this first strategy to be used at an early stage of the process, when the company is focused on generating material. It would be beneficial for the writer and the company to have at least an outline for the play as well as a series of ideas for scenes and characters at this stage.

- The writer, performers and director should take one of the scenes and discuss it, fleshing out any details that will help inform the devising process. (Alternatively, if they do not yet have any outlines for scenes, they can discuss a premise for a scene collaboratively.) The following might be some questions to consider:
  - What are some possibilities for things that could happen in this scene?
  - What function does it serve?
  - Which characters are or might be involved?
  - Where might it fall within the framework of the entire play?
  - What are some possibilities for setting?
  - What is the style of writing/devising/performance?
  - Whose perspective is it from?
  - Are there any physical or sonic elements that might be useful to incorporate, like props or songs?
  - Which elements could be physicalized? Which could be vocalized?
- This scene is discussed thoroughly so that everyone understands the possibilities for the devising process. While devising is by nature often unpredictable, it is useful for the entire group to attempt to have a shared understanding of what elements might be involved.

- The performers can then devise the scene, engaging with a style of and approach to the devising that is entirely dependent on the experience and preferences of the performers and director(s) and on the nature of the play in development.
- The scene is recorded and/or noted by the writer.
- The scene is discussed with the group, allowing everyone to ask questions, bring up any issues and make suggestions for a revision of the scene. This process can be led by the writer, director, performers or an organic result of the group process depending on the nature and hierarchy of the company and the project.
- The process can be repeated as many times as desired by the group.

2) Call and response II

This second strategy is designed as a continuation of the previous one, intended to facilitate the development of a text that has emerged from this scripting and devising process, at a later stage in the process. It is similar to 'call and response I' in terms of the structure and tasks but is intended to encourage the writer and company to engage with the collaborative aspect both of the dramaturgical development of the written and devised material, while also engaging with both the writer and performers' independent creative agency and potential input.

- The company starts by reading through an existing draft of the play text developed by the writer after 'call and response I'. The writer, director and performers can then pinpoint a number of scenes that they would like to develop, revise and/or extend.
- Choosing one of these scenes, the group talks through the possibilities for development and exploration; the writer can take this opportunity to discuss any dramaturgical issues that have arisen during the writing process or pose suggestions for devising. The following might be some questions to consider:
  - What isn't working dramaturgically and needs to be changed or cut?
  - What needs to be expanded?
  - What ideas and themes could be explored?
  - Which characters could be explored and pursued further?
- The director and performers can then respond to the writer's thoughts, adding in anything they believe would be useful for the development of the scene. (This particular aspect of the collaboration can be adjusted to suit the hierarchy of the company and the needs of that particular project.)
- The performers read through the scene again, keeping the concerns and suggestions of all in mind, allowing themselves the opportunity to try to think of possibilities for deviation from the script.

- The performers then devise through the scene, using the text as a starting point and creating their own alternative developments, perhaps even changing the plot or perspective and involving new characters or cutting old ones (to name but a few suggestions). These interventions can be the result of the performers', writer's or director's ideas, or a combination of all three. For example, the director can ask for the performers to diverge from the text at set points in the existing scripted scene.
- This process can be repeated as many times as desired by the company, with the writer returning to the existing text each time to gain an understanding of what developments in the devising process might help the project move forwards.

4   The Writer/Director

Now that I have presented two distinct approaches to writing and collaboration used by Shared Experience and Filter Theatre, in this chapter I will compare and contrast two further methods that these companies have used to work collaboratively within the writing process. Chapter 4 will explain the model of the writer/director as a working method of text-based collaboration with a writer/director. In Part I, I will examine the first variation of the writer/artistic director by using the process that Shared Experience's Artistic Director Polly Teale use to create *Brontë* (2005) as a case study. In Part II, I will consider the second variation of the commissioned writer/director through an analysis of the process that writer/director David Farr developed with Filter to create *Water* (2007). This chapter will consider the similarities and differences between these two variations of the model of the writer/director, especially the ways in which authorship is influenced by the distinction between the process of a commissioned writer/director and one who is an artistic director. As in Chapters 2 and 3, towards the end of this chapter, I will lay out a number of practical strategies inspired by this model of working intended for the use of the reader in making their own approach to the writer/director model.

Part I   The writer/artistic director: Polly Teale

Brontë, written and directed by Teale, was first produced for a regional tour in 2005 which culminated at the Lyric Hammersmith Theatre in London. It was subsequently revived in 2010 for the Watermill Theatre in Newbury, Berkshire, and again in 2011 for the Tricycle Theatre in co-production with the Oxford Playhouse. However, it is important to note that Nancy Meckler directed those subsequent productions, so when I refer to the production that Teale wrote and directed, I am referencing the 2005 version. It is also important to note that movement director Leah Hausman choreographed the 2005 production, while

Liz Ranken choreographed Meckler's 2010 and 2011 versions. *Brontë* was the third play in a trilogy written and directed by Teale, which included an adaptation of Charlotte Brontë's *Jane Eyre* (1997) and *After Mrs. Rochester* (2003), an adaptation of Jean Rhys's *Wide Sargasso Sea*, itself a postcolonial response to *Jane Eyre*. Similarly to *War and Peace*, the authorship of the final production of *Brontë* is complex and layered; the source texts which informed the script were written by the Brontë sisters (including their letters as well as their novels); the dramatic text was written by Teale; the movement was created initially by Hausman and then by Ranken, both of whom created an important visual narrative for the text, and Teale (and then later Meckler) shaped the staging and the production team's creative input as director. What made *Brontë* different from *War and Peace* is that Teale became more of an auteur than Edmundson had been; by writing and directing the play, Teale shaped not only the dialogic but also the physical and visual aspects of it, increasing her authorial influence over the material but also over the collaborative process itself with the cast and creative team.

Brontë is Teale's imagining of the lives of the Brontë sisters in their childhood home in Yorkshire, where we are shown how they created their vivid novels amidst the darkness of their life with their repressive father and alcoholic brother. *Brontë* deals with the lives of Charlotte, Emily and Anne Brontë, the authors of, respectively, *Jane Eyre*, *Wuthering Heights* and *The Tenant of Wildfell Hall* (among others), novels whose characters are conjured up throughout the play. Teale constructed the play on the basis of well-researched but also imaginative speculations revolving around the question of what the circumstances and events were which inspired those three isolated women to write novels so rich in their descriptions of human experience. Teale said what shaped the text was

> the idea that these three spinsters – and I'm using that word consciously because I think they would have felt like spinsters in that society – how their life experiences were so limited and, as far as we know, they had no sexual experience – how they'd written some of the most passionate and even erotic literature of all time.[1]

Brontë tells the story of the three sisters, beginning with their childhood growing up with their brother Branwell under their father's strict supervision; we see each sister develop as a writer and achieve literary success, only to die at relatively young ages. Teale not only dramatized the day-to-day lives of Charlotte, Anne and Emily but also adapted brief moments from each of their novels, inviting the audience to draw their own conclusions as to how these sheltered and isolated women – leading lives of rural domesticity in nineteenth-century Yorkshire, caring for their aging father and alcoholic brother – wrote such richly imagined texts. The action takes place within the parsonage, juxtaposing the reality of the Brontës' lives with the fantastic, physicalized realizations of the characters from their novels. The story of the sisters' artistic and emotional development is illuminated and intensified by these moments of adaptation, blending the lives of the historical figures with the fictional ones.

Teale believe that the most efficient process of working was for her to play the roles of both writer and director for all three plays in the trilogy, as she had conceived of the driving theatrical forces that would shape the movement and text;[2] The process that she used while developing *Jane Eyre* was hugely influential in the way in which she scripted the other two productions; Teale developed a theatrical concept, wrote a partially drafted script and then experimented with approaches to staging and physicality in a workshop, working alongside performers and Ranken – like Hausman, arguably her most important collaborator in this model of the writer/director process. Teale used the play text as a basis for her process, but in contrast to the writer-as-co-creator model used to create *War and Peace* with Edmundson and Meckler, she was able to explore ways of authoring the production with her team of a movement director, performers and designers. She began by working with a partially written draft in order to discover ways of integrating the physical with the dialogic elements of the play. Because she was functioning as both writer and director in this model, once Teale had drafted a partial script, she conducted workshops so that the movement director (Hausman in the case of the 2005 production of *Brontë* and *After Mrs. Rochester*, and Ranken in the case of the 2010–2011 production of *Brontë*) could contribute ideas for staging the source text; as with Edmundson, this stage of the process allowed her to see the different themes and visual motifs which recurred in the script and possible ways of staging and physicalizing. It also allowed the movement director to devise a physical language with the performers that would later be used in the final production. Once a draft of the play text was completed, it was used in rehearsal as a framework within which Teale, the performers and Hausman could devise physical scenes and gestures which were designed to illuminate the narrative's hidden underbelly and the characters' inner thoughts and emotions, much like the relationship between text and physicality in *War and Peace* and *Stockholm*. This developmental process was especially important in creating *Brontë*, arguably the most complex production in the *Jane Eyre* trilogy as a result of its highly intertextual nature.

Teale's role

Teale's process of working as a writer/director differed from the writer-as-co-creator model in which she and Meckler engaged when working with Edmundson as detailed in Chapter 2 in that she shaped the visual and spatial nature of the production while she scripted the text as a writer/director, trying to seek a balance between the physical and the written. Teale incorporated exercises and methods she learned from and created with both Meckler and Ranken, altering them to suit the needs of her process. Designer Angela Simpson remarked that Meckler 'makes sure her team is secure and everything is in place' before rehearsals – in other words, that she had all her meetings with the writer, movement director and designer early on in the process so that she knew that the script, movement and design were ready to be implemented and so that she could devote her energies during the rehearsal period to working with the actors.[3] In contrast, Simpson noted that Teale continued the discussion about how the production was evolving as it developed with the production team, keeping everyone in conversation with each other throughout the processes, from research and development to rehearsal.[4] While the central collaborative relationship in *War and Peace* was between Edmundson and both Meckler and Teale, the central collaborative relationship in *Brontë* was between Teale and Hausman, as Hausman helped Teale to discern which 'expressionist techniques' and concepts 'fuel[led] and [fed]' the play and which 'capsize[d]' it, through a series of devising sessions with the performers (both those involved in the initial workshop and those involved in the final production).[5] In this way, Hausman became a kind of dramaturg for Teale within this model of collaborative practice, helping her compose the different elements of the production.

Research and development

Teale's auteur-driven approach to the sharing and dissemination of research was especially important for *Brontë*, as it was not a straightforward adaptation for Teale but rather an intertextual labyrinth of possibilities for a narrative engagement; like *War and Peace* and *Stockholm*, the shared research process united the creative team in terms of the ideological, structural and aesthetic direction of the production. The initial development of the *Brontë* text in 2005 mirrored that of previous works written and directed by Teale in that Teale was the main arbiter of the source text(s) and assisted in her interpretation, adaptation and staging by a creative team whose ideas informed her own. After a three-month research process in which Teale gathered information about the Brontë family, reading their novels and poetry, excavating biographical and historical material (pertaining not only to their lives but also to the area of Yorkshire and time period in which they lived) and visiting the Brontë house in Haworth, she wrote a partial first draft of the text. Teale shared much of the research with other company members – such as Hausman, designer Angela Davies, composer Peter Salem and the performers – in order to create a shared vision for the production, allowing everyone involved to understand the historical and biographical background of the Brontë sisters' narrative. This shared understanding allowed the creative team to be able to respond to the source and research material with a certain amount of artistic autonomy while also deepening the collaborative process through discussion and experimentation. Teale's choice of research material influenced the team's way of thinking about the subject matter, and in turn, their response to the material influenced her approach to the scripting process.

Collaborating with her company as a writer/director afforded Teale the opportunity to realize the kind of elaborate, visually driven stage adaptation that necessitated the creative input of performers, a movement director and designers. In the *Brontë* text, Teale wanted to represent the work of the Brontës within the context of their lives, by constructing a feminist, historical, materialist-driven hypothesis regarding their relationships to one another and their experiences as women living in Victorian Yorkshire, subjugated to the demands of the men around them. The main conceit that Teale developed as a writer/director in order to allow the different novels, hidden thoughts and dreams of the Brontë sisters to coexist in a theatrical way, which was facilitated by a physical score devised by Hausman and the performers, was that of creating different 'ghosts' from the novels' characters to 'haunt' the sisters, a mechanism that she had begun to develop during *Jane Eyre* and *After Mrs. Rochester*, productions which also emerged from this model of working.[6] Teale said that in each work she wrote for the company, she set out to create a 'device that [would] allow them ... to explore, to excavate, express the hidden world' of the characters' inner lives.[7] While adapting *Jane Eyre*, she became intrigued by the 'mythic power', 'danger and eroticism' and 'terrifying rage' of Mr Rochester's wife Bertha Mason from *Jane Eyre*, and by what she imagined to be Charlotte Brontë's 'repulsion and attraction to her own creation,' as well as what that character symbolized for Charlotte.[8] As a writer/director, Teale was free to explore this hypothesis not only through her adaptation of the Brontë novels and scripting of their narrative in the form of the text but also through her direction of the production, especially the way in which she collaborated on the physical score of the piece with Hausman. Ranken said she used elements from Rhys's *Wide Sargasso Sea* when she choreographed *Jane Eyre*, physicalizing the character of Bertha with 'empathy', depicting her as someone judged unfairly by society, forced into confinement and alcoholism, which clearly had an effect on Teale from the beginning of the creation of the trilogy.[9] The figure of the 'madwoman in the attic' and all the sociocultural associations behind it became the conceptual through-line for all three productions, facilitating Teale's exploration of the work of Charlotte, Emily and Anne Brontë through a feminist lens and, at the same time, pursuing what she believed was one of the central objectives of the company: to 'make physical ... the interior world of feeling and memory and imagination'.[10] In *Brontë*, Teale drew a parallel between the character of Bertha, Charlotte's madwoman in the attic, and the writer's personal experiences.

Teale's main goal for the initial three-day workshop for *Brontë* that she led with Hausman and a group of performers was to try out different approaches to staging sections of text that she had written in order to see if they would not only convey the narrative clearly but also physicalize the central metaphor of the play: the 'ghosts' of the Brontës' characters that inhabited the Howarth Parsonage. She noted that 'the scenes need[ed] to be very honed and sprung and muscular' in order to allow her and Hausman to guide the performers through physical improvisations which would ultimately become the productions' physical score.[11] Therefore, rather than improvising dialogue (as Guy

Retallack did with Filter in the first stage of *Faster*) she collaborated with Hausman to direct the physical sequences devised by the performers (a model closer to the one used by Bryony Lavery for the development of *Stockholm*); the movement director used the written text as a framework to inform the exercises that she developed to create stylized, expressionistic physical sequences. For example, in *Jane Eyre*, Bertha not only existed as a character in her own right but also emerged as a physicalization of what Jane was feeling, communicating Jane's thoughts through heightened, stylized physical action. 'There's quite a big idea behind that that you're trying to express theatrically. And I'm not sure that's something that actors could improvise their way into. Somebody has to take hold of that and say, how do we make this work?'[12] Teale believed that the script could provide parameters for the physical expression of dramatic devices in the way that the source text provided parameters for the entire production; she worried that if the performers were asked to devise dialogue in response to this concept, then it would be too difficult and ultimately unsuccessful. (This attitude towards collaborating with performers to physicality rather than dialogue reflects Meckler's preference as well.) In creating the physical sequences for *After Mrs. Rochester*, Hausman directed the performers to consider different 'energies' and elements of their characters, such as hot or cold, or fire or water, then asking them to do simple tasks such as cross the room while embodying that energy.[13] Ranken said that in working on *Jane Eyre* and in developing the motif of Bertha as Jane's emotional life, she gave the performers directions such as 'physicalizing the colour red' and considering 'the idea of confinement, the different stages in Bertha's journey in becoming more towards almost an animal state'.[14] Teale wanted Hausman to create an expressionistic physical language for *After Mrs. Rochester* and *Brontë*, so the movement director used an expressionistic approach to the choreography with the performers. Teale explained that the workshop was 'incredibly useful' for her as a writer because while she was writing the text, this concept was 'actually quite difficult to visualize and imagine fully when it [was] on the page', to understand what would be illuminating and what would be distracting, confusing or overwhelming for the audience.[15]

As a writer who was also an artistic director, Teale was in a position to write her texts with the company's style and ethos in mind by embedding the physical images into her writing, but this approach was challenging because it was more difficult to be objective as a writer/director about the way the physicality and the text worked together dramaturgically than as a writer collaborating with a director.[16] Although Teale and Meckler often worked separately from each other on different projects, they were also mutually dependent collaborators who gave each other insight into the productions on which they were working. Teale turned to Meckler for dramaturgical advice for the *Brontë* text before rehearsals began, as she often did when she both wrote and directed a project. In the 2010 production of *Brontë*, Meckler directed and Teale

Shared Experience's *Brontë*, 2011 © Robert Day

solely played the role of the writer, coming to rehearsals to make adjustments to the script. Teale commented that one of the greatest changes was Meckler's helpfully suggesting significant cuts to the text, allowing the movement to play a more prominent part in the narrative – giving the performers, in Teale's words, 'more breathing space' as some parts of the 2005 text proved to be cumbersome and difficult to perform five years later.[17] Teale said she believed that one of the most difficult tasks as a writer was to leave enough room for what was 'unsaid' between characters, which reflects what Lavery, Scott Graham and Steven Hoggett said about developing the *Stockholm* script. While writer–company collaborative practice lends itself to productions combining text and physical composition because it facilitates the generation of spoken, written and corporeal language (either simultaneously or in parallel), it is also imperative to have an outside, dramaturgical perspective to make sense of the different elements of creative input from the various collaborators involved in the process.

Source text and play text

In *Brontë*, Teale combined excerpts from *Jane Eyre*, *The Tenant of Wildfell Hall* and *Wuthering Heights* with letters and poems written by Charlotte, Emily and Anne in order to provide an insight into the minds of the sisters, whose personal lives have remained relatively unknown. In this way, she became responsible for adapting fictional and nonfictional source texts as well as constructing a narrative of her own – an approach to adaptation close to the one used by Stephen Brown on *Faster* than by Edmundson on *War and Peace*. Teale functioned as a writer/director in order to structure the text and staged the production in order to invite the audience to discover these stories (fictional, real and imagined), emphasizing the constructed, speculative nature of the story. This method of depicting the Brontë sisters' lives and adapting their novels contrasted with what Teale called the 'dreary, repetitive, uneventful' and exterior lives of 'drab domesticity' with the inner lives of 'soaring, unfettered imagination'.[18] While *War and Peace* began with the actor playing Pierre begin *War and Peace* as a modern-day British visitor to the Hermitage in St. Petersburg, *Brontë* began with a prologue with some of the characters in modern dress; the actors playing Charlotte, Emily and Anne begin *Brontë* as contemporary young women researching the lives of the Brontë sisters before they donned early Victorian costumes. The three anonymous women address each other and the audience, asking, 'How did it happen?' and saying, 'Three Victorian spinsters living in isolation on the Yorkshire moors', in order to introduce the characters they are about to play, as well as introduce Teale's central question regarding the Brontë sisters.[19] Teale noted that she began the play in this way in order to emphasize the fact that the play was 'a response to the Brontë story, not a piece of biography', so that the audience recognized that they were looking at this story 'through the filter of time'.[20] Her use of the word 'response' signals the unusual nature of this adaptation and its emphasis on the physical/visual as well as the textual/dialogic.

By drawing attention to the constructed nature of the story, the audience is alerted to the fact that the play is a response to the work of the Brontës and existing biographical material, rather than a realistic portrayal of their world. The play is held together by the narration of Charlotte, Emily and Anne, but these three characters also transform into the three anonymous, contemporary women discovering the Brontës' family history in the prologue and epilogue, and at intervals throughout the play, characters from the Brontës' novels. For example, Branwell often made an appearance in each writer's story-in-progress, serving as Heathcliff in Emily's *Wuthering Heights* or as Arthur Huntingdon in Anne's *The Tenant of Wildfell Hall*, suggesting that he, as one of the few young male figures in their lives, served as a model for the alcoholic, emotionally abusive male characters in their novels. In one of his drunken outbursts, Branwell tells his sisters, 'I used once to be loved by a beautiful woman. But she had a husband and he had a gun,' while reaching out aggressively to fondle Anne, making his sisters increasingly uncomfortable with the lines, 'Tell her ... I think of her night and day. Her flesh, her smell, the deep, dark places where I drank'.[21] The overall effect of *Brontë* was one that indicated that the audience was not simply watching a dramatization of the sisters' lives but was also bearing witness to their memories, imaginations and inner lives. Teale believed that the authors' imaginations were the key to understanding their lives, and so finding a way of dramatizing their 'inner world ... where they were really themselves' was crucial because 'otherwise, you'd just be looking at the surface of their existence'.[22] *Brontë* had a cast of six performers playing the parts of 12 characters, both historical figures and 'ghosts', characters from the sisters' novels. While the performers playing the father, the brother and Cathy/Bertha enter and exit the space, the performers playing Charlotte, Emily and Anne are mostly present, waiting at the edge of the wings – just visible to the audience – even after they have died, as if they are watching over each other.

Teale's play depicts the Brontës' canonical novels and their personal history in a way that explores notions of subjectivity and experience not only through dialogue but also through physical presence. The narrative focused on Charlotte, Emily and Anne's relationship not only to their work but also to each other, painting a picture of three women who relied on each other for creative and moral support, depicting their memories of childhood and fantasies through physical expression. Within the restrictions of the basic parameters of the narrative and characters of the source texts, Teale engaged with movement created by the performers and the movement director in order to reinvent and comment on this text by exploring the hidden or underdeveloped aspects of the story which interested her: 'The private experience of the characters.'[23] Like *Stockholm*, the text bears the imprint of the movement directors and performers' creative input through visual conceits and physical sequences developed within this writer/director model. For example, '*Lights change. Two months later.* CHARLOTTE *arrives home in coat and shawl with luggage. She sneezes.* ANNE *gives her a hanky as she continues her story*'.[24] This aspect of the text indicates a fluid, stylized passage of time, indicated by visual elements such as a change in lighting, music and costume (themselves created by Teale's design team); this approach not only underlines the surreal and constructed nature of the world of the play but also indicates an endlessness to the tedium of the sisters' lives, the only respite from which were the moments in which they write and escape from their day-to-day tasks. This approach to collaboration and writing facilitates Teale's particular brand of adaptation, allowing for the interruption of the depiction of the Brontë household with the short adapted scenes from the Brontës' novels, the imaginings and fantasies springing forth from the world around them. Similarly to Edmundson's transitions in *War and Peace*, Teale's approach relies on repeated visual motifs in order to facilitate both the narrative and the central themes in the production without having to depend too heavily on exposition.

The most prominent motif in the text, around which Teale structured the narrative, is the use of the metaphor of the haunted, tormented fictional characters as visual representations of Charlotte, Emily and Anne's hidden fears and desires, or what Crouch calls, 'a "split" in the heroine – a division between warring aspects of the character's subjectivity ... deconstruct[ing] and interrogat[ing] the heroine's public and private identities ... [t]o reveal hidden tensions and conflicts'.[25] The characters who most embody this motif are Cathy from Emily's *Wuthering Heights* and Bertha from Charlotte's *Jane Eyre*, representing Emily's intense emotional and spiritual connection to the surrounding moors and Charlotte's repressed inner sexual passion.[26] For example, as Charlotte writes to her teacher Mr Heger (played by the performer playing Charlotte's father as well as Mr Rochester), Bertha appears and begins to control Charlotte physically. Charlotte then gives in to her repressed inner desire for Mr Heger as Bertha comes on stage, crawling along the floor and grabbing on to Charlotte, *'no longer young and beautiful, but ravaged by years of madness and incarceration'*.[27] The character of Bertha (which Teale refers to as one of the 'ghosts' in the 2005 text) represented Charlotte's hidden, shameful longing as well as her creative writer's imagination. Teale created this sequence by weaving together her own imaginings, physical sequences devised by the performers and Hausman (and later, Ranken) and one of Charlotte's letters written in 1845 to her boarding school tutor in Brussels, Constantin Héger – an older, married man for whom Charlotte harboured an unreciprocated and secret infatuation (in this context serving as a kind of model for the Mr Rochester realized in Teale's adaptation).[28] Charlotte writes to herself onstage, reading aloud,

CHARLOTTE. Dear Sir. Day and night I find neither rest nor peace. For three months I have waited and still you torture me with no reply. Nothing. Not a morsel. Not a mouthful. It is cruel. The poor need little to live. They ask only for the crumbs that fall from the table. Deny them this and they die of hunger.[29]

While Charlotte struggles with writing this letter to Monsieur Héger, crossing out words, the tension building inside of her, we see that *'BERTHA is behind CHARLOTTE, wild with longing and frustration.'*[30] Suddenly, Charlotte, possessed by the spirit of Bertha, bursts out with 'I love you. I love you. I love you. You can't do this to me. If I was a dog you wouldn't do this to me. I wish I was your dog so I could follow you and smell you and lick your shoes and have you beat me and...' while

Bertha throws herself to the floor in pain and frustration, a symbolized embodiment of Charlotte's own thwarted passions.[31] In Charlotte's *Jane Eyre*, Bertha is completely dehumanized, being described as a 'beast' nearly as large as Mr Rochester (in comparison to the childlike Jane), and does not speak but rather growls like 'some strange wild animal', 'athletic' and full of 'virile force'.[32] In Teale's adaptation, Bertha is portrayed as a constituent part of Charlotte's personality, representing her repressed, shameful desires – an abused woman, locked away, rather than a subhuman creature.

In the author's note for the 2011 publication of the text, Teale explained that Bertha was represented in three phases throughout the play, expressing different stages of Charlotte's social and intellectual development: at first, in her childhood, Bertha represented Charlotte's fantasy of what it would be to be a beautiful grown woman; she then became 'an expression of the part of Charlotte (sexual longing, rage, frustration, loneliness) which she wished to disown, conceal from others'; and later, in the second act of the play, once *Jane Eyre* has been published (in the play), Bertha became the evil and immoral 'antithesis' of Charlotte's imagining of herself as Jane Eyre, the 'good angel'.[33] Govan, Nicholson and Normington explain that the adaptation process 'demands the development of metaphor' and that 'companies that

Shared Experience's *Brontë*, 2011 © Robert Day

work in this genre often seek to open up the texts to new interpretations. The cultural status of the sources is challenged, often inverted
or politicized'.[34] Teale examines the historical-biographical material as
well as the source texts through this psychoanalytic lens, this metaphor
of the characters as elements of the authors' psyches, in order to make
her intertextual approach to the play dramatically viable and appropriate for Shared Experience as a company with a tradition of physical
interpretation. In doing so, Teale is challenging the concept that Jane is
the outright hero of *Jane Eyre* and Bertha is the monster who attempts
to destroy the man she loves, standing in the way of her future; instead,
she re-envisions Bertha as a victim of Victorian morality and repression.

The role of the writer/director and text

Like *War and Peace*, the authorship of *Brontë* can be seen in layers; the
source texts (letters, novels and poems) written by the three Bontë sisters
were adapted into a dramatic text by Teale, the movement sequences
were devised by Hausman and the performers, while Teale 'authored'
the production by bringing together the textual and the physical language. Meckler note that Teale's adaptations are like 'auteur pieces'
because she follows her own vision, supporting the text she writes with
staging that she has conceived herself.[35] However, this interpretation
of Teale's work is not entirely accurate – her vision also relies on the
ideas and material generated by her collaborators, such as performers,
designers and movement directors. Interestingly, Teale believes that her
approach to working as a writer/director has been influenced by her
tenure working within the company because 'the Shared Experience
approach means that the pieces need to be shaped and formed quite
very specifically in order to use this expressionistic approach', linking
the identity of the company to a particular theatrical style and linking
that style to her approach to making work.[36] Additionally, the nature
of Teale's role as a writer/director on *Brontë* is influenced by her intention with respect to adaptation process, which was to make the narrative and the experience of the characters relatable to contemporary
audiences while retaining what she believed was the essence of the
time period and culture in which the novel was written – a reflection
of what Teale refers to as 'the Shared Experience approach'. In order to
do this, she investigated the emotional and psychological motivations

of the characters by creating a narrative that pulled together the writings of Charlotte, Emily and Anne Brontë (which constituted their public-facing identities) and also their private lives, both imagined by Teale and evidenced by their letters. She collaborated with the performers and Hausman in order to make this tension between the public and the private visible to the audience through what Ranken called the 'metaphysics' of the physical language of the productions.[37] Teale created a mise en scène that would support her vision by exploring the source texts and research about the Brontës in discussions with her creative team, collaborating with her designers and Hausman in order to develop visual motifs for the production; Teale's collaborative process allowed her to change the script as a result of discussions with her creative team, workshops and rehearsals.

Part II   The commissioned writer/director: David Farr for Filter

In comparison to *Faster*, *Water* was a more streamlined collaborative process that involved both devising material as an ensemble and writing text independently. Writer/director David Farr met Filter Artistic Director Tim Phillips in 2005 because Phillips had arranged a meeting with the Lyric Hammersmith Theatre's previous director, Neil Bartlett, as a result of the success of *Faster*. By 2006, Bartlett had left the Lyric and Farr was the new artistic director; Farr agreed to work with Filter on a new project after seeing the result of three weeks of research and development in which Phillips, Dimsdale and Roberts were involved: a 45-minute scratch performance consisting of a series of devised scenes. Farr commissioned Filter to create a new piece based on the work that they created during the development week, initially paying them each an authorship fee and signing them on as writers.[38] It was agreed that Farr would act as a writer/director, and John Clark and Jon Bausor were hired as lighting and set designers, respectively. Broadly speaking, the devising process and rehearsal process were two stages of work involving the larger artistic team, with Farr helping to structure the project while scripting and directing it. In total, starting from the first research-and-development period, the whole process took 18 months. Although Farr commissioned Filter as the artistic director of the Lyric, I refer to this model of working as the commissioned writer/artistic director model because Farr – unlike Teale – was collaborating with a company for whom he was not the artistic director.

The process of creating *Water* was markedly different from the process used to create *Faster* in that Filter was able to modify their approach to working in order to negotiate the company hierarchy with respect to the role of the writer (and in this case, the writer/director) more successfully in response to a more clear-cut agreement, a stronger vision for the production and the aid of a more experienced writer. In response to Farr's acknowledged specialized skill of scripting and directing in a devising context, Filter was clearer in their contractual agreement with him as well as in their decision to share the authorship of the project. *Faster* was a learning experience for Filter, and when they set out to create *Water*, the company knew that they wanted to work with someone like Farr, who was experienced in writing, directing and devising, who would be able to provide a stabilizing force for the project, much like the combination of Retallack and Brown did for *Faster*. Phillips explained that the company's relationship with Farr worked well primarily because Farr was a writer as well as a director, so he was able to construct a narrative using the different scenes the company devised, simplifying the whole process of transferring devised work from the rehearsal room to a script. Phillips said, 'A lot of [Farr's] job was figuring out … how to get from one scene to the next …. We can do it, but we're not writers. How to stage it … putting it together is more of a specialized job'.[39] What is interesting about Phillips's statement is that while in the context of *Faster*, the idea of using a 'writer' on the project made him wary, in the context of *Water*, the idea of using a director who was 'more writer than a director' was attractive because Filter had come to consider it more efficient than devising without a writer. Phillips enjoyed working with Farr, not only because he was a skilled writer and director but also because he allowed Filter the freedom to generate material while structuring the devised scenes into a coherent narrative framework. This process is similar to the writer-as-company-scribe model, but I argue that it is a distinct approach because of the impact of Farr's expertise as a director on the project. In working with Farr, Filter had hired not only a writer/director but also a dramaturg to oversee and coordinate the devised and written material. Here, I turn to Cathy Turner and Synne K. Behrndt's definition of a dramaturg as 'someone who helps keep the process open, while at the same time being aware that decisions have to be made in order to shape the material towards performance'.[40] Kate McGrath, who had performed the role of drama-turg for *Faster*, was not involved in *Water*, leaving Filter with the task of finding someone who could fulfil the role of dramaturg. For Farr to consider the staging and the narrative of the production simultane-ously, it was inevitable that he would also play a dramaturgical role for the company, as there was no dramaturg assigned to the production. (It is interesting to note that in the programme, Farr is listed as 'director' rather than 'writer/director' and the only other signification of author-ship is a credit that *Water* was 'created by Filter'.)

As a result of Filter and the Lyric negotiating the collaborative pro-cess together in a contractual as well as discursive fashion, the process of creating *Water* was established on more formal, precisely defined terms than *Faster*. Although Dimsdale, Phillips and Roberts tend to perceive single-authored work as less dynamic than purely devised or partially devised/partially scripted work, Phillips conceded that the job of scripting and/or performing the role of dramaturg on a devised pro-ject was 'specialized' and that he, Dimsdale and Roberts were not able to perform these particular roles. *Faster* had been a challenging experi-ence of bringing together devising and writing, of developing a produc-tion and a process at the same time with a group of practitioners who were not familiar with each other's tastes and methods and were not completely clear about the objectives for the production. Since Farr was regarded by Filter to be an expert not only in directing and writing but also in combining a scripting process with a devising one, the company became more comfortable in working with writing and text in their col-laborative process. In this way, the writer/director model afforded Filter an added sense of trust that facilitated both the creative process and communication among the collaborators.

Research and development

Since there was no formal, preconceived methodology for the gen-eration and composition of the production, Filter and Farr relied on a flexible system of checks and balances in order to keep miscommu-nication to a minimum; it was agreed between Filter and Farr that a combination of research, discussion, devising and writing would be the primary means of composing the production and script. As a semi-decentralized company, Filter combined the centralization of the top-down company hierarchy with the decentralization of collaborative creation and devising. Phillips explained, 'We really felt our way through it much more than any other show we've done'.[41] *Water* was an original production which revolved around three narrative strands about a diver, a political advisor and two estranged brothers. Farr was responsible for the bulk of the scripting and the text, while (similarly to *Faster*) the themes, aesthetics and approaches to staging had been decided during the research-and-development period, from which the characters and storyline stemmed. *Water* dealt with the stories of Joe, a cave diver; Claudia, a government worker; Graham, an environmental officer; and Peter, Graham's father. The play combines the personal with the political, investigating each character's story, focusing on his or her increasingly self-inflicted condition of isolation while also drawing from themes such as globalization and climate change. Since the scope of the piece was so broad at this point, the company divided the research as to what topic would concern each company member's character. Dimsdale developed and researched material pertaining to his character, the diver, while Roberts did the same for his character, in preparation for the devising sessions with Farr, Phillips and performer Victoria Mosely (who had been involved with *Faster*). Within the devising process, Dimsdale, Phillips, Roberts and Mosely were guided by Farr in the form of what Phillips called 'semi-structured improvisations'.[42] Farr, Dimsdale, Phillips and Roberts had ongoing discussions about the progression and direction of the production, the background research they were doing, what they believed was missing and what they wanted to eliminate. Throughout the project, Farr maintained the outside eye of a dramaturg in order to maintain a sense of balance and structure amidst all the writing, researching and devising that the company was doing both together and independently of each other. 'The dramaturg is there to facilitate someone else's vision, or maybe more accurately is there to facilitate the production's vision'.[43] Farr not only was able to be an external organizing presence for the company as a writer but was also as a director to facilitate the company's vision for the production as it emerged.

According to Farr and Filter, there was a strong autobiographical element to the *Water* text, which was a result of one of the company's approaches to the devising process but also a by-product of the negotiation of the authorial power shared between the commissioned writer/director and the company. Dimsdale explained that one of the techniques Filter used early on in the devising process to develop the characters was that of hot-seating, or the cross-examination of one performer playing a particular character by the rest of the company in order to answer a series of questions about their character, an approach to character development through devising.[44] In order to keep a record of the developments made during the hot-seating process, someone within the group (generally Farr) would record the performer's responses to the questions and then incorporate that material into the developing script, either developed into a monologue or as a contribution to a scene in the form of dialogue. It is unsurprising that much of the material generated for *Water* turned out to be semi-autobiographical for the company members, as they based the characters on themselves or people they knew. Through the contributions of autobiographical material, the devised, improvised and written contributions were able to be distributed relatively evenly between Farr, Phillips, Dimsdale, Roberts and Mosely, whether they contributed in the form of improvised, physical or written composition. In this way, no one person working on the production was an 'expert' in any particular subject – everyone in the company had a given topic to research but was also at liberty to improvise (or in Farr's case, to write) using personal experiences. While Farr had the advantage of being able to maintain a kind of dramaturgical perspective on the development of the project, the performers had the advantage of working with material that was individualized to them and readily accessible during improvisation sessions.

The use of autobiographical material in the devising process functioned not only as a way to generate scenes but also as a bridge between what the performers wanted to achieve in terms of character development and what they needed Farr's specialized skill set as a writer/director to do. Being encouraged to delve into personal information in order to construct characters and a narrative during the devising process gave the performers a starting point from which to create characters with which they could become comfortable within a relatively unstructured devising process. Farr's relationship with each performer differed according to the nature of their involvement in the production and also their own inclination and ability to write. Farr worked closely with Dimsdale and Roberts to create the characters of Joe, Graham and Peter, helping script and edit from the accumulated improvised scenes, pieces written alone by Roberts and Dimsdale and excerpts from their combined research material. Roberts stated that since he was not a writer, he worked closely with Farr and that Farr's role was to, 'together with me, try to find the voice of Graham and the voice of Pete the father, but the voice that would sit comfortably with me the actor'.[45] Farr was able to help Roberts discover a character through structured improvisations that was both meaningful to him and suitable for him as a performer that he was not able to script himself, as well as later transfer the devising to the written script. Govan, Nicholson and Normington explain that 'Autobiographical performance is a distinct mode of working with an emphasis on a self-reflexive, creative methodology' and that the 'tensions' inherent in staged autobiographical content 'are explored and even exploited for theatrical effect'.[46] The material that the company produced was fruitful for Farr, as it allowed him to experiment with the balance between the similarities and the differences between the characters and the performers who created them within the script. The element of autobiography is often highlighted within the script in Farr's use of self-reflexive language, which gives the impression that the dialogue used is intended to remind the audience that what they are watching has been created collaboratively by Filter. For example, as the play begins, Dimsdale addresses the audience directly as himself before he becomes his different characters, saying, 'Hi, welcome to the Lyric Hammersmith, I'm Ollie. We'll be taking you to a lot of different places tonight, but we'll start by going back twenty-six years and travelling 4,725 miles west from here'.[47] When Graham meets his half-brother Kris for the first time, who is a DJ in Vancouver, the radio station depicted onstage plays the music of Cathead, Phillips's band.

In contrast to *Faster*, *Brontë* and *War and Peace*, as it was an original work, the process used to create *Water* was more similar to that of *Stockholm* in that Filter had started by researching, discussing and devising material around a theme and then developed characters and a narrative. For *Water*, however, the central argument of the production came later in the development of the project, as a result of Farr's role within the process both as a facilitator/dramaturg and also as a writer. Farr explained that he developed what he referred to as a 'thesis' while reading a book called H_2O about the properties of water which had been given to him by the company; he proposed to the company that they could centre the entire production around the way in which the oxygen and hydrogen atoms that comprise a water molecule bond and 'whether or not we have the ability to literally behave like water, to reach out and be sociable and use each other, rather than being individualistic'.[48] As a result of this discovery, Farr was able to help Filter construct a strong but flexible narrative framework around a dramaturgical concept. Farr explained that Dimsdale's plot strand of the diver and his great dive into a deep cave 'became a metaphor for individualistic human striving onwards and onwards' and that the 'notion of making contact with other human beings … became central'.[49] In developing this line of thinking, Farr was able to facilitate further developments in the devising and scripting process, organizing the ideas the company was producing without discouraging or confusing them. I again turn to Turner and Behrndt to illuminate Farr's role:

> Here, the dramaturg becomes a kind of artistic advisor, who looks to develop and deepen the conceptual approach through suggesting practical solutions as to how the theme could be explored. There is a simultaneous engagement with research and finding practical ways into the work.[50]

In devised work, an overarching metaphor, often constructed by the dramaturg, becomes important to frame the work created and to assist in the development of a narrative. Farr helped facilitate the research and devising that Dimsdale, Phillips and Roberts were doing by suggesting an ideological framework for the production that was simple enough to allow for a variety of different characters and narrative strands but complex enough to create a strong overall message. In creating this ideological and dramaturgical framework, Farr developed a structure which could accommodate the devised material, texts written by various members of the company and ideas that arose from group discussions.

Writing, scripting and devising

Within this writer/director model, *Water* was composed of three kinds of material: written, scripted from the devising and physical approaches to staging. Farr made a distinction between the work he scripted that was taken from the both devised scenes and exercises and the work he had written outside the devising process by saying that he believed the work devised for the production was more personal, about the characters' emotions and relationships, while the written work was more of a political nature.[51] Emma Govan, Helen Nicholson and Katie Normington explain,

> Devising performance is socially imaginative as well as culturally responsive, and articulates between the local and the global, the fictional and the real, the community and the individual, the social and the psychological. ... Devised performance is an agency of both personal self-expression and community or civic activism.[52]

The process of devising is often as eclectic as that which Filter developed to devise *Water* because it is a flexible form of creation, and as Govan, Nicholson and Normington explain, it is one that can bridge a number of different subjects and styles of performance. Phillips commented that in producing a show that centred on water, the company – and Farr especially – believed they had a political responsibility to engage with the subject of climate change and rising water levels. They approached global warming as a metaphor, rooting the politics in the personal, semi-autobiographical narratives so as to make the more politically driven aspect of the production seem more intrinsically related to the main narrative.[53] Farr focused on developing the characters' emotions and relationships with the actors because he believed, from previous experiences, that it was too difficult to try to devise politically informed scenarios with a group of people – that everyone in the room had to be equally well informed about the subject matter in order for the improvisations to be accurate and fully developed, which would have required more time for everyone to have done the necessary research.[54]

Since Farr was operating as a director as well as a writer, like Teale, his close collaborations which informed the aesthetics and composition of the production included the designers as well as the performers (by which I also mean Phillips, who created the soundscape on stage each night). The result of collaborating with designer Bausor from an early stage in the project was that he lent another dimension to the way in which the story was developed; he focused on inscribing the space in order to establish an aesthetic and a series of dramatic conceits, using visuals and proxemics to assist Farr and the company in constructing a narrative and using a design-centred approach to create expositional shortcuts. Farr believed that the design scheme of *Water* encouraged the company to develop the characters and the story alongside the practical conceits of how one should depict the world of the play. He called creating a narrative or characters from an image 'working backwards' and gave as an example the scene on the squash court where the character Peter is playing a game of squash with a colleague who encourages him to apply for a job in Vancouver.[55] Towards the beginning of the project, Phillips, Bausor, Dimsdale and Roberts came up with the idea of two characters playing squash at the beginning of the period of development and figured out how to stage it; at first, Farr rejected the idea because he did not believe that it had a useful place in the story, but as the company pressed him to consider the scene further, he incorporated it into the production, devising around the concept of a squash game. Farr reflected that one of the benefits of working collaboratively with Filter was 'having an armoury of visual ideas ... subconsciously create[d] in the dark ... but with a sort of sense that you've got a theme'.[56] This compromise between structured and unstructured work allowed Filter to create images, characters and ideas around a theme without feeling hampered by the pressure to create a cohesive story right away. This creative process was also a useful negotiation of power and creative control between Filter and Farr. Because Filter could come up with dramatic conceits and ideas in the beginning and as a commissioned writer/ director, Farr could mould the raw material into a text later on in the process. Farr's dramaturgical overview, which called for the company to continually consider the way in which the project would function structurally balanced Filter's desire to work conceptually, laterally and visually. Since Farr enjoyed collaborating with practitioners who were more inclined to 'create visually' than he was, he valued Bausor's skills in the way that Filter valued his, allowing Bausor a certain amount of authority to design and devise various ways of staging the production.[57]

A result of including Bausor in the development of the narrative was that the nature of the script is such that each scene is relatively brief and the locations within the play change constantly; *Water* shifts back and forth rapidly between the perspectives of Graham, his father Peter, his ex-girlfriend Claudia and Joe the diver. The way in which the company decided to stage this particularly episodic production was to begin with a base of a minimal set that conveyed a stark, contemporary and even cold appearance with a heavy emphasis on shadows, silhouettes and clean lines. This minimal space allowed the company to shift locations rapidly, flying in screens, frames and pieces of furniture from above. Transitions were facilitated by images and sounds that were able to shift in order to signify different locations, cultures, time periods and atmospheres. For example, when Graham finds an X-ray of his father's lung, it is projected onto a large screen, which then facilitates the transition to a scene revolving around Joe the diver; the projection of the lung functions as a signifier of the cancer from which Graham's father Peter died, as well as to foreshadow Joe's death by drowning during a dive, reinforcing repeated themes of water, isolation, sinking, separation, loneliness and death. The performers in the different narrative strands of the play – although all sharing and passing through the same physical space, like ghosts – do not acknowledge each other or connect dialogically. The text, soundscape, staging and design complement each other, blending and weaving together as the audience is continually reminded of the loneliness of the contemporary human condition made lonelier by modern technology. The result of this style is that each character's emotional experience is underscored and heightened as the play shifts back and forth from scene to scene and moment to moment between realism and more stylized forms of representation. The most frequent directorial and authorial technique used to achieve this effect is the form of direct address. For example, the audience is taken back to Vancouver University in 1981 where Graham's father, Peter, is giving a lecture on marine biology and rising water levels. Peter uses the metaphor of human relationships to demonstrate how hydrogen atoms bond to form water particles, emphasizing the role of cooperation in fighting climate change:

> How successful we are in our reaction to these challenges may rely on our ability to be like water. To reach beyond our own selves and bond with those around us. But are we capable of doing so? Or are we destined to be increasingly solitary, alone, and unbonded, constantly pushing further and further as individuals, placing the planet on which we live under intense pressure and leaving us unable to connect both with each other and the world we live in.[58]

Peter's lecture stands alone as a monologue, going on for another short paragraph, addressed to us the audience as if we are the audience in the lecture hall at the university, feeling the intensity of this character's challenge to his students. This monologue stands alone from the rest of the dialogue in the play, emphasizing its thematic and narrative significance.

Filter's *Water*, 2007 © Simon Kane

In addition to Farr, Bausor and the performers involved in the devising, Phillips's work on the sound design for *Water* represented another authorial influence within the process. While Bausor created visual cues and design concepts to facilitate the narrative and scene transitions, taking the place of lengthy exposition, Phillips's use of sound functioned similarly. Phillips used a combination of realistic and more abstract, non-representational sound in order to create settings and atmosphere for each scene, as well as merging two different sounds together to create a new scene or indicate a shift in the mood of the moment; for example, in an early scene where Graham is at home in Norfolk, the sound of his typing on the computer morphs into the sound of raindrops outside, connecting the themes of isolation and water aurally. Phillips's choices in sound design indicate that Filter is concerned with the power of suggestion and the economy of subtle parallels rather than lengthy exposition and extensive dialogue. This approach to staging is reminiscent of Teale's collaboration with Hausman and how they engaged with movement in order to express the unspoken subtext of *Brontë*. About her own work, American director Anne Bogart says, 'I find it more interesting to trigger associations in the audience than psychologies'.[59] Filter aims to create work that makes room for the audience to make thematic connections through the details of set and sound design, in addition to performance. In both *Faster* and *Water*, Filter focused on a sound-driven approach and a method of staging to suit the narrative of each so that the writing, design and performance style serve the story, illuminating the central intellectual argument of the piece along the way. Phillips says Filter is concerned with developing engaging methods of staging in order to accommodate the 'layers of performance', the way in which the sound, movement, set and dialogue are integrated into the production in order to create what he refers to as 'a total experience'.[60] As a result, the two stories (about a man who goes in search of his family and a deep-sea diver attempting to break the world record) are created by piecing together the details or fragments of stories, allowing the audience to be active in putting together the narrative and in understanding the secondary, political message about the dangers of global warming.

Conclusion: authorship and the role of the writer/ director

The authorship of *Water* is twofold: those responsible for the origination of the material for the project but also those who had the most influence regarding the final editing and structuring of the material. Dimsdale, Roberts and Phillips are the authors and legal owners of each Filter production; the final product is a reflection of the vision of the central artistic directorship, but one which could have been realized only with the help of outside artists. Filter's method of composition is structured in such a way that the artistic autonomy of the writer is limited and the writer's work regulated by the company's semi-decentralized hierarchy. The authorship of *Water* is shared between the directors, writers, dramaturg, designer and performers, as both written and non-written applications of creation of material were important to the genesis and structuring of each piece. Although Dimsdale, Phillips and Roberts had the final say in what was eliminated and what was kept in the final production, the stability and consistency of their relationship with Farr allowed him a nearly equal authorial position. Farr fulfilled Filter's role of the commissioned writer/director, able to make his own contributions while incorporating the scenes that the company devised, accepting Filter's final editorial decisions while unifying the work into a tangible, written whole and directing the company within the production along the way. Filter depended on Farr as an organizing, authorial presence in order to help shape, guide, and create material for the text for performance for *Water*, maintaining a balance between the chaos of creation and the order of writing and dramaturgy integral to their process.

Part III Practical strategies

Scripting and staging

Drawing from both Shared Experience and Filter's processes as framed by the writer/ director model, the following practical strategies are designed to aid the writer/direc- tor in generating material pertaining to the scripting of the production as well as its staging, allowing the two elements to develop in a reciprocal fashion. Each strategy gives the writer/director an opportunity to generate and develop material with differ- ent types of collaborators. They are designed to be used to develop a new play from its earliest stages, gradually moving towards negotiating a process based on a more substantial performance text. These approaches can be applied to a process involving a new play or an adaptation of an existing source text.

Building a character

The following strategy is designed to aid a writer/director and performers with whom they are working to generate material in a character-driven approach. This strategy is most appropriate for the beginning of a collaborative process when very little mate- rial has been written or scripted, but there is a general sense of the concepts, charac- ters and stories involved in the project. It is, essentially, a combination of the 'research/ exploration' strategy from Chapter 2 and a general hot-seating process.

- Once the group has settled on the themes of the project and/or basic structure of the narrative, the writer/director (or the group together, depending on the preferences and hierarchy of the company) decides which performers will focus on developing which characters.
- Each performer is then assigned the task of researching *around* the character, examining source material that could help inform the role. For example, if the

character is a photographer, then that performer will research different photographers and decide who might make an interesting point of reference. If the character is a Soviet spy, the performer will then research the Soviet era and the KGB.

• The performers then bring in their research to the writer/director and company and present their findings, discussing possible directions in which to go and how those decisions might impact other characters as well as the narrative of the piece. The writer/director and performers can then use this discussion to inform their decisions regarding the nature of each character and how to focus the work being written and devised.

• As a next step, the writer/director and company can guide each performer through a hot-seating process, asking them questions as their characters in order to make discoveries in a spontaneous, organic and discursive fashion. The writer/director can either record this process with a video or take notes throughout.

• The writer/director can then extrapolate information gleaned through the hot-seating process in order to sketch some ideas for scenes, creating short premises or outlines. The performers can then use these sketches to devise material together, with the support of the writer/director.

Sound and vision

This strategy is intended to enable a writer/director to generate material in collaboration with performers, a movement director and a sound designer. It can be adjusted to be used either before any text has been written or as a response to a draft in development. This particular approach is suitable for a process involving a movement director or choreographer.

• The writer/director meets the sound designer/composer and the movement director to begin considering the ways in which the story can be told through sound and physicality. This process can begin when the script is in draft form or when the writer/director is at the beginning of the journey with the text and has only an outline of a story or a series of ideas. It is important to note that the latter will most likely produce a more collaborative process of working, involving other members of the company more deeply in the generation of material and ideas for the play text.

• In the case of a project in the stage before a draft of the play text has been written, the three collaborators can discuss narrative and other possible ideas. This is an opportunity for the writer/director, choreographer and sound designer to suggest possibilities to each other that might impact each other's spheres of influence within the production. For example, the choreographer might ask the sound designer or composer if it is possible to consider a particular quality in the soundscape that might facilitate a certain quality in the movement. (The same meeting can be had in the case of a script already in draft form; the discussion is likely to be more specific and focused, allowing the collaborators to refer to specific scenes and characters.)

- The following might be some questions to consider:
  - What is the general tone or feeling of the piece?
  - Who might be the central characters?
  - What is the setting(s) like?
  - What sort of performance space will the company be using? Is this a touring production? Is it site-specific or site-responsive?
  - What might some sounds or music associated with the piece be?
- The sound designer or composer goes away and takes some time to composes a piece of music or soundscape for a scene or segment of the play (in the case of the play existing in the form of a draft) or in response to an idea (in the case of the project being in a script-less stage).
- They then bring this element of sound into a workshop setting where the writer/ director, movement director and performers are present. The performers can then listen to the sound/music and find ways of responding to it, either organically or in response to direction from the choreographer (depending on the needs of the project and the company's preferred way of working). In the case of an existing play text being available, the company can engage with this process in response to the scene or segment of the text with which the sound designer was working when creating the sound/music.
- At this stage, the company can reflect on the relationship between the sound, movement and any existing text, focusing on developing and adjusting the work to suit the project. For instance, the writer/director might realize that the soundscape or piece of music might better suit a different segment of the play, desiring a different quality for that particular scene or moment. This decision will then influence the movement score. By the same token, the writer/director may make new discoveries about the text during this process and be inspired to write a new scene or rewrite old ones as a result.
- This approach can be repeated throughout the development and rehearsal process of the project and be adjusted to accommodate the needs of the production.

Inner and outer

This strategy is inspired not only by the working methods of Shared Experience but also by those of The Open Theater, which I discussed in Chapter 1. It is intended to explore the dichotomy of the internal workings of a character's fears, objectives and desires and the outer façade of that character in order to discover physical, emotional and dialogic possibilities for the piece. This approach can be attempted at various stages in the development of a play text or in the adaptation of a source text. It is geared towards generating material through writing and devising that will not only illuminate different aspects of the characters in the piece but also enable both the writer/director and the performers to have creative agency through a collaborative process. (It can also be modified to incorporate the input of a movement director or choreographer.) Ideally, this strategy will allow the writer/director and performers the opportunity to explore the characters in the piece more thoroughly. It would be useful for the writer/director and performers to have a discussion about each character before beginning, investigating different aspects of their speech, physicality, behaviour and relationships to each other.

1. The writer/director writes a scene that gives a glimpse into the characters' inner selves, their most private, hidden fears, desires, impulses and secrets. The performers play the scripted scene and when the writer/director claps their hands, the performers switch from playing this inner self to improvising physicality and/or dialogue relating to the external façade of the character.

2. The writer/director writes a scene that gives a glimpse into the characters' respective outer selves, where their external façade or public self is most prominent and their private, secret fears and desires are hidden. The performers play the scripted scene, and when the writer/director claps their hands, the performers switch from playing this outer self to improvising physicality and/or dialogue relating to the inner, hidden life of the character.

3. After completing the first two parts of this, the performers can then devise one physical gesture that represents the inner, private versions of their characters and another that represents the external, public versions. This gesture can be tied to a particular impulse discovered in the improvisations, to a moment in the script or a general concept relating to the character. As with the 'gesture' strategy in Chapter 2, the gestures in this case can be small or large, rooted in realism or stylized. The performers then work their way through any scripted scenes that the writer/director would like to explore, finding ways of incorporating these gestures as they go. The writer/director (or movement director) can then guide the ways in which these gestures are used, asking the performers to exaggerate more or minimize their movements, finding moments in the scenes where the gestures might serve the story and the characters' journeys.

5   The Writer as Poet

Chapter 5 will present a fourth model of collaborative writing: the writer as poet. This model considers writer–company collaboration by approaching writing as another element to be developed and integrated into the theatre-making process, rather than the central or guiding force. The writer as poet model can be seen in relation to Chapter 3's writer-as-company-scribe model in the sense that both processes rely on a more director-led rather than writer-led approach, the difference being that writer as poet has grown out of an ensemble-driven process. In this chapter, we will examine the relationship between Kneehigh's then-Artistic Director Emma Rice with writers Carl Grose and Anna Maria Murphy within Kneehigh's *Tristan and Yseult* (2003, 2014–2015). In examining this process, I hope to uncover the ways in which text and the writers functioned, particularly the ways in which poetry was generated and then used within the production as text for performance. As in the preceding chapters, after investigating this model of writer–company collaboration, I will present a number of practical strategies extrapolated from this model of working intended for the use of the reader in creating their own approach to the writer-as-poet model.

Part I   Anna Maria Murphy and Carl Grose for Kneehigh

Kneehigh was established by Mike Shepherd in Cornwall in 1980, run by Bill Mitchell from 1995 to 2005 and Rice from 2005 to 2012. The company was run jointly by Shepherd and Rice from 2012 to 2016, after which Shepherd returned to running it alone. In contrast to companies like Shared Experience and Frantic Assembly, their focus is not on new writing and facilitating the work of writers, per se, but rather on making new performance and engaging with writers and texts on a case by case basis, according to the perceived needs of the production. Although the company now tours nationally and internationally, it grew out of the tradition of theatre-in-education, providing a service to the communities in rural Cornwall. Kneehigh has the distinction of being the sole company in this study based outside London, and the setting for their work is significant to both their collaborative process and also the content of their material. The company's work can be described as being guided by an ethos of popular theatre and performance, engaged in discovering different ways of adapting both traditional and contemporary stories from a variety of sources that have become part of regional (*Tristan & Yseult*), national (*Brief Encounter*, 2008) and international folk culture (*Hansel & Gretel*, 2009). Kneehigh creates touring productions based on original and adapted material as well as pop-up, promenade performances under the subheading of the Kneehigh Rambles, developed by Murphy and also work for the company's nomadic theatre space, The Asylum. Similarly to the other companies in this study, Kneehigh has a core staff of producers, managers and administrators and draws from a large pool of performers, writers, designers, musicians and technicians on a project-by-project basis. The work the company makes and the process it uses are informed not only by its origins but also by the fact that members of the company are often flexible in their roles and in their involvement with Kneehigh. For example, Mitchell designs productions for Shepherd and Rice, but during his tenure as artistic director, he directed Rice as a performer, and Shepherd often performs as well. Shepherd and Rice's remit evolved from making theatre for the communities around them to treating their national and international audiences as members of a larger community. Catherine Love and Diana Damian describe the work as focusing on 'locating a certain universal and playful morality in their architecture', that it is 'diverse, yet always in the spirit of playful celebration; a sort of contemporary carnivalesque.'[1] Kneehigh's approach to adaptation is more similar to Teatro Vivo (which I will explore in the next chapter) than it is to Shared Experience; the company draws on popular stories, myths and fables as the basis of their productions and stages them using circus techniques, physical theatre, song and dance in order to reach those who might not normally attend the theatre as well as seasoned playgoers. Rice links the company's work to the primitive human instinct to engage in social and religious rituals, and she believes that the purpose of their work is to help audiences feel that they are a part of a larger community through storytelling.

Kneehigh's history and identity as an ensemble has shaped their process of working as much as the directors' and writers' tendencies as practitioners. Grose and Murphy were both involved in the company as devising performers before they worked as writers, which suggests that they had a deeper, more comprehensive understanding of Kneehigh's ensemble-driven process and ethos than would an outside writer. Duška Radosavljević's defines 'ensemble' as a theatre-making group 'ultimately geared towards acknowledging the centrality of the actor/ performer's contribution to the process of theatre-making'[2] and the 'ensemble way of working' as an ethos of collective, collaborative practice in which company members make 'the same kind of contribution' through devising or make 'distinct kinds of contribution towards the same artistic outcome', such as writing, directing, composing, designing or performing.[3] Both the company's process and the work it produces are eclectic and playful; they have engaged performers who also work as musicians, circus performers, aerialists, jugglers, singers and dancers to devise and perform the productions; the work itself has been staged in tents, village halls, castles, quarries and harbours, in addition to more conventional theatre spaces. In this ensemble approach, Kneehigh pulls from a variety of performance skills in their productions, creating roles to display performers' aerial work, musical talents or even magic tricks, embedding their distinct personalities and ethnic or national identities in the text. For example, in *Tristan and Yseult*, the role of Yseult was originated by Éva Magyar, a Hungarian performer; Yseult's foreignness is signalled through the use of Magyar's translation of parts of the text into Hungarian, which remains un-translated for the English-speaking audience in the text and the performance.

Kneehigh has collaborated with a number of other writers, such as Tom Morris, Nick Darke, Annie Siddons and Tanika Gupta, and Rice herself has adapted the script for several productions as a writer/director (both alone and in collaboration with Morris). However, in this chapter, I will focus on the writings of Grose and Murphy because of the unique approach to collaboration that they have developed with Rice by engaging with poetry and focus on the ways in which it positions the text with respect to collaborative writing. I believe it is useful to make a distinction between dramatic writing and poetry, as the material written by Grose and Murphy for *Tristan and Yseult* adheres to a particular rhythm, meter and/or rhyme scheme and engages in symbolism in a way that much contemporary writing does not. Grose met

Shepherd as a teenager on a regional youth-theatre project and began working with Kneehigh as a performer soon afterwards; his first writing project for the company was as a co-writer with Murphy on *Tristan and Yseult* (2003, 2005, 2013–2015), which led to work on later productions, such as *The Wild Bride* (2010), *The Umbrellas of Cherbourg* (2011) and *Hansel and Gretel* (2009). Murphy began her work with the company as an untrained performer doing theatre-in-education projects in the mid 1980s and first wrote for Kneehigh in 1993 when she wrote a part that she herself played in a Wild Walk promenade piece, which eventually led to further writing for the company, including productions such as *Tristan and Yseult, The Red Shoes* (2000, 2003, 2010), *The Bacchae* (2004), *Don John* (2008) and *Midnight's Pumpkin* (2012).

Summary of Grose and Murphy's role

In making *Tristan and Yseult*, Rice chose to work with writers to create text, rather than adapt the work herself, and explains that she 'cast' Grose and Murphy in the role of the writers, as she cast the performers, designers and musicians, choosing each practitioner for their particular style and voice; she believed that it was important to work with both because they each had a distinct contribution to make in their writing.[4] Their backgrounds as performers are especially important to their relationship to Kneehigh in that they have developed the capacity to understand the importance of play and playfulness in the work, the process of a kind of call and response between the director and the various practitioners with whom they work in the rehearsal room. The writing was split in various ways between Grose and Murphy – one writer concentrating on some characters, the other concentrating on other characters and sometimes the two overlapping or writing scenes or sections together. Grose worked in the beginning with Rice to find a structure for the text that would allow the director's vision to be reconciled with the source material. Grose and Murphy brought sections of material (poems, monologues, songs) into the research-and-development period, working with Rice, the designers, musicians and performers to discover possibilities not only for the text but also for the staging. While scripting scenes for the play, Grose and Murphy also wrote songs, on which they collaborated with the company's musical director, Stu Barker. By time rehearsals began, the writers were able to bring a rough draft of the text into rehearsals, which was then altered and rewritten as needed in collaboration with the director, in response to the contributions from the rest of the company.

Creating a foundation for the work

While many of the models in this book engage with a research-and-development period designed to serve the writer's process and generate material for or to explore possibilities for staging the text, the process which Kneehigh employs at the beginning of and throughout their rehearsal process is intended to serve the company and encourage the ensemble to come to an understanding regarding the nature of the show, to ask questions, to produce initial, instinctive responses to the story that Rice or Shepherd have chosen to adapt. The role that the writer(s) play in this process is not to respond by generating a draft of a text from which the company works as a starting point for the production (as a writer would for Shared Experience or Frantic Assembly), but rather to become a part of the ensemble and connect with the company's responses to the story, as well as respond to the director's needs with respect to the text – how the director perceives the text as functioning within the process at that point. Although this model could be considered similar to the writer-as-company-scribe model in the way that the writer is expected to respond to the needs of the company, the writer-as-poet model engages with the text as one component among many in the collaborative process and is less reliant on the writer to develop the narrative. At the beginning of the process, the company comes together to write their first instincts regarding the story, what they believe the themes and key moments might be and what they anticipate might cause problems; this piece of paper stays up on the rehearsal room wall and 'forms the agenda' throughout the rehearsal period – a physical symbol of the ensemble ethos of the company.[5] A typical rehearsal period for Kneehigh is five weeks with a five-day research-and-development period, which would involve roughly five or six performers, the writer(s), the director, musical director and designers. Grose notes that the company often has a rough idea of the set in place and gives the performers an opportunity to play games and improvise around that set in order to allow the constructed space to inform the work that is generated.[6] Performer Joanna Holden (who was in Kneehigh's

2010 production of *Hansel and Gretel*) explained to Radosavljević in an interview that Kneehigh used a number of approaches to devising with which she was familiar from working with other ensembles such as Told By An Idiot and V-TOL Dance Company, which she described as 'rough theatre', 'broad brushstrokes, an outline, and then carefully filling in the details.'[7] The director asks the performers to use props and costumes to get an idea of their characters and the ways in which they might interact; this approach then gives the writer(s) ideas for possibilities that they can then incorporate into the text they generate and also prepare to construct a text that will be able to accommodate the ideas for staging, music and physical sequences that may come out of the rehearsal process later on. Rice says that if she has set the foundation for this process well enough, she is left with 'a huge palette from which to start creating' and the ideas that come out of the R&D process from the company will all contribute to building the world of the play.[8] Grose and Murphy are often in the rehearsal room in order to engage with the collaborative development process and later, during rehearsals, be able to respond to the changes Rice needs them to make to the text.

For *Tristan and Yseult*, Grose and Murphy worked largely with poems as the basis of their text partly because this medium allowed them to work in a flexible way, facilitating the ensemble aspect of the collaborative process. During the research-and-development week, Grose and Murphy brought in poems, songs and monologues they had written to try out with Rice and the performers, responding to the workshopping of the material and any material generated by improvisation.[9] Some of the poems they wrote were able to be transformed into songs with the help of Barker if Barker and Rice believed that poem lent itself particularly to music. Using the medium of poetry allows both Rice and Barker the flexibility to decide which aspects of the text will function as dialogue and which will function as songs, which as Murphy notes, is important to decide early on in the process not only so that the performers can have time to learn the music, but also so that the songs can be an integral aspect to the story.[10] By writing poems that can stand alone as thoughts, concepts or moments in the piece, Grose and Murphy enable Rice to split practitioners within the ensemble into pairs or small groups within the rehearsal barns, assigning them tasks in respect to trying out material so that the time is used efficiently and work is continually being created and developed. While Rice ultimately oversees this process, she allows the practitioners within the ensemble (writers, designers, musicians or performers) artistic autonomy to create short pieces that can then be brought back to her to watch. Stuart McLoughlin, a performer who has worked with Kneehigh, explains that Rice asks practitioners to make her 'an offer', which she then reviews and shapes with suggestions, and that the general feeling in the R&D and rehearsal rooms is one of structured, focused experimentation as well as openness.[11] Instead of workshopping a play text whose integrity is contingent upon its wholeness, Grose and Murphy develop their piecemeal interpretation of the story, which is then woven into the ensemble process during the R&D period, and further developed in the time between the R&D and rehearsals. This approach to writing also facilitates the division of labour, allowing Grose and Murphy to work on the text without having to be in the same room together.

The text is a reflection not only of the various interpretations and retellings that emerged from the process of adapting the original Tristan and Yseult myth but also of the authorial arrangement between Grose, Murphy and Rice. The production is an adaptation of the medieval Cornish legend of a doomed affair between Yseult, an Irish princess, and Tristan, a French knight who brings Yseult back to King Mark of Cornwall as a prize from a battle with the Irish king; the pair are eventually discovered, Yseult returns to King Mark and Tristan marries Whitehands, but both Tristan and Yseult die at the end. Grose and Murphy's poetry reflects the layered nature of the source material, conveying a variety of cultural influences on the play and the way in which Kneehigh plays with time shifts and timelessness. Grose explains that he and Murphy included different styles of poetry, which added 'a classical feel, a musicality of text' and 'elevate[d] the language out of the domestic'.[12] In terms of the acknowledgement of authorship, in the credits for the production, Rice is listed as adaptor and director and Grose and Murphy are credited as writers: Rice is the one making the final decisions regarding the material used and the way that material is interpreted and dramatized.[13] The production was intended to be rooted in medieval folklore but also informed by a pseudo-1950s aesthetic and inspired by the films of Quentin Tarantino, which Rice believed would give the story a more contemporary feel.[14] In the initial writing process, Grose generated material in response to his independent research on the original legend and also worked with Rice in order to find ways of telling the story.[15] He and Rice cut roughly two-thirds of the original story, which contained 'the more fantastical Medieval elements' such as 'dragons and lepers', in order to serve Rice's more contemporary vision: he was inspired to start the play with the death of Tristan and work back to the beginning in the next scene by Tarantino's *Reservoir Dogs*, where the character of Mr Orange is shown in the beginning and explained by the end of the film.[16]

Murphy's approach to the work was less structural and more instinctual than Grose's – she created her poetry that fed into the script from generative foundation exercises such as creating boxes and notebooks filled with inspirational objects and material. One of the central strategies Murphy employs when writing is a 'kenning', a poem formed by any number of stanzas, each stanza being a kind of riddle with two describing words, often used in Old Norse and Anglo-Saxon poetry.[17] Murphy believes this approach is useful because it allows her to describe characters quickly and simply but also because it serves a second function of facilitating her work with Kneehigh's educational and community programmes, especially for those involving children.[18] For example, *Tristan & Yseult* opens with a speech that includes a kenning for the Love Spotters, a kind of Greek chorus of unloved people who comment on the play's narrative:

LOVE SPOTTERS

We are the unloved.

We are the Love Spotters.

Passion watchers

Kiss clockers

Love is at arm's length.[19]

The kenning influences this speech by simplifying their uncertain role in the play for the audience and, as Murphy notes, cuts to the 'essence' of these characters, working in figurative language that builds on the eclectic, visually and sonically rich design elements of the production.[20] Murphy works quickly and generates a large amount of material, which is perhaps why she is comfortable with Rice's exercising her editorial authority over the text, keeping anything that she believes contributes to the telling of the story she has envisioned and getting rid of anything that does not. Since Murphy has been a member of Kneehigh for many years and began as a performer, she understands the process and knows the rules before she has even begun working on the text, admitting that this process does not always work for all writers involved with the company. The poems that Grose and Murphy created contribute to Rice's palette of material generated in the research-and-development period, which she is then at liberty to include how and when she sees fit. Murphy uses these approaches to map out the story in different ways, approaching writing in instinctual rather than strategic ways – as an exploratory journey – a style of working that is closer to Rice's than Grose's.

Kneehigh's *Tristan and Yseult*, 2015 © Steve Tanner

Poetry in motion

Tristan and Yseult was originally developed as a site-specific production to be performed at Rufford Abbey in Nottinghamshire and Restormel Castle in Cornwall, both ruins exposed to the elements; there is an expansive, exuberant quality to the production, as if the original medieval, open-air setting for it was preserved, even when the production was adapted for indoor theatre venues.[21] The set design, which had been a major contributing factor in the development and rehearsal processes from the beginning, was versatile and accommodating but also emphasized particular motifs from the text that represented Rice's adaptation of the story and Grose and Murphy's realization of that adaptation. The set was part-ship (masts, rigging, hammocks and gangplanks), part-1950s nightclub (fringed curtains, smoke, a neon sign) with a central circular platform upholding a ship's mast from which performers hung props and costumes and swung from ropes. The show was staged in a three-quarter round with gang planks and staircases framing the space, allowing entrances and exits at different heights and angles and enabling the actors to observe each other and engage with the audience at different times throughout the performance. The Love Spotters also functioned as musicians, and although the band kit was placed on a platform at the back of the space, they had the freedom to move, sometimes playing their instruments surrounding the central circular platform, weaving in and out of the audience. A combination of live and recorded music played throughout the majority of the production, either underscoring speeches and physical sequences or becoming a focal point for the audience through song and dance. The physicality of the performers also played a significant role in the production, telling moments of the story corporeally rather than through the text alone, using aerial work, dance and movement sequences, lending the narrative a fantastical quality and suggesting the greater themes at play: the complications of human emotion and the pain of loneliness and love alike.

The challenge for Grose and Murphy, working within this model of writer as poet, was to honour the essence of what Rice and the company believed to be at the heart of their adaptation and also weave in their own ideas and preoccupations. The text had to be comprehensive enough to realize Rice's vision for the adaptation and the concepts generated in the R&D period by the ensemble – giving the company a substantial framework for the facilitation of material to be generated in rehearsals – but it also had to be flexible enough to respond to the company's input. The metaphors Rice uses to describe her way of working and the role of the text within it are illuminating; she speaks of the writers' 'feeding in their poetry'[22], 'creating the palette of colours', gathering the 'harvest' of ideas and 'landing ... lots of beautiful planes'.[23] As many of the pieces they wrote were developed in response to certain ideas, often as individual units, they were flexible enough to be deconstructed, cut or shifted to another place in the larger play text. Grose and Murphy allowed Rice, Barker and the performers to experiment with staging and structuring the material, as well as adjusting the tone of the speeches, to reflect the influences on the production.[24] The director relied not only on the text to tell the story but also on the performances, music and design, which was why all these elements begin to be developed from the earliest stages of the process: 'This physical world holds meaning and narrative, it is as much a story telling tool as the written word.'[25] Rice believes that 'plays' 'prescribe too much' and limit her thinking about the production and of what can happen in it, and as a result, the text is treated as another evolving element in the process, like the music or the costumes, layering into the ensemble-driven collaboration, rather than serving as the primary source of inspiration.[26]

Similarly to the other play texts in this book, both the dialogue and the stage directions of *Tristan and Yseult* reflect the particular abilities, tastes and tendencies of the director, performers, musical director and members of the design team. Rice animated the text with music, singing, dancing, a circus-inspired piece or a physical sequence. For example, when Tristan and Yseult fall in love on the boat from Ireland to Cornwall as a result of drinking a love potion, the character of Whitehands says, 'But in my experience, a love potion is just an excuse for wild abandonment with one you already love.'[27] The stage directions read like poetry – they are suggestive but minimal, leaving room for Rice and the performers' interventions:

> *TRISTAN and YSEULT play with the bottles and with the idea.*
>
> *They drink the potion and the wine.*
>
> *The Dance of Intoxication.*
>
> *TRISTAN AND YSEULT swing on the ropes, kiss and finally collapse together, asleep.*[28]

Tristan and Yseult swap the bottle with the potion and the wine bottle back and forth in a game that grows wilder and wilder until the two are dancing with each other, flying through the air on ropes and then, finally, embracing.[29] Similarly to the physical work created by Frantic Assembly and Shared Experience, the physicality is supported by the text but adds visceral dimension to the performance that 'presents romantic passion as a force that makes lovers levitate ... and then sends them crashing to the earth'.[30] Simon Harvey, an artistic associate of Kneehigh who has worked as Rice's assistant on a number of productions, observes that in *Tristan and Yseult*, the text is 'more poetic', with scenes that have a freeness, an openness about them; both the dialogue and the stage directions engender interpretation from the director, designers and performers because the text was shaped in rehearsal with the intention of accommodating the company's input into the production.[31] Rice prefers to use the text as a starting point for any devising she asks the actors to do, rather than work from scratch, partly because she often works with performers for whom English is a second language, who are not comfortable improvising dialogue in English, and also partly because many of her performers are more articulate physically rather than linguistically; poetry facilitates this kind of devising process because it allows the performers to interpret the work, rather than more direct, concrete language allows.[32] Although it is not indicated in the published text, sections of the script are intended to change from night to night through improvisation, allowing the performers both the security of the written text and also the possibility of artistic autonomy.[33]

Grose and Murphy's conception of the dramaturgy of *Tristan and Yseult* reflected Rice's preoccupation with collaboration as working with a pallet of colours; the different voices and styles that the writers brought to the project created distinct characters and also helped to realize Rice's eclectic adaptation. Grose and Murphy's unique voices created a particular language for each character, reflecting the varied nature of the staging, music and design scheme. Grose explains that he wanted to 'let the style of the poetry tell the story',[34] that the different styles were intended to suggest a different voice for each character. For example, Frocin speaks in nursery rhymes and limericks to give him a 'stunted', 'nasty' and 'childish' tone, and Rice asked Grose to write King Mark in iambic pentameter to elevate him in status and style from the other characters.[35] From time to time, Grose interrupts

Kneehigh's *Tristan and Yseult*, 2015 © Steve Tanner

the verse to inject a dose of contemporary language to ground the speech in the modern world in which Rice is ultimately situating the production. For example, when we meet King Mark in his court, he sets up the story for us in a fairy tale fashion:

KING MARK

At birth, I'm told, Fate bestowed on me three things:

The first being that I was born to be King,

The second was a heart that keeps good pace,

And the third, the gift of a friendly face.

KING MARK takes his sunglasses off and looks at the audience.

Two out of three ain't bad.[36]

Grose breaks the style of King Mark's speech but also the rhyme scheme as well in order to draw our attention to one of King Mark's central attributes, his fearsome appearance. Murphy was given the task of writing the 'voice of the loveless and the broken-hearted', so she wrote a series of monologues and poems exploring those themes within the story, which she found both helpful and freeing, as she had never written a structured performance text before *Tristan and Yseult*.[37] In the last scene of the play, for example, Whitehands stands next to the dying Tristan, who is waiting for Yseult, and says, 'the loved attract love,/ If you are already loved, more love just seems to come/ your way./ Whereas us – the unloved – must take Fate in our/hands.'[38] Murphy's poetic, intimate language complements Grose's more technical, structured work by drawing in the audience through the play's broader themes of love and relationships in a personal fashion.

Conclusion: writers' dynamic within the company

The writer-as-poet model allowed Grose and Murphy to generate material not only in collaboration with but also in response to Rice and her ideas for the production; Rice explains that her relationship with the writers is similar to that of her relationship with the performers, that their obligation is to be interpretive and responsive as well as creative – they are part of a larger ensemble rather than the primary creative influences on the production.[39] Kneehigh is a company that relies on an ensemble-driven, collaborative dramaturgical process; as a result, Rice acted as director, adaptor, dramaturg and composer, arranging the elements of the production in order to serve her vision. Rice believes that Grose and Murphy played an essential role in the project but says that 'the authorship ... lies with me', that 'There is a musical landscape that I work on and then the words inhabit that and breathe life into that vision.'[40] Grose agrees that Rice is the author of the production and that she 'respond[s] better to text as a texture', rather than text as primary force, as it allows her to work more instinctually and physically, rather than having to be bound to what he calls a 'script-in-hand, academic approach' to rehearsing.[41] Although he acknowledges this mindset of the avoidance of a more conventional approach to playwriting – such as creating a series of scenes that then become a script can be frustrating for a writer – he is able to work in this way because he understands Rice and Kneehigh's ethos, having worked with them for many years.[42] Kneehigh does not have a particular model for working with writers that they apply to every production, because the material for each project might necessitate a different way of working and a different engagement with text. Claire McDonald writes,

> The practice of contemporary theatre dramaturgy asks us to consider texts in and for performance in a re-imagined way. The new dramaturgy does not proceed from text as a *known* set of procedures, but instead explores what those procedures might be. ... In the new dramaturgy, text moves closer to texture, and to the notion of fabrication as a material practice.[43]

While Grose and Murphy played a similar role within *Tristan and Yseult*, their approaches to writing and collaborating with Rice were not only distinct but complementary. Grose, who describes himself as a 'technical' writer, carefully navigated his way through the story, researching the background of the legend and its various adaptations, methodically reading and re-reading the source text and drafting sections of text over and over in an attempt to find 'the voice of the show',[44] the 'tonal quality of the language'.[45] Grose was selective in terms of what he chose to pass on to Rice so that he could believe that he had already exhausted the possibilities for this poetic voice before she contributed her input and guided him through the next phase of rewriting. He also found it useful to start by writing songs before the non-lyric texts, as he found the song writing to be quicker and more instinctive, and it provided central moments in the plot around which he then wrote other texts.[46] Murphy preferred to write a poem that encompassed the entire story in order to create a simple structure within which to work, a kind of map that would help her plot a course through the rest of the project before she wrote the individual speeches.[47] In contrast to Grose, Murphy tended to write quickly and instinctually, sending Rice the bulk of her work and allowing her to pick and choose which pieces of text she wanted to continue to develop.[48]

This process of writing allowed each writer a certain amount of autonomy in terms of not only the content of the work they produced but also the process in which they engaged as writers; each writer was able to adhere to an approach to writing that was both comfortable and productive but also one that took Kneehigh's particular system of collaboration into account. Rice actively encourages engagement with this model of writer as poet; she often asks a writer to write the 'song or the poem or the sonnet' of a character or moment in the story because she feels it allows the writer more freedom, rather than feeling the weight of being responsible for the entire production.[49] In asking Grose and Murphy to write her songs and poems, Rice allowed for space within the text for other interventions and contributions from the designers, musicians and performers.[50]

One of the most challenging aspects of this kind of collaboration is control of the written material and coming to a mutual understanding of the way in which that authorial control operates within the company with respect to the text, as the process foregrounds the director's authority rather than the writer's. The model of writer as poet is exemplified by the process of creating *Tristan and Yseult*; it is predicated on the foundation of an experienced ensemble of practitioners who have a collective understanding of how authorship operates within each production. Rice explains that the writer's presence in the rehearsal room is important so that the whole company can have the opportunity to experience 'the same moments of surprise or revelation or improvisation', thus gaining a shared understanding of the possibilities and the problems that may be arising from the process, which, in turn, aids in minimizing conflicts between her and the writers.[51] She goes on to admit that her relationship with writers such as Grose and Murphy is 'tricky' and can sometimes produce tensions because she is in control of the production, which can sometimes conflict with the fact that the writers are autonomous artists with their own voices, but that her long, ongoing relationships with both of them makes the process easier and the communication more fluid.[52] Murphy was available to attend rehearsals more frequently than Grose was and thus had more exposure to the work devised by the performers and also Rice's direction of the work; this might have been a difficult rehearsal period if Grose and Murphy had not trusted each other and Rice.

In an ensemble-led process such as this, it is paramount that the writers involved have a comprehensive understanding of what their roles entail, what the agreement is between themselves and the director and how the work they write will be treated before the process begins. This is a significant element for a tried-and-tested collaboration such as the one between Grose, Murphy and Rice, but it is even more crucial for a writer or director who has not worked in this way before or an external writer who has been commissioned for the first time by a company that has their own method of collaboration and a history of working together. Former National Theatre Literary Manager Sebastian Born explains that within the context of a collaborative devising company, the writers with whom they work must have a clear understanding of the expectations regarding the nature of their work and their stake in the authorship of the piece; once that 'invitation' is on the table, the writer can then be in a strong position to decide to commit to the project or not.[53] Collaborative companies and writers with a history of working together are much less fragile than one-off commissions between companies and writers who are not already acquainted and have to work to develop a foundation of trust, understanding and communication from which to work.[54] Grose notes that while his experiences with Kneehigh have been positive and have resulted in largely successful productions, 'devising isn't the be-all, end-all, joyful, collaborative way for people to make theatre' and can be especially challenging for a writer because 'one is asked to discover the show along the way', which can have a number of possible outcomes, such as the company continually requesting rewrites during the rehearsal process or the agency and influence of the writer within the project dwindling until their input is negligible.[55] Whether the writer is a commissioned outsider or has a long-standing relationship with the director in question, there is no way of guaranteeing a smooth process for a writer–company collaboration working with this kind of ensemble or director-led model, but the possibility of a productive process becomes more likely if all parties involved clearly agree on the roles of the writer and the text from the beginning. Especially if the authorship will ultimately be shared, it is important to understand not only the agreed-upon process and the roles within that process but also who bears the responsibility of making the final decisions.

Part II   Practical strategies

The model of the writer as poet can be seen as a way for a writer to collaborate with an ensemble, especially if the project is director led and the writer is working closely with the director. It can also be considered as a possible model for a director working with an untrained or less experienced writer, or a writer for whom writing for performance is not a primary or familiar mode of working, as this particular approach allows for a significant amount of input and guidance from the director. These strategies have been inspired by the process Grose and Murphy developed with Rice while making *Tristan and Yseult*.

Poetry as play text

Inspired by Kneehigh's approach to devising as framed by the writer-as-poet model, the following strategies are designed to help a writer generate and implement poetry within a director-led collaborative process. They are designed to be used in two ways: (1) either within the context of a devising process or (2) as an approach to writing material in the form of poems, as a response to a prompt of some kind (whether it is research material, source material to be adapted or a directive from another collaborator, such as a director). This approach can be used as a way of working with multiple writers or a means of generating material that will then be shaped by a director within a rehearsal or workshopping process later on.

1) Writing the voice I

This strategy is designed to encourage the writer to explore the voice of a character in an expansive, poetic but simple fashion in the form of a kenning, as used by Murphy. It is designed to allow the writer to generate material around a particular character within a structure. This approach can be used as a starting point for further writing in order to think through a character by using metaphors and images, or it can serve as the dramatic text in and of itself, to be explored in workshops and rehearsals with a director and performers.

- The writer(s) chooses a character to focus on.
- They of a number of two-word descriptors for the person they are describing without naming them specifically. This can either be the character describing themselves or one character describing another. (For example, Murphy's Love Spotters.)
- They can then incorporate compound words and figurative language, using the form of the kenning as an opportunity to experiment with style and imagery.
- The following might be some questions to consider:
  - What are the central elements of the character's persona?
  - What is their status?
  - What is their background?

- Do they have a particular physical or psychological quality you'd like to investigate?
- What is their relationship to other characters?
- What is their relationship to the world of the play?

- The writer(s) should consider different aspects of that character that not only relate to the themes of the play and the narrative (if one has been conceived yet) but also stand out as visual tropes.
- The kennings created can then be tried out in the rehearsal room by the director and performers in different ways in order to understand what functions they might serve in the play. For example, a kenning can serve as an introduction of a new character. They can also be used as a springboard for devising for the performers, encouraging them to investigate different characters to create scenes, monologues and physical sequences. For instance, if one character uses a kenning to introduce another, the group can then investigate that new character by using the qualities relayed in the kenning.

There should be an understanding between the writer and the company before the writer begins the work whether the kennings will function as part of the dramatic text or as a springboard for devising, the distinction being that the latter treatment might potentially mean that the work will be used and discarded. Although writers, directors and performers' opinions regarding a piece of writing can shift and change throughout a collaborative process (as can the writing itself), some kind of preconceived agreement as to the treatment of the text can help to avoid conflicts surrounding the role of the text and its permanence or disposability.

2) Writing the voice II

This second strategy builds on the first by taking the concept of exploring the voice of a character through the kenning and expanding upon it to include other forms of poetry as inspiration. The style of poetry chosen should reflect the nature of the character and aid the writer in discovering a form of expression for that character. For example, a kenning is a simple poetic form that tends to embrace a kind of folk language that is suggestive of, for instance, fairy tales. In contrast, a form of poetry, such as a sonnet, will have a different effect on the way the characters express themselves.

- The writer(s) can repeat the previous approach, replacing the form of the kenning with another poetic form. Some suggestions are a sestina, haiku or limerick, but they should feel free to experiment with style and rhyme scheme to suit the character and project.

- The writer(s) can consider what that form will ask of the language used. Some elements to consider include repetition, rhyme scheme, length, rhythm and tone.
- As in the kenning, they should attempt to incorporate imagistic, figurative language, using the form of the poem chosen as an opportunity to experiment with style and explore possibilities for the characters and the world of the play.
- Considering the questions suggested in the previous approach may be useful in gaining an understanding of the characters to be developed.
- Like the kenning, these poems can then be tried out in the rehearsal room by the director and performers in different ways in order to understand what functions they might serve in the play. For instance, the poems can be used in order to allow the director and performers to investigate different characters by building scenes, monologues and physical sequences.

3) Poetry as response

This third strategy also asks the writer to use a poetic voice in order to generate material, but this time the starting point is the performance space. This approach is intended to allow the writer to respond to material generated by a design team, in collaboration with a director. It can be used within the context of a purpose-built performance space, a set created for a non-performance space or a site-specific production (for example, some of the spaces in which Kneehigh has worked, such as the castles for which *Tristan and Yseult* was originally created). It can also be used to respond to a set that has been designed in advance of rehearsals that has particular spatial characteristics.

- Once a space has been chosen for the performance, the writer should walk through it with the director and designers (stage, set, lighting, sound and costume).
- Alternatively, if a set has already been created for the production, the writer can explore that space with the director and designers to try to come to an understanding about its inherent possibilities and limitations with respect to the production and play text.
- The writer and company can then consider the particular properties and dimensions of the space, as well as what its distinguishing features are (such as atmosphere, aesthetics and lighting).
- The writer and company can then discuss the ways in which the story can be told in that space, expanding upon what can be conveyed visually, physically and verbally and try to set down some central features of the production as parameters within which the text can work. One suggestion would be to explore which areas of the space might represent different locations or episodes within the story.

- If the production is site-specific, site-responsive or interactive in some way, the writer should consider where the audience might be placed and how this will influence the text. It may be useful to try to come to an understanding with the director and designers about the placement of the audience and if there might be any moments of interaction with the audience.
- If there is singing or live music, the writer should come to an understanding about where the singers and musicians might be located throughout the performance and how this could impact the text.

These two approaches to writing can be approached as a solo activity for the writer or in collaboration with the director and performers depending on the nature of the project and the company.

- Building on 'writing the voice I' and 'writing the voice II', the writer can then write the voice of a character in the form of a poem as a response to a particular visual or spatial characteristic of that space. It might be useful to approach different ways of having the character interact with that space.
- If the situation of the audience is a particularly significant feature of the production (as with interactive performances), the writer can attempt this strategy again, this time writing the voice of a character in a poetic form as a response to the placement of the audience. It might be interesting to experiment with some audience–performer interaction within the text, allowing for audience response or even intervention.

6   The Multiple Writer

Chapter 6 presents the fifth and final model of collaborative writing: The multiple writer model. This final model is designed to consider a way of working wherein a company has commissioned multiple writers to create a script for a production that will involve a significant amount of devising, workshopping and discussion, in addition to the writing itself. The multiple writer model is, on one hand, unique within this book because it is the only case study that I have chosen to include that engages with multiple writers, devising, adaptation, site-responsive work and audience–performer interaction; on the other hand, it also reflects a number of elements of the other case studies. It is similar to the writer-as-company-scribe model in that it involves the combination of writing and material devised by performers in a director-led process. It is comparable to the writer-as-poet model in that the director has a strong authorial presence within the process. While the text does not necessarily need to be the central guiding force, depending on the stage of the project, the writers can be highly influential, so there is also a comparison to be made with the model of writer as co-creator. In this chapter, I will examine the relationship between Teatro Vivo with writers Vic Bryson, Michael Wagg and me within the making of *The Odyssey* (The Albany Theatre, 2012). I will examine the ways in which text and the writers functioned during the process, particularly how the challenges of adaptation, devising, promenade theatre-making and audience–performer interaction were met. As I have done in previous chapters, after I have explored and deconstructed this model of collaborative practice, I will present a number of practical strategies inspired by this model of working intended for the reader to use in developing their own approach to the multiple writer model.

Part I   Vic Bryson, Michael Wagg and Sarah Sigal for Teatro Vivo

Teatro Vivo was established in London in 2005 by Artistic Director Sophie Austin as a company with a remit of creating both new work and adaptations and of working with existing play texts, with an element of audience interaction, in non-theatre spaces and outdoor venues:

> Our aim is to inspire people to contemplate the nature of human engagement by creating performances that encourage a sense of play for all who experience them. We collaborate with artists from all backgrounds to open up the possibilities of what theatre can be and encourage non-professionals to participate in our process allowing us to share and learn skills and wisdom. We explore the environments that we work in to ensure our productions become an essential part of the community and a source of inspiration and entertainment for all.[1]

Teatro Vivo's approach to creating work is expansive and changes to meet the needs of each production because their mission is multi-faceted: to work with new and existing stories, to engage a variety of interdisciplinary collaborators, to produce work for unusual sites and to enlist a participatory approach to all their productions. The structure of the company is such that Austin is artistic director and is supported and advised by artistic associates Kas Darley, Catherine Hooper and Mark Stevenson, who are also performers and producers working on company productions. Teatro Vivo has created productions in public parks, libraries, supermarkets and even whole neighbourhoods, working with a large base of collaborators such as performers, designers, writers and musicians. They have produced work such as *Here But There* (2006–2007), a play loosely inspired by Anton Chekhov's *Three Sisters* by Gabriel Bisset-Smith; *Supermarket Shakespeare* (2008–2010), a devised production inspired by William Shakespeare's sonnets; and *Hothouse* (2008–2009), a tango-inspired performance devised by the company. Austin has directed the majority of the company's work, and although most of Teatro Vivo's projects have been devised by a pool of freelance performers, the company has engaged a number of internal and external writers in the past to write texts. It might be useful here to compare the ethos and company structure of Teatro

Vivo to that of Kneehigh in the previous chapter, returning once again to Duŝka Radosavljević's definition of ensemble as a theatre-making group focused on the 'centrality of the actor/performer's contribution to the process of theatre-making'[2] and a kind of collaboration wherein all company members make relatively significant contributions to the process.[3] Although not all collaborators in every Teatro Vivo production are asked to make an equal contribution, Austin does concentrate on enabling a collaborative process whereby all participants – from performers to designers – offer input throughout, through their own creative practice or discussions. Radosavljević explains that, 'The 21st century ensemble takes into consideration ... different attitudes to tradition and innovation, changing conceptions of leadership and authority, and varying artistic vocabularies.'[4] The company is highly reliant on the devised work of its performers and also of the various local practitioners with whom they work in different communities (both amateur and professional) but also, ultimately, on Austin's direction and vision for each production.

Teatro Vivo's work is eclectic, and, similar to Kneehigh, can be described as embracing a kind of folk approach in order to stage stories in ways that are engaging but also accessible to audiences. Also like Kneehigh, the company is not specifically focused on producing new writing and working with writers, but rather works on existing plays, stories and myths and then challenges, questions and/or deconstructs their original meaning by staging them in unfamiliar, incongruous or surprising venues; for example, when they set out to adapt *The Odyssey*, they knew that the urban environment of Deptford would inform and bring new meaning to their interpretation of Homer's epic. This approach to making work enables Teatro Vivo to bring their work to new audience demographics (in terms of not only people who have not previously seen their work but also those who might not otherwise see theatre) and also collaborate with amateur practitioners living in the communities in which they work, deepening the connection to the area. Although Teatro Vivo does not identify primarily as a site-specific company, it may be useful here to situate them in the field by applying Mike Pearson's definition: 'If site-specific performance involves an *activity*, an *audience* and a *place*, then creative opportunities reside in the multiple creative articulations of *us*, *them* and *there*.'[5] Pearson is articulating a philosophy that is applicable to Teatro Vivo's work – namely, the boundaries between performers and audience members are intended to maintain a kind of flexibility. This relationship is facilitated by use of unconventional spaces because these locations allow a different kind of movement of and proximity between performers and spectators than that which is generally available in more conventional theatre spaces. Stevenson explains the dynamic within the relationship between the texts that the company chooses to adapt and the unusual or unexpected sites that it chooses as the setting for that adaptation: 'One of the great things about exploring a classic text on a high street is the resonances that it brings out from contemporary society.'[6]

The company aims to facilitate the notion of community engagement and expanded access to performance through what Pearson calls the 'multiple creative articulations' of performers (whether professional or amateur), spectators and sites for performance, engaging with writing and text on a project-by-project basis. While Austin makes the final decisions regarding the productions which she directs, decisions about new projects, venues and communities in which they work and new collaborators they engage are collective decisions within the company among Austin, Darley, Hooper and Stevenson. Company members also perform in Teatro Vivo productions and are endowed with a significant amount of creative agency by Austin, often devising entire productions. Like Kneehigh, they are also flexible in their roles from production to production, sometimes contributing only to workshops without participating in the final piece or, for example, acting as a performer in one production and writer in another, as Wagg has done. Although Teatro Vivo does not work with writers for every production, Austin acts as a director/ dramaturg, developing the dramaturgical structure of the piece and its relationship to the space or venue at hand throughout the workshopping and rehearsal processes. In addition to Bryson, Wagg and myself, they have worked with writers such as Fiona Whitelaw, Emma Warren, Mark O'Neil, Gabriel Bisset-Smith and Jaspre Bark in the creation of new work and have adapted and deconstructed texts by Shakespeare, Chekhov, Bertolt Brecht, Lewis Carroll, Charles Dickens, the Brothers Grimm and Homer. In their publicity and programmes, the writer has been credited in a variety of ways depending on the company's relationship to them and the text, the writer's relationship to the text and the level of input from the writer. For example, *Lovers and Liars* (2006) is credited as 'an interpretation of William Shakespeare's *Twelfth Night*' with 'contemporary words by Emma Warren', whereas *The Odyssey* is credited as 'inspired by Homer' and 'a new interpretation by Vic Bryson, Sarah Sigal and Michael Wagg'.[7] This fluidity of accreditation reflects Teatro Vivo's variety of approaches to working with text, be it extant or newly written.

Meeting the company

In the summer of 2011, I became involved with *The Odyssey* essentially because the needs and interests of Teatro Vivo overlapped with my own interests as a writer. I met Austin at a networking event for writers and directors at the Young Vic Theatre. She told me her company was looking for writers to collaborate on a multi-writer, promenade adaptation of *The Odyssey*, which piqued my interest not only because I had studied Homer but also because I was curious about ways in which site-specific and promenade productions can be made. Austin was seeking writers with whom she could collaborate because the company had produced a completely improvised, 20-minute scratch performance of *The Odyssey* earlier in the summer for the Sydenham Arts Festival; while she believed the idea had potential, she and Wagg believed that 'good writing would be essential to this piece so it felt important to bring writers in as soon as possible' – knowing that it would be a considerable undertaking, both for the company and the writer – and that developing the collaborative relationship early on would be crucial.[8] The following month, in September, I attended a meeting where some of the other members of Teatro Vivo and some other prospective writers discussed some initial concepts for the project and how to proceed in the collaboration. The meeting was intended for Austin and the other company members to develop some of those ideas and discover new ones, as well as come to an understanding about the writers present – who they were, what their instincts were regarding *The Odyssey*, their previous writing experiences and their opinions on collaboration.

For one reason or another, I was the only external writer from that evening who decided to come back to work with the company; I was interested in seeing how I could contribute to their process and how they would accommodate me artistically and authorially. While I had worked as a commissioned writer, a writer within a collaborative process and a writer alongside devising performers, I had not previously worked with site-specific performance, nor had I adapted an existing text. As a result, I felt able to abdicate a certain amount of authority to the company in order to become involved with what was a potentially interesting and rewarding project. From the perspective of the company, they believed it would be beneficial to commission writers to collaborate on a script for the production because they knew that *The Odyssey* would be a complex and large-scale production with multiple sites, characters and storylines necessitating the 'cohesiveness' of 'an authorial voice' for the individual scenes and overall dramaturgical structure; however, they knew in advance that they were seeking writers who, although new to the company, would be willing to be part of the overall collaborative, creative process, rather than 'an overseer'.[9] Although it was a risk for a company to work with an external writer like me (Bryson and Wagg had already worked with Teatro Vivo), they believe that the risk was worthwhile in order to create a text that would be robust enough to sustain a long, epic journey through the streets of London but also porous enough to accommodate the devised input of the company. Austin explains that although she had commissioned Bark and Bryson to adapt *Romeo and Juliet*, the process was different in that 'they took a character each and rather than collaborate, they worked separately to come up with two very different takes on the *Romeo and Juliet* narrative', each working closely with the performer for whom they were writing rather than collaborating with the entire company.[10] She continues that the process of commissioning writers 'became very important' because she wanted 'a writer's rigour to elaborate themes and explore ideas further' than the company previously had when working purely in a devised, writer-less process but also because she knew that her envisioned scale of the production would necessitate more than one writer.[11] Austin wanted the process of commissioning to involve more formal discussions and meetings with prospective writers because she knew it was going to be an unusual and highly collaborative process, and 'not for everyone'.[12]

Summary of Bryson, Sigal and Wagg's role

Creating *The Odyssey* within this multiple writer model was a complex process that involved an ongoing negotiation of individual interpretations of the source material in the form of Homer's epic, the space within and the sites outside The Albany Theatre, the combination of written and devised material, the role of the authorship of three writers and a director and the dramaturgy that facilitated the audience's journey through Deptford. Bryson, Wagg and I attended a number of workshops to allow us to try out speeches and scenes from *The Odyssey*, working with Austin and the performers to find possibilities for the staging and interpretation of Homer's text within the environment of The Albany and the area of Deptford. Partway through the process, we staged a scratch performance of the work to a small, invited audience on site, which greatly influenced the way in which we proceeded with the process. Although Bryson, Wagg and I were given a certain amount of freedom in terms of our respective visions for the characters and the story, Austin made the final decision in terms of the excerpts we chose to stage from Homer's original text, the journey of the audience and the nature of the audience–performer interactions. The play text was divided up among the three writers largely by character; each of us was responsible for a number of characters, and sometimes we shared scenes. The writing was shared among the writers and the director via Dropbox, and rewriting continued throughout the rehearsal period and into the run of the production. Ultimately, the sites we used had a significant impact on the process and final product, influencing our concept, characters and overall structure.

Research and development

The first workshop

Two months after our initial meeting, the company held a day-long workshop to try out sections of the text that Bryson, Wagg and myself had written, as well as to find ways of staging a number of unwritten ideas. In preparation for the workshop, Austin asked Bryson, Wagg and me to come up with ideas for scenes, written scenes and monologues, anything we could think of to tell the story and find a way into the text. Austin designed the workshop to create not only a sense of structure for all the concepts and written work we wanted to explore throughout the day but also a sense of trust – that we could explore ideas in a focused fashion in a large group of practitioners comprised of those who had worked with the company before and those who had not. Afterwards we were divided into three groups, and instructed by Austin to find ways of telling a third of *The Odyssey* as a small group, having only 10 or 15 minutes to devise a short piece. In a similar fashion to Kneehigh's ensemble-led approach to adaptation (rather than a writer-led approach, like Shared Experience's), Austin found instinctual responses from the company to the story useful in developing an interpretation that could later be developed through writing and devising. We then worked in small groups on scenes and monologues, the writers and Austin moving among the groups to consult with performers and help them work through the texts. Austin wanted to see what we chose to submit to her performed in the workshop without any input on her end, in order to see what naturally, instinctively interested us; in turn, we began to draw conclusions about what intrigued Austin, in terms of both style and content. The seemingly disposable, infinitely adaptable nature of the text created by the writers was to become a theme throughout the process.

The next segment of the day was led more by writers, as Bryson, Wagg and I brought ideas for scenes or concepts revolving around characters to pairs and small groups of performers, and those groups then devised and developed approaches to these unscripted ideas. This process felt less certain than the phase before, where we were able to work with texts, but for me, having worked through the scenes and monologues I had scripted and having seen the texts that Bryson and Wagg had written, I had a better idea of what I wanted to develop with the performers from my file of as-yet unscripted ideas. Despite the fact that we were involved in an early stage in the collaborative process, there were a number of concepts for scenes and interpretations of characters that evolved throughout the day that found a permanent place in the final script. Everyone was communicating well enough to be able to listen to individual practitioners' instincts and consider all possibilities presented to the group with a surprising level of trust and respect, considering that the nature of the project was still relatively undefined. In terms of the dramaturgy of this large-scale collaborative process, whenever we discovered an idea that felt in some way effective or exciting, we discussed it and noted it down, feeling a sense of satisfaction that we might have found a piece of the puzzle. In *Dramaturgy in the Making*, Katalin Trencsényi explains,

> Dramaturgy is the action through which meaning is created by the recognition and arrangement of patterns. This act of composition or construction in the theatre today is understood in the context of the performance as a dynamic and durational whole.[13]

We continued to arrange patterns of words, gestures and themes and then attempted to figure out how to incorporate them into a possible dramaturgical framework of the production. Although Bryson, Wagg and I were not yet sure what would ultimately be kept, the process itself took the pressure off us as writers from bearing the burden of having to conceive the production on our own. It also established the idea that the creative agency would be divided between the director, writers and performers in various ways and that the work created would arise from a number of different ways of working such as discussion, devising (in large groups, small groups, pairs and individuals) and writing.

Research and initial engagement with texts

From this point forward, the streets, shops and public spaces of Deptford began to play a significant role in the dramaturgical process. After the one-day workshop, Austin took Bryson and Wagg on a walk through Deptford in order to see the possibilities for the sites that the company might be able to use for the production; I was away at the time, but I had a discussion with Austin about the walk and the spaces that Austin and the writers were considering using, in addition what Austin wanted me to write in response to the workshop. She wanted to make sure that we the writers kept not only the physical space but also the character of Deptford in mind while we developed our vision for the adaptation. Wagg viewed the sites as possibilities, as offering 'suggestions' for his writing and as a 'challenge to think again':

> Working outdoors in busy, urban places means that it's not always possible to develop ideas in situ, or to anticipate all possible blockages. So the challenge I think is to make something for a specific place, that is responsive to it, but that is loose enough to be moved and flexible enough to be re-made very quickly elsewhere if necessary.[14]

He brings up a crucial point about writing for a site-specific production: in the beginning, the locations to be used might change and the text has to be adaptable enough to respond to the site but also open to alteration in case one site for an individual scene is replaced with another. (At the time, Teatro Vivo was negotiating with various vendors around the neighbourhood to see who would be willing to host scenes from the production throughout the run.) Homer's *Odyssey* is a lengthy, much-adapted text, rich in multiple narratives, characters and symbolism; similar to the challenge that Helen Tennison faced when she adapted *War and Peace*, we knew we would have to eliminate much from the original in order to be able to create a script for a two-hour-long production. Therefore, the additional constraint of the necessity for taking into consideration the promenade aspect of the production, the specific sites and the audience's journey was useful for us in terms of finding an approach to writing that would satisfy Austin and the company – it narrowed our brief and shaped our thinking considerably. Bryson agreed with this, saying, 'It was difficult for me to write a scene without a physical context – once I knew "where we were", then the motivations would flow in that context.'[15]

This period after the first workshop and before the second marks the beginning of the ongoing conversation that Austin, Bryson, Wagg and I conducted largely via email and Dropbox, in which we sent thoughts, character sketches, scenes, monologues and fragments of research or inspiration (such as articles, songs, images, books, films and TV shows), allowing each other's contributions to inform our writing. Bryson, Wagg and I wrote short pieces independently, focusing on attempting to explain or define a particular understanding of a moment, episode or character from *The Odyssey*. We each tried out a combination of writing new pieces and rewriting older ones that had been explored in the workshop. We kept a number of email threads going that revolved around ideas; we had so many discussions going at once that we had to start to adhere to the rule of making a separate email with a new subject heading for each new topic, character or dilemma. This process of cross-pollination not only brought our writer/director group closer together but also facilitated the development of a conceptual foundation from which we were able to develop a collective understanding about the nature of the script and our vision for the adaptation. Wagg notes that 'Practically, Dropbox was very useful for sharing ideas, reference points and text in progress' and suggests that 'some sort of central depositary to keep it all manageable is a good idea', adding that even the references we had made and the scenes we had written that were edited out of the final draft of the script were 'essential tasters' that contributed to the project and our thinking about it.[16] Austin believed that this sharing of inspiration was 'important to aid our understanding of the world we were all trying to create'; she cites the American television series *Homeland* as an example of an especially useful reference point for the group, as the first season was being aired during this phase of the project and 'helped us to realise the contemporary potential to the story'.[17] *Homeland* helped facilitate our understanding of *The Odyssey* and *The Iliad* as texts relevant to twenty-first-century society in the sense that it presented us with an alternative, contemporary Odysseus – Sergeant Brody, an American soldier held hostage for many years during the Iraq War, returning home to his family. As a result, from this point onwards, we began to view Odysseus as a war veteran attempting to return to civilian life, which proved to be key to our interpretation of the source text.

The multiple writer model facilitated a kind of layered approach with respect to the different ideas and pieces of text that we the writers developed independently and also together to create what we called the 'master script' for *The Odyssey*. Bryson notes that 'there was a feeling from the start that we had permission to plunder any texts, rather than being true to the one.'[18] She took the approach of examining a summary Austin had sent us of what she believed was germane to the story we were telling in our production and compared it with her own close reading of Homer's *Odyssey* in order to understand what might be missing from our version. This is an example of how this process of layering (conversation that informed conversation, text that informed text, conversation that informed text, references that informed conversation) enabled the group to explore notions of the audience's role and journey character, plot, adaptation, staging and the way in which the promenade aspect of the project would function concurrently. In *Ensemble Theatre Making*, Rose Burnett Bonczek and David Storck write,

> something special can happen when you get people to function effectively as a group. They become more than just the sum of individuals: a new entity is born; greater accomplishments are possible. It's a super-force that heightens our capabilities as individuals and serves to illuminate the furthest potential of human endeavour.[19]

We learned that as long as we worked to maintain the flow of communication, this kind of gentle push and pull of independent writing, collaborative discussion, group writing and the sharing of work created an organic balance of agency among ourselves and also between ourselves and Austin.

The second workshop

The next phase of the development of the project was a three-day workshop in January 2012 where Austin had taken stock of the material we writers had gathered over the previous two months and set specific tasks to accomplish for herself, us and the performers involved. She sent out a document in advance for all the participants, which included the aims of the workshop, goals for the production, synopsis of our adaptation and an act-by-act breakdown of the dramaturgical structure. In her brief, Austin wrote that the company was setting the production 'in an urban community to highlight the contemporary relevance of the story' and also connecting with local artists and community groups through involvement with the production, thus making the audience central to the telling of *The Odyssey* and connecting 'mythical elements' with 'domestic relationships of its central characters'.[20] The concept and general narrative structure of the production were in place, but the content and interpretation of Homer's *Odyssey* were still to be decided.

This workshop was designed to allow an open but intimate forum for the writers, Austin, her assistant Hooper and a group of performers to discuss questions that remained unanswered (what would be the role of the gods? are we in Deptford or Greece? do we need guides for the audience?) and also to explore different interpretations of some of the mythical characters that Odysseus encounters, such as the Cyclops, Circe and Calypso, partially through workshopping written material and partially through devising from ideas. The adaptation process as conceived by Teatro Vivo within this multiple writer model was informed by a more democratic, performer-oriented process than other contemporary companies in this study, more reminiscent of work created by companies such as The Open Theater, which emerged in the 1960s and '70s. We explored different characters and scenarios from *The Odyssey* by pairing each writer with a single performer or a small group. As in the first workshop, we developed text we had created and also worked with unscripted ideas. Some texts, scenes, ideas and monologues were explored in our small groups, and others were performed for the company at large, depending on what we believed was important for and appropriate to the process. For example, the concept of how we would represent the maids and the suitors in Penelope's house was examined as a large group: we discussed concepts that could inform these characters collectively; Austin set up a series of structured improvisations;

and then Bryson, Wagg and I made notes while we observed the scenes that were devised. Combined with the notes we took, these improvisations then became material for the scenes we later scripted. Representations of individual characters such as Circe, the Cyclops and Calypso were assigned to individual writers working with individual performers or performer groups by Austin. Different groups would often try various interpretations of the same character, and then we would watch scenes and monologues written, devised or partially written and partially devised back to back, conceived by different groups. We had small showings of work and discussions around the different approaches to the adaptation, questioning what each interpretation of each episode on the story would imply dramaturgically within the context of the whole production. Whereas the first workshop was designed to allow the company to explore ideas relatively freely, this second workshop was designed to focus more specifically on questions and possibilities that Austin, Bryson, Wagg and I had discussed in the previous month. Katalin Trencsényi defines this kind of 'new drama development' as being centred on creating 'an environment where a new piece of theatre can be conceived, developed and grown', which is achieved by allowing the writer 'to see, hear and test the work', as 'The aim is always to enhance the performability of the work.'[21] During this phase, we were aiming to explore the intersection between our ideas, pieces of writing, research and the liveness of the devised work the performers created, whether directly or tangentially related to our ideas.

The third day of the workshop centred on exploring the character and layout of the neighbourhood of Deptford surrounding The Albany Theatre and the shops, pubs, cafes, parks, bridges, roads and community centres within it in order to come to an understanding of the ways in which the promenade aspect of the production could function with respect to both the text and the staging. The whole group spent the morning walking around Deptford, taking notes on the nature of different sites and what scenes or episodes might be served by being staged in them. Considering the play as a living, moving entity, in situ, with an audience involved in the telling of it, enhanced and challenged the work we had done over the past two days and also the writing we three writers had created and shared in the previous two months. At times our surroundings facilitated the process, giving us new ideas and new contexts for the characters and the plot we were constructing; for example, the character of the Cyclops took on a new, less menacing and more pitiable form in our minds as a homeless man camping out underneath railway arches, searching for his lost herd of sheep in a barren urban context. At other times it challenged us and posed new issues, such as that of the positioning and journey of the audience; we realized that even with a small group of people, it was going to be difficult to get everyone from place to place in a way that was both organized and well timed and also in keeping with the themes and style of the production. It is useful to consider this approach to collaborative working as falling under the umbrella of what dramaturg Milan Zvada terms 'interactive dramaturgy':

> While one-way dramaturgy is preoccupied mainly with play text analysis, characters, adaptation, and semantic interpretations (referring to psychological and narrative theatre background), interactive dramaturgy deals with performance as a complex interactive process with an intended effect. Nevertheless, interactive dramaturgy too makes use of one-way dramaturgical methods as they ideally coexist in practice. ... [I]n an interactive approach, a focus on the structural elements of performance is supplemented with a focus on the process. Interactive dramaturgy is concerned mainly with the fact that the theatrical world is being constructed gradually and purposely to evoke certain kinds of responses in the audience, yet keeping its thematic, narrative, or psychological principles more or less integrated.[22]

I do not necessarily agree that dramaturgical practice can so easily bifurcated into integrative/interactive and text based, but in this context it is useful to consider Zvada's point that interactive dramaturgy is a kind of approach to the construction and composition of the elements of text and production that not only considers the text/performance itself but also exhibits a 'focus on process' and the evocation of 'responses in the audience'. By the time we had reached this stage in the workshop, our dramaturgical approach was certainly interactive and integrative in that we were seeking ways of applying the material we had written and devised in the previous days to the concepts of promenade and interactive performance. While Austin, Bryson, Wagg and I had been discussing these particular aspects of our version of *The Odyssey*, this walk through Deptford compelled us to confront them in a more immediate way.

The scratch performance we staged at the end of this workshop period gave everyone who had been involved a working idea of the kind of production we were trying to create, the possibilities therein and the challenges that it presented and would continue to present to us. During lunch, Austin selected a series of scenes and monologues that she believed to be interesting and effective, and she quickly pieced together a dramaturgical framework that would allow the company to explore our version of *The Odyssey* as a site-responsive, interactive and promenade production. Drawing from the previous days' work, she chose different groups' interpretations from various episodes from *The Odyssey* (both from scripted and devised scenes), cast the characters we had explored and situated these episodes in different locations around Deptford. Working from this selection of material and sites, she then mapped out a rough journey for the audience. She invited an audience of friends, former collaborators, current collaborators (such as the designers with whom we would be working) and members of the Teatro Vivo board. This element of this workshop proved to be vital and gave us a sense of how the production would later work; it enabled us to understand Deptford better – both the layout of the town and the possibilities for performances and audience interactions. The fact that Austin was managing the composition of the scratch performance reflected a balance of creative agency between her and us as the writers because it allowed us to take a step back from the material we had been developing with the performers and gain an insight into Austin's vision for the production.

At this point in the process, the space and the audience within it had become what Pearson calls an 'organizing principle'[23] for the dramaturgy and continued to have a major impact not only on the adaptation we were writing and devising but also on this multiple writer model of working. It is worth asking a question that Pearson believes is germane to site-specific performance: 'How does it *disperse* itself within and in relation to a particular architecture or environment?'[24] Dispersal seems to be an appropriate word to use in the context of the scratch performance; the material we had written, devised and partially scripted/partially devised was dispersed as soon as the performers activated it out on the streets, in the parks and under the bridges of Deptford that evening in a kind of unleashing of all our creative energies. In this moment, what Pearson terms the 'stratigraphy' of the production (borrowed from the field of geology, by which he means 'layering material'), unfolded and opened out to us, both to the makers and also to the audience of the scratch production, folding back again on itself to encompass the geography and psychogeography of the neighbourhood and its architecture.[25] After going to Penelope's house and meeting Penelope, Telemachus, the maids and suitors, the audience were given the task of trying to find Odysseus by piecing together his journey by talking to the gods and monsters that he encountered along the way. The interaction of the audience with the layering of the material we had created onto the site revealed to the company the practical needs of the production, the possibilities for both character development and staging and the potential holes in the narrative.

Pre-rehearsal collaborative writing

The writing process after the scratch performance that involved Bryson, Wagg and myself can be characterized as a targeted, action-based approach to collaborative writing. One of the most important elements to this phase in the process was an outline of the production that Austin devised for the three of us, which she had based loosely on the scratch performance. The outline mapped out the entire production, including plot points for long scenes (to be written collaboratively), shorter episodes (to be written individually), locations for each scene; possible journeys for the audience and suggestions of which writer should attempt which scene, episode or character, although she also stated that the writing assignments were suggestions that could be queried if necessary. (This is reflective of the writer-as-poet model in which Emma Rice directed Carl Grose and Anna Maria Murphy's writing with respect to particular moments and characters within the adaptation of *Tristan and Yseult* that she had conceived.) The kind of dramaturgical approach we applied to our collaboration can be illuminated by the definition of dramaturgy developed by the 'Dramaturgy at Work' open workshop and seminar at the University of Roehampton (Dance Department), as discussed by Konstantina Georgeiou, Efronsini Protopapa, Danae Theodoridou, Simon Bayly and Nina Power in February 2015; they define dramaturgy as 'working on actions' and 'encounters in distinct dramaturgical practices'.[26] Although this definition was developed as a starting point for a conversation about the relationship between performance, dramaturgy and political activism, the concept of dramaturgy as 'working on actions' is useful in this context because Austin was applying the notion of actions and action points to organize the outline of the production and divide the labour of the writers, maintaining each individual writer's autonomy while also helping us explore possibilities for collaboration and synthesis. As a result of this highly structured, action-based mode of collaboration, our work during this period fell into two categories: collaboratively written ensemble scenes and individually written episodes.

While Bryson, Wagg and I tackled the individually written scenes and speeches as we had been working (by writing drafts, sharing them on Dropbox and discussing changes via email), we approached the prospect of writing long, ensemble-driven scenes collaboratively, which was more daunting and demanded more careful, strategic thinking. The three of us took comfort in the dramaturgical outline presented by Austin, but we were hesitant about how to proceed and worried about creative infringements. Bryson expressed in an email what we were all feeling:

> I wanted to voice my feeling that it might take us some time to find out how we work together and that we might try things, then try something else, then try a different way. ... And, to be honest, I fear it being a frustrating and turbulent process as well as a rewarding and stimulating one. I think for me that's okay.[27]

What helped the collaborative process was this kind of open communication; we were able to express our feelings openly yet tactfully, about the ideas, the writing and the process, in the intimate space that existed around the three of us. It was challenging, continuing to write in a directed, purposeful fashion, knowing we had to contribute unique voices but also find a way for the language and the themes of the play to be consistent. Bryson suggested that in the ensemble scenes, we each develop a character and create a voice for that character, explaining that 'Just as different characters have different agendas and voices, so do we' and calling this approach 'character-led action'.[28] She believed it would allow each of us to do some thinking and planning for each character individually, share these musings via email and Dropbox and then write what we came to call the 'Post-it note moments', small episodes within longer scenes that could be moved around or changed as needed – which could be considered scene-led action.

Towards the beginning of this process, in order to map out the introductory scene where the audience met Odysseus, Penelope, their son Telemachus, Euryclia the housekeeper and the maids and suitors, we had a meeting to design briefs for each of these characters, using a combination of free-association and strategic dramaturgical planning; this groundwork allowed us to develop a shared understanding of the nature of each character and how they could diverge from and complement the others. Each writer took responsibility for writing one maid, one suitor and a main character (such as Telemachus, Penelope or Euryclia), developing that character individually; inserted them into a short 'Post-it scene'; and then put these Post-it notes together to form the larger, ensemble scene. For example, one suitor was intended to be an alpha male, another was a scheming gambler and a third was an Odysseus aficionado. In an extension of this action-based dramaturgy, my suggestion was an amalgamation of Austin's approach of outlining the play and Bryson's character-led action – that is, creating a detailed outline of the ensemble scenes so that each writer had a shared understanding of 'what exactly is happening from moment to moment' in order to script the characters' dialogue and action in a specific, agreed-upon fashion while still having the freedom to develop a particular character's journey within the scene.[29] We would each develop monologues and short scenes around these characters and then share the material with each other. After seeing how the other writers were developing the other characters in the ensemble scene, we were then able to go back to our own text fragments and amend various lines and developments in the plot to create a sense of consistency and continuity. Wagg notes,

> To have three writers felt beneficial for this particular project. The challenge of bringing this huge sprawling story and all its literary baggage to some sort of shape was far easier to meet with teammates by your side. ... With a team of writers, we had the comfort of being able to let one of us off the leash for a bit, to go and push at something, while others were able to hold the ground and make sure the team as a whole continued to serve the piece; by which I think I mean to serve the characters by feeding the actors. This happens beyond the writing team as well, throughout the company, this push and pull.[30]

Teatro Vivo in rehearsal, 2012 © Sophie Austin

We were incorporating such a volume of disparate material (devised scenes, notes about the audience journey, images from the sites around Deptford, suggestions from Austin, text we had created previously) that a collaborative, action-driven, organized writing process felt like a productive way to reflect on and process it all. Claire McDonald describes this type of dramaturgical approach as 'connective tissue that connects experiments in writing with performance form,' noting that 'the etymology of dramaturgy suggests work, or composition, in relation to action.'[31] Through a structured, action-based method of collaboration, we had found a way of linking our ideas about the production to the actual writing process.

Role of the text and writers in rehearsal: the writer/director/performer collaboration(s)

The rehearsal period challenged Bryson, Wagg, Austin and I and the cast to find approaches for combining the text and devised material and to address issues of staging, the use of the different sites around Deptford and the audience's journey during a limited rehearsal period. One of the main issues we faced was that of maintaining fluid communication despite the fact that not all the writers could attend every rehearsal; Wagg and I were present for the majority of the rehearsals (as Wagg was also in the cast), but Bryson was unable to attend as often, partly due to the fact that her partner, Stevenson (playing Odysseus), was needed nearly daily in rehearsals and the two had to share child-care responsibilities. The problem with a lack of writer availability was that when Austin and the performers had questions regarding the text, sometimes changes had to be made without the writer present, which was necessary for the sake of time but frustrating for the absent writer. In contrast, during the development and writing process, all changes were debated, consented to and eventually mutually agreed on, as there was more time and fewer people involved in the process. Additionally, keeping track of all of the changes was also extremely difficult. Edits and additions were added to the master script daily, and sometimes performers wrote sections themselves, or devised sequences that were never fully written down. Inevitably, the writers who were present more often had more impact on the script and the production gener-ally, which, as Bryson noted, endowed the process with an element of 'randomness', in contrast with the planned, methodical nature of our collaborative writing process.[32] What we came to realize as the rehearsal process progressed was that the writers' role in the process had not been clearly defined and we tested different approaches as we went along, which was unsurprising as none of us had ever worked with this kind of model. While this practice functioned well before rehearsals when we had more time and the collaboration was limited to the three writ-ers and Austin, it became more difficult within the pressurized con-text of the rehearsal room and the added complexities of working the text around the sites we had chosen and the improvisation that would be needed when the performers interacted with the audience. Austin explains that her 'greatest challenge came with working with eight dif-ferent spaces on one show' and figuring out 'how to work with the space and how the space can inform your storytelling and affect the audience journey'.[33] Since *The Odyssey* was not being staged in a con-ventional theatre space, the director's job was even more complex and demanding than it would have been had her only challenge been to create a single production from the texts of three different writers and devised material from a whole cast of performers.

Another challenge we faced was the reconciliation between written and devised work, which sometimes worked in tandem and sometimes seemed to be at odds.[34] Similar to Filter's experience working within a model of a company-scripting writer collaboration on *Faster*, Austin and the performers wanted a text that was both solidly dramaturgically constructed but also porous and flexible enough to accommodate interventions from the audience or indeed even passers-by. Wagg explains in an interview that the performers not only had to be comfortable with the material they were performing but also had to feel a sense of ownership over it so that they could improvise in the event of an unexpected occurrence, and he explains that the role of the writer was to make the performer feel 'as armed as possible' – in other words, well prepared with written text from which they could deviate through devising, if necessary.[35] However, it was more difficult for the performers to improvise around a part that had been written for them than a fully devised role, especially within the context of *The Odyssey*, because they have to take into account the writers' preconceived ideas about the scene or the character, as well as the adapted source material from Homer's stories (both *The Odyssey* and *The Iliad*) and references that we the writers had researched and incorporated into the writing. Stevenson believes that although it was a significant methodological shift for Teatro Vivo to work so extensively with writers, it allowed the performers to 'have a more poetic and nuanced narrative than we would have come up with through devising alone', and it enabled them to 'have some larger multi-character scenes, something that is much less easy in devised work'.[36] While working with text was more difficult for the performers in terms of having a sense of ownership over the material, it facilitated the creation of a more complex dramaturgical structure and also a shared understanding of the journeys and objectives of the different characters – a process which Katalin Trencsényi refers to as the shared dramaturgical work characteristic of devised processes.[37] Stevenson goes on to add that since *The Odyssey*, Teatro Vivo has increased the amount of written material in subsequent productions.[38]

The primary method of working that Austin developed in order to bridge the gap between the written and the devised was the process of pairing a writer with a performer (for monologues) or performers (for scenes) to develop his or her character(s), working through text together in order to work out anything that was inconsistent or difficult to perform or that necessitated alteration to reflect the site or interaction from the audience. Austin would then watch these pieces and give further suggestions for changes. The director explains that her role going into rehearsals necessitated organizing a tremendous amount of written material, which she preferred to see as a single piece of work written collectively by a 'team' of writers, rather than taking into account which section had been created by which writer. This was sometimes problematic for us as the writers: while we understood that Austin was working in a way that was effective in terms of time and in terms of developing a dramaturgical understanding of the script as a whole, we had invested so much time in observing each other's authorial boundaries during the writing process (as Austin admits) that we felt a sense of ownership over our individual pieces of writing.[39] She continues that having writers in the rehearsal room 'was a real gift' because it meant that we, Austin and the performers 'were able to shape the writing as we went along' and concedes that 'I certainly don't think every writer could be part of such a process. You need to be egoless, generous and think on your feet.'[40] Authorial negotiation was ongoing throughout the rehearsal period. For instance, performer Jason Eddy played the role of Achilles, which I had written; we worked together on his monologue with Jason reading through the text with me, making suggestions for changes and developments and even improvising small sections. Our collaboration carried on into the evening after rehearsal as we emailed ideas back and forth to add to the speech and then bring the changes into rehearsal for the next day. This phase in the rehearsal process was both one of the most fruitful and yet also one of the most challenging: we as the writers had to relinquish a certain amount of control over our work; the performers had to navigate Austin's suggestions, their own concerns about how the writing was functioning in performance and also the writers' peccadillos; and Austin was faced with tying each separate episode together to form a cohesive journey for the audience. The director believes that the benefit of this close collaboration between the performers and the writers was that it allowed the latter 'to have a greater sense of ownership over their characters, and so when improvisation was called for in a scene, they were entirely comfortable slipping in and out of the text.'[41]

The flexibility of this model of working allowed for the inclusion of a variety of other creative agents (apart from the writers) that supported the dramaturgical process. When we encountered moments in the production that would invite a significant amount of audience interaction, Austin asked the performers to devise the necessary scenes and characters independently. For example, Scylla and Charibdis were created by

Rebecca Peyton and Natasha Magigi in order to serve as characters who guided the audience from site to site while also telling them stories about Odysseus, which were sections of narrative from the original Homer that we had not adapted. (Stevenson calls these interludes 'something between a scene, a monologue and impro with a moving audience'.[42]) Additionally, Austin arranged a community chorus – a number of local volunteer performers who played music, sang and recited poetry, posing as godlike figures who helped direct the audience from site to site between scenes. She also decided to split the audience into four different groups, each group seeing one-half of the stories being performed, in addition to the beginning, end and interval (which was in itself a series of performances). This approach gave the performers more freedom to interact with the audience and the spaces around Deptford, in addition to taking the burden off the writers in terms of having more material to generate and incorporate into the production. Having smaller groups of audience members to shepherd through the streets meant the production could move more quickly and cover more material from Homer's epic. Josephine Machon explains that a 'vital component' and 'defining feature' of immersive and participatory theatre must be 'the physical insertion and direct participation of the audience member in the work.'[43] We as the writers were not truly able to understand how the production would function and how we would need to structure it until we tried out scenes on site, with a test audience.

Teatro Vivo's *The Odyssey*, 2012 © Tom Broadbent

Conclusion: writers' roles within the process

Although the production was a success and the writing was valued, our role as writers and the role of the text remained unresolved to some extent, even into the restaging of *The Odyssey* three months after the initial run at The Albany. One of the ongoing issues for the writers throughout rehearsals was the lack of time to discuss the script and the changes that were being made or that needed to be made. Especially within the context of a company that largely produced devised material that was intended to be shaped and revised rapidly and on its feet, from the director and performers' point of view, it was practical and efficient to critique a writer's scene and ask for revisions to be completed as quickly as possible; from our perspectives as the writers, it was often difficult to expose our work to criticism in an open forum and then find a way to present something markedly changed, incorporating specific suggestions, in a short amount of time. Personally, I was never able to edit a scene in only an hour or two; after working through changes in rehearsal (usually with Austin and then one-on-one with the performer(s) involved in the scene), I needed to go home and work on it alone afterwards in order to have time to reflect on the material and be able to incorporate the necessary changes. Referring to the writers, Stevenson reflects, 'Sometimes it felt like they were mass material generators for the performers to try out, which occasionally made them feel less like collaborators than they could have been.'[44] In the end, it was difficult to negotiate the time that the writers needed to develop and discuss the script with the limited time we had to produce the play. Austin herself often had to think on her feet and respond quickly and instinctively to the text in order to keep the process running smoothly and on schedule, in addition to navigating each performer's and each writer's particular concerns and tastes. Our solution was to instate morning writers' meetings with Austin in the hour before rehearsals began, which allowed us to tell a writer who had not been present the day before what changes were being considered and each person to discuss the text in 'a less public forum'.[45] In a rehearsal room full of people eager to move the process forward, we the writers were more inclined either to feel pressured and rush through changes in the writing or to balk and become resistant to those changes. In *Ensemble Theatre Making*, Rose Burnett Bonczek and David Storck write that a strong foundation for an ensemble (which is what we had essentially become by this point) can be facilitated by 'self-awareness, listening, flexibility, and openness'.[46] The added writers' meetings with Austin in the morning not only gave us the practical benefit of discussing rewrites and dramaturgical stumbling blocks that had arisen in rehearsal but also reproduced the intimate group of four in which we had collaborated before rehearsals began, which reinforced a sense of trust and clarity of communication.

Although it became routine for the writers and the director to resolve more minor questions in collaboration with performers in rehearsal, any major structural issues that were left in question were not easily solved in this flurry of the rehearsal and production process, as they necessitated not only more time but also more discussion between we the writers and Austin. The final scene in the play proved to be the most difficult to resolve, as the whole company felt a kind of duty to bring together all the different strands of the production and find a way of mediating between the original Homer and our own complex adaptation. We had failed to find a time for the writers and Austin to meet to go over any potential changes before the restaging of *The Odyssey* three months after the initial run, which meant that Austin made changes to the ending in order to resolve some issues relating to the message of the play that she believed were lingering independently of the writers, by 'amalgamating two versions from two different writers that were written independently without knowledge of each other'.[47] By the time we explored these changes in rehearsal, there were still some issues relating to this new ending, but as we had little time to re-rehearse and address a number of other pressing changes (such as the waning quality of the evening light from June to September), so the ending was never fully resolved.

In 'Who is the Dramaturg in Devised Theatre?' Teresa Stankiewicz reflects a common view about devised dramaturgy: 'In devising, dramaturgs might be specifically assigned or in the form of true collaboration everyone might serve as dramaturg.... It seems unimportant who plays the role of dramaturg as long as the dramaturgy is accomplished.'[48] However, for our situation, it was important who was making dramaturgical decisions, regarding both the devised and written material, as authorial integrity and authorial control were embedded in these dramaturgical decisions. Teatro Vivo had largely previously created productions that were devised and often credited in a collective fashion as 'devised by Teatro Vivo', so in some ways, perhaps the company as a whole never fully adjusted to a new, more authorially differentiated ethos. Although we tried a slightly different scripted version each night of the performance, we were never able to script a satisfying ending – possibly because we had not resolved such a crucial moment in the play earlier and more collaboratively. At this point, Austin said she viewed the text as the product of a collective voice, which is how it likely appeared to the outside world, despite the fact that Bryson, Wagg and I knew who contributed which sections, sometimes down to a line or an idea. Austin explains,

> I don't think we necessarily cracked the best way to discuss and work on the different scenes if a writer wasn't present during rehearsal and we didn't keep a good record of the changes that were made – in fact the final script that we have probably isn't the final script that was performed on the final day of the last show. There is something wonderful about that – this was a live and moment by moment process where no show would be the same. The writers had to give up an ownership of their individual moments which was hard I think.[49]

Though we believed that this sense of ownership necessitated many discussions, long working processes and many redrafts, it benefited the production because it allowed us as the writers to create a text that wove different ideas, locations, source material, stories and tonal qualities together. We essentially lost clarity and focus in terms of what we were saying about Odysseus, his relationship with his family and his journey because we hadn't followed through with the collaborative process we had developed throughout the creation of *The Odyssey* for the final scene of the play. Here it is useful to recall Grose's reservation regarding the difficulty of establishing control and authorship with respect to written work within a non-writer-driven collaborative process: it can be challenging, and it is important to form an agreement regarding the role of the writer and the text at the beginning.

In the end, we learned to balance the collective voice of the production with that of the individual voices – of the writers, performers and director – and later, that of the audience. We often took advantage of the fact that we were writing an adaptation and used both *The Odyssey* and *The Iliad* as a kind of touchstone to help bring together our voices, something to which we could return to when we believed we were losing our way. Bryson, Wagg and I explored the idea that Homer 'was not necessarily one man, but may have been a collection of various voices, itinerant poets singing and eventually scribbling their tales', that *The Odyssey* has developed an identity only as a fixed text by a single author over thousands of years and many translations.[50] While performing *The Odyssey*, Wagg wrote in his blog,

> Many voices have made our story too. Not only three writers and Teatro Vivo, who are a collective, but the people of Deptford who've signed up as a community chorus of gods, the fellow-travelling audience, and the folk who stumble through the story blissfully unaware that they've just passed a whirlpool and a six-headed monster outside the People's Choice. ... Sometimes the audience try to derail us. It's our story just as much as yours they seem to say. We are Homer.[51]

Part II   Practical strategies

The following practical strategies are designed to enable multiple writers working on a project to script a text in collaboration with a director and performers. There is a similar dimension to the strategies from Chapter 3 (writer as company scribe) in that they are intended to facilitate a combination of writing and devising, incorporating the material generated in the rehearsal room into the text, and vice versa. Additionally, there are similarities to the strategies from Chapter 2 (writer as co-creator) in that both focus partially on adaptation through collaborative writing, and in fact, some of the strategies from Chapter 2 can serve as useful initial approaches to adaptation work and can be combined with some of the exercises below. I have divided these approaches to working into categories that address the various challenges that Bryson, Wagg and I faced while working on *The Odyssey* so that the multiple writer model can be applied to these particular scenarios.

Writing in a collective

The following strategies are intended to help a pair or group of writers find approaches to writing together, whether in collaboration with a company or purely as a writing group.

1) Outlining

- In collaboration with the director (and possibly the dramaturg if there is one involved in the process), the writers come up with a comprehensive outline of the entire play. (Of course the performers can also participate in this part of the exercise, but it is likely that the more participants involved, the slower the process will be.) This outline should be as thorough and detailed as possible; the vaguer the outline is, the more decisions will have to be made later on, during the scripting and devising process, necessitating a lengthier, more drawn-out process. While it is ideal for the writers and director to have a collective understanding of the nature of the story and characters before the outline is created, it is possible that this will emerge through the outlining process.
- Either the director can then assign short scenes/episodes within the outline to the writers or the writers can decide among themselves who will take which scene/ episode.
- Longer scenes/episodes can later be broken down into individual segments and then be assigned to different writers (as we will see in the following exercise).

Unless one writer has less availability than the others and has specifically requested less involvement, there should be an attempt to give all writers involved an equal amount of writing in order to create a sense of ensemble writing and collective ownership over the text.

2) Outlining and colouring in

- In the same fashion as in the outlining in the preceding exercise, the writers draw up an outline of a single scene in as thorough and detailed a fashion as possible. This exercise is especially suited to long scenes with multiple characters.
- The scene is then broken down into 'beats' (significant, individual moments) by the writers together. The writers and/or director then decide which writer will take which beat of the outlined scene to script.
- Each writer writes their beat, in accordance with the outline of the scene, paying particular attention to the function of that beat, how it develops, where it falls within the scene and which characters are involved.
- One the beats have been written, the writers share their work with each other, reading the beats in chronological order. Each writer should take note of the similarities and differences between the beats, coming to an understanding within the group of what can be developed and reconciled in order to maintain consistency

within the script. This can be done with the writers alone first and then with performers and the director, as it may help the writers to reconcile any obvious issues among themselves before entering a rehearsal room.

* The writers should take particular note of the ways in which the characters are depicted in the different beats, how they have been interpreted by the different writers and how this will affect their journey through the scene. It will help the performers later on if the writers make sure there is as much consistency as possible in this sense.

Working on site

The following two approaches are designed to assist the writers in writing collaboratively for a site-specific, site-sensitive and/or promenade production, working with the text on site and responding to the given sites when writing. They are intended to be carried out after an outline of the script has been produced and the writers and director have a sense of the story they are telling and the structure of the text. (These strategies can be applied to any collaborative process involving a writer intended to create a site-specific production and can be adjusted to suit a process with a single writer.)

1) Mapping I

* The writer(s) can explore the site that the company plans to use for the production and, together with the director, make a list of possible locations that could be interesting to use for performance.
* They can think through the locations within the site and compare them to the list of scenes within the outline of the script, matching up scenes with locations that might suit each other.
* Once a few different possibilities for situating different scenes have been conceived by the group, the whole company can then walk through the site and think about how the audience's journey from one location to another could impact the structure of the text.

2) Mapping II

* Once the writers have explored the site and paired different locations within it with possible scenes, they can then experiment with writing different versions of these scenes for different sites.

- For instance, a writer may be deciding between two sites for one scene. They can write a draft of the scene for each site, thinking about how the space and its possibilities for the performers and the audience might impact the integrity of the scene. The following might be some questions to consider:
  - Which site is more interesting?
  - Which is more appropriate to the production?
  - Which is more likely to serve the project?
- Once all the writers have gone through this process, they can compare notes with each other on what they have discovered about the site and its effect on the project, characters and individual scenes. This can then enable the writers and director to come to an understanding about how to structure the text with respect to the site.

3) Exploration

The approach below can serve as an alternative to the exercises above, to be used as a way for the writers and director to explore a site as inspiration to form ideas for a script. It can also be applied to a situation wherein a company is choosing from a number of sites for a production but have not chosen one yet; it can be useful in helping the company find a site which throws open the largest number of possibilities for scripting and performance. This approach would be most useful for a project wherein the text has not yet been written.

- The writers should repeat the process of exploring a site intended for the production, as explained in the previous exercise, taking notes on different areas and spaces — what kinds of stories, atmospheres and possibilities they suggest. One suggestion is for everyone to sketch or take pictures of any sites they find particularly inspiring.
- Especially since the text has not yet been written at this stage, the writers should take care to consider any particular features of the building or site that could add new spatial dimensions to the production, such as balconies, staircases, bridges, tunnels and platforms.
- The writers should consider the layout of the site and think about possibilities for guiding an audience through this space; how might these possible journeys influence the story and the structure of the script?

Adaptation

This last group of strategies combine approaches to adaptation of non-dramatic source material for performance with a multiple writer collaborative process. If, like

The Odyssey, the production in question is both an adaptation and a site-specific or promenade performance, these strategies can be carried out before, after or along-side the previous ones that relate to site exploration.

1) Fountdation building

- Along with the director, the writers can discuss the aspects of the source material that feel significant to the production: themes, narrative strands, characters, atmosphere and visual motifs. (Some useful, complementary exercises to use from Chapter 2 might be 'Performing the source text' and 'Character journeys'.)
- As in the 'Research/exploration' exercise in Chapter 2, individually, each writer can create a list of inspirational material that they feel relates to those aspects of the source material (such as poems, other books, articles, TV shows, films, songs, pictures) and share these items within the group, either in person or via an online sharing platform.
- Each writer can then attempt to write a scene, monologue or fragment of text inspired by one of the sources in this file of inspiration (either their own or someone else's).
- Consider combining a poem and a song or an article and an image and allow these items to influence your interpretation of the adapted source material; this will give you an idea of the ways in which different ideas from the group can be combined.
- When the writers share their work, the objective should be to see which themes and ideas have recurred throughout the excerpts of texts in development. It might be useful to gain a collective understanding of what the writers share in terms of interests and where they diverge conceptually and creatively. Another element to consider is what each writer has challenged and what has been maintained with respect to the source text and its adaptation.

2) Character building

- Each writer takes a character from the source material the company is adapting.
- The writers, director and/or performers then discuss the characters chosen and how each person in the group views them. As in 'character journeys' from Chapter 2, the following might be some questions to consider:
    - Who is this person?
    - How do they see the world?
    - What are their distinguishing characteristics?
    - What do they want?
    - How do they change?
    - What is their journey?
    - What is their relationship to the other characters?

- Each writer should then write a monologue for their character, responding to a particular moment or episode from the source material. A performer can then work with each writer, progressing through the monologue and sharing their thoughts about the character and how they come across in the text, as well as possibilities for revision.
- These possibilities can then be discussed with the director and the rest of the group before the writer revises the piece. It will be useful for everyone to share the work as a whole so that there is a collective understanding about how the writing is emerging and about the approaches that each writer is taking.
- The writers can then redraft their monologue based on changes suggested in this writer–performer collaboration later on.

Conclusion

The role of the writer

The five models of working for a writer in a collaborative process which I have presented throughout this book can now be observed through a slightly different lens: what are the possibilities for the role of the text? The role of the text can be categorized in three ways that relate to the quality and level of influence on the collaborative process:

- **The guiding force.** Whether the model of working is one that is led by the writer, the writer/director or a collaborative agreement between the writer and the company, a number of case studies in this book demonstrate ways of working wherein the text is the guiding force throughout the process. In the case of *War and Peace*, the initial concept for the production was agreed upon by the writer and the company, but the text was written before rehearsals began and guided much of the work generated for the production (such as the staging, design and movement score). Although ideas for *Stockholm* were initially developed through discussion and movement-led workshops, Bryony Lavery's narrative, characters and dialogue shaped and informed the resulting production. Writer/director Polly Teale was the central driver behind *Brontë*, but she had written much of the text and had sketched the main theatrical conceits before rehearsals began.
- **The supporting force.** In the second case, other productions demonstrate a process in which the text was a supporting element rather than a guiding one. The text generally serves as a secondary driver within a collaborative process when there is a good deal of director- and performer-centred generation of material. The text is more likely to be created in response to the needs of the production and the company rather than for its own sake, such as *Faster*, which served to crystalize concepts and develop a cohesive narrative from material from the devising process. Another example of this is *Tristan and Yseult*, where the writers wrote the text in response to the director's

needs and conceptualizations, giving voice to the characters already existing within the original source material.

- **The integrated force.** In the third case, the text sometimes serves as a guide and at other times as a support for the material conceived and generated by the rest of the production team. This characterizes the role of the text within a process that is not necessarily led by the writer, but rather one in which the writer or writer/director plays a significant role, working alongside the director and performers who also demonstrate considerable artistic agency in the generation of material. The text for *The Odyssey* is representative of this tendency in that Vic Bryson, Michael Wagg and I were commissioned to script the production in conjunction with a multi-part workshopping process, incorporating the director's concepts and material from devising sessions. *Water* is a different example in that David Farr developed the text he was commissioned to write alongside the devising process in which he led the company, allowing the devised material to inform the text and vice versa.

In many ways, the role of the writer in a collaborative context is infinitely variable, changing from project to project, depending on the needs of the company, the writer and the agreement established between the two entities. Claire MacDonald explains, 'the expanded field of writing does not ... proceed from writing, but *with* writing, and from writing's engagement with other practices.'[1] The methods which Kneehigh, Filter, Frantic Assembly, Shared Experience and Teatro Vivo have used to work with writers and writer/directors demonstrate a tendency towards creating a shifting and flexible process that allows for a certain amount of negotiation between the commissioned writer and the company in order to serve the production and artistic goals of the collaborators involved. Describing the process he negotiated with Filter when working on the text for *Faster*, Stephen Brown learned that 'the writer needs to be in a sort of zig-zag with the company', which he facilitated by 'feeding ideas' into their discussions, stepping back from the devising process, returning to the rehearsal room, observing the work, writing text and then sharing what he had written with the company.[2] A writer can be a practitioner within a company and one who also plays another role, such as a performer, as in the case of Michael Wagg's functioning as both a writer and a performer in *The Odyssey*, or a director, as in the case of David Farr for Filter's *Water*. A writer can also be a practitioner who serves in a role that is distinct from the rest of the company but who also is charged with the writing of a text, such as Bryony Lavery's role in the creation of *Stockholm*, or the driving force behind the conception and execution of the project, such as Polly Teale for Shared Experience's *Brontë*.

Authorship

How might authorship be impacted by these models of writer–company collaboration? The relationship between the writer's role in the process and the authorship of the piece are interdependent. The role of an individual writer can change from company to company and production to production (depending on the goals of both the writer and the company and the requirements of the production); texts produced by writers and writer/directors such as Helen Edmundson, Bryony Lavery, Stephen Brown, Dawn King, Ollie Wilkinson, Polly Teale, David Farr, Carl Grose, Anna Maria Murphy, Michael Wagg, Vic Bryson and I have been the product of the writer's contributions but also, to varying degrees, of the shared creative agency of an entire production team. The written and non-written applications of theatre-making are developed to suit the objectives and aesthetics of the project in question, so the authorship of the work can be shared to varying degrees among the collaborators involved. National Theatre Associate Director Ben Power feels that as collaborative processes involving writing, devising and dramaturgy continue to shift and change, a sense of 'shared ownership' has begun to emerge, as well as 'the dissolving of barriers between the traditional functions of writer, director and other creative artists.'[3] This is not to say, however, that the authorship cannot evolve organically from the process, nor that all collaborators involved would necessarily find the dissolution of role-related boundaries desirable. As writer Clare Bayley explains in her chapter on writing and devising, 'the question of authorship can be problematic, so to avoid bad feeling later on, it's important to clarify this before you start.'[4] With the exception of *Faster* (a case in which the authorship of the production and the text shifted throughout its development), the authorship and accreditation were agreed to at the beginning in the case studies in this book.

The concept of authorship within a collaborative context can be complex and sometimes even contentious, as different people can be considered responsible for a number of significant elements from stage to stage of the development of the project in question: the origination of the central concept, the performance material (textual, physical, devised and written) and influence regarding the final editing of the material. Furthermore, authorship reflects the way in which each company's hierarchy and the writer's or writer/director's role influences the compositional process. For example, regarding Shared Experience, the authorship of the writer or writer/director and the authorship of artistic director(s) and the movement director are reciprocal; in the case of *War and Peace*, although Edmundson was the author of the text which influenced the staging and movement, Nancy Meckler, Teale and Liz Ranken were the authors of the highly influential staging, movement and concepts that shaped the text. Teale was the primary author of *Brontë*, but Leah Hausman (as the movement director in the 2005 production) and Ranken (as the movement director in the 2010 production) contributed to this authorship greatly by composing the movement that created another dramaturgical dimension to the production. Frantic Assembly's concept of authorship is similar to Shared Experience's in that there is a reciprocity between the written and the physical score. Scott Graham and Steven Hoggett have created what has become the company's approach to making work, and thus, they greatly influence the work of the writers they commission; they also establish the central theme for every production, which the writers then develop into a narrative, around which the directors devise movement with the performers. The writers produce the texts, sharing the authorship with the directors, and the performers contribute to the authorship of the choreography in the devising sessions during rehearsals. In the case of *Faster* and *Water*, Dimsdale, Roberts and Phillips contributed to the authorship by establishing the central theme for each production before the devising process began and by approving all the final decisions made to the production and the text. In *Tristan and Yseult*, Grose and Murphy are the authors of the text, but Rice is the author of the concept that drove the adaptation and the staging of the production. With *The Odyssey*, the authorship is even more complex, as Bryson, Wagg and I all contributed to the originating concept, text and devising, but many performers generated material through devising, and Austin originated the concept, conceived the staging and had the final say dramaturgically.

Best practice

In many ways, best practice for writer–company collaborations is much the same as best practice for any kind of theatre and performance-making. However, the potential for disagreements, misunderstandings, miscommunication and violation of creative and authorial boundaries can increase with the amount of input and number of contributors on a collaborative project. For those interested in applying these models of working and practical strategies to their own artistic endeavours, I offer some thoughts on best practice.

Clarity in the initial agreement between collaborators regarding delegation of roles, the hierarchy of the company and its effect on the decision-making process, and an open discussion of the expectations of the collaborators involved is key to creating an efficient collaborative process. A clearly expressed contract can provide a foundation for a flexible approach to solving any problems that may arise in the development or rehearsal process, as it gives all parties involved a series of guidelines on which to fall back. 'It's incredibly important that you and ... the writer know exactly where you stand before going into the process', commented Oliver Dimsdale when asked about Filter's relationship with writers.[5] The clearer the initial agreement between the writer and company (and in fact, any practitioner working on the project) is, the more productive the process of working will be for all involved. Emma Rice says, 'You can't negotiate who's in charge halfway through. ... I think that's really establishing what the chain of command is.'[6] Hierarchies within companies and within writer–company collaborations also tend to dictate processes of working and modes of communication and decision making, so clarity is vital regarding the ways in which collaborators understand their respective positions so that working processes can evolve and the collaborators can obtain their artistic objectives. Bryson suggests that it is not only especially important to agree on roles within the process but also to continue to clarify those roles throughout.[7] The responsibilities that fall within those roles are a crucial point to discuss at the beginning of the project. For instance, is the writer responsible for scripting the entire text? Will there be a dramaturg assisting on the production? Will the director be responsible for running developmental workshops? Will the performers be expected to produce any scripted work as well? Out of a discussion of roles and obligations may come another regarding the process used to make the work or at least a general timeline for the project, including deadlines for drafts of scripts, dates for workshops and rehearsals and any meetings that might be necessary. It is also important to come to an agreement regarding how the work will be credited in any published material and how any resulting profits will be shared.

It is equally important to keep the channels of **communication** open throughout the process of working. Bryson suggests that one 'Make time for the creative team to meet outside the actual rehearsals.'[8] As we learned when making *The Odyssey*, if a process is lengthy and complex and involves a large number of collaborators, it is easy for the discussion of the material and how it is evolving to fall between the cracks during a busy and pressing rehearsal period. A series of discussions before, during and after the workshops and rehearsals (either in person or via email, though a combination of the two is likely to be practical) helps facilitate the creative process and allows the collaborators to address any questions or issues that may arise, rather than waiting until it is too late to address them. This kind of sharing of information can also help to maintain the expectations established at the beginning of the project as well as keep track of how the material for the piece might be evolving and changing. Rice attests, 'If you've had all of the right conversations, then everybody knows what's happening and you never need to worry.'[9] By the same token, it is also imperative that writers not lose their sense of voice or autonomy within a collaborative process; while it is important for writers to be flexible and willing to negotiate with their collaborators, it is equally important that they feel they can express their opinions and make a case for their choices regarding the work they have written.

Openness, trust and respect. Collaboration can be difficult for a writer by virtue of the fact that collaborative processes of theatre-making are often less clear and/or streamlined than solo-authored performance writing – there may be more voices involved, more collaborators to satisfy, more systems of checks and balances and more needs to meet. As with any creative process, the principles of open-mindedness about the process and trust and respect for one's collaborators are paramount. Deviser Joan Schirle argues that 'By creating a shared space, generating and manipulating models, and using outside resources and strategies, the capacity for making decisions is expanded.'[10] Bayley admits that although there are 'many pleasures to be found in devising new work' for a writer, there are also many 'pitfalls' because 'each writer and company will make up their own rules and conventions about their process,'[11] but Bayley suggests that a 'state of generosity' that accompanies open-mindedness and open-heartedness can provide a writer with 'a greater breadth of experience and a larger set of skills' while working collaboratively.[12] A clear initial agreement and ongoing and robust discussions surrounding the work will help to develop a sense of respect and trust within the company, especially if the practitioners involved do not have a previous history of working together. By the same token, collaborators who have worked together before should be vigilant in maintaining the same level of trust and respect rather than making assumptions based on previous experiences.

Documentation. Finding a system for documenting discussions, workshops, rehearsals, drafts of texts and devising sessions can be beneficial for a number of reasons. Graham and Hoggett video every devising session with their performers so that they may be able to watch the material created at the end of each day and decide what to keep in the production, but recording workshops and rehearsals might be helpful for writers as well in order to be able to reflect on the work being developed with the rest of the creative team. On *The Odyssey*, we kept the threads of emails going back and forth between writers and the director as well as drafts of scenes from the script in Dropbox so that we could refer back to them when necessary. I believe that the process of documentation is useful not only practically but also psychologically for collaboration: for instance, if you as a writer know that a draft of a scene you have written is saved in a shared file, you may be more comfortable with accepting and implementing suggested changes, knowing the earlier version is still in existence. Additionally, the more material that is developed and documented and the more people there are making contributions to discussions, workshops and rehearsals, the more organized the creative team needs to be, as it can be easy for drafts of texts, notes and ideas to get lost in the fray.

What is the future of collaboration?

When I set out to study writing in collaboration and also to make collaborative work as a young writer in 2005, the theatre and performance industry in the UK was benefiting from generous Arts Council funding under Tony Blair's government. However, as I write this conclusion, the funding situation has changed dramatically since the election of Cameron in 2010 (as well as his re-election in 2015), and its impact on theatre-making today is worth considering. As writer Fraser Grace explains,

> That theatre, and especially new plays in the theatre, are under threat, is not in doubt. When the playwright Fin Kennedy published his report *In Battalions* in 2012, the surveys he conducted painted a grim picture of the situation in the UK. In spite of the huge and conspicuous successes like *A Servant of Two Masters* or *Jerusalem*, recessionary pressures were hitting the industry hard, and the playwrights' corner of it especially so.[13]

In Kennedy's report, which Grace cites, he has found that a number of dramatic cuts to funding for arts funding in Britain has resulted in the cancellation of productions; the production of fewer new plays; significant cuts to theatre companies and venues; a decrease in commissions for writers; shorter runs for productions as well as shorter rehearsal and R&D periods; and compromised (if not entirely eliminated) community and youth outreach programmes – to name but a few.[14] In *Arts Index: England 2007–2014*, actor, director and the chair of National Campaign for the Arts (NCA) Samuel West writes, 'our arts sector … is having to rely more and more on earned income rather than public funding'[15] and goes so far as to say that the NCA is concerned that 'we have now reached a tipping point where further cuts to funding will permanently damage how the sector supports society.'[16] As the financial support shown for the theatre industry under the Labour Government from 2003–2008 encouraged innovation and expansion of theatre-making practice in the UK, as well as the creation of new work, the cuts to funding from 2010 onwards have impeded the continuation of this kind of growth. Alex Mermikides and Jackie Smart write, 'The stability of a company …, which is determined to a large extent by its funding situation, inevitably impacts on its structure'.[17] As the company hierarchy informs the model of working and thus the resulting text and production, it is not only the structure and stability of a company that is impacted by its funding prospects. The impact that these cuts have had on new writing and collaborative theatre-making is especially noteworthy, as it has become less expensive to produce revivals of older plays that need no long periods of development involving readings, workshops, meetings and the like. Joe Sumison, artistic director of the Dukes Theatre in Lancaster, notes that funding cuts also have the side-effect of demoralizing practitioners and challenging their 'perception of their own value'.[18] In an already competitive and poorly paid industry,[19] this psychological component of the fight for survival can impact the nature of the collaboration; time spent on fundraising and grant writing distracts from creative work, and the pressure to find funding sources can add pressure to an already stressful process. Collaborative working models – especially those involving lengthy devising and or/ developmental periods – sometimes demand more funding than less collaborative modes of making work in order to pay the creative team involved to participate throughout each stage of the process. Although ensemble practice can be ideal for collaborative work (so that the same directors, performers, designers and writers can work together again and again, developing a shared language), it is a difficult (if not nearly impossible) goal in the UK, as ensembles are costly to maintain; it is unusual that a company can afford to be able to employ more than a skeleton staff of an artistic director(s) and an administration team (or lone administrator).

However, collaboration – both within individual productions and across the industry – is and will continue to become more important than ever in this climate of significantly compromised funding structure where so many companies and practitioners are struggling to continue to produce work. We will have to find new partnerships and alliances to make up for the gaps in our budgets. For example, at 'Cutting Edge: British Theatre in Hard Times' (a conference organized by the British Theatre Consortium and The Writers' Guild of Great Britain), Bolton-based Octagon Theatre Artistic Director Elizabeth Newman stated that in order to keep the theatre running after a series of stringent funding cuts, the Octagon established a number of partnerships with external organizations such as 'Bolton at Home', an organization that provides social housing.[20] The principles of collaboration and best practice approaches developed for making work can be applied to the process of seeking producing partners, as well as individuals and organizations willing to exchange goods and services, which in turn could result in the discovery of new methods of writer–company collaborative practice. Nevertheless, this is not to say that these collaborations are or will be easy to pursue. Newman adds that the creation of these kinds of partnerships is difficult and time-consuming, often taking time away from the actual process of theatre-making.[21] Royal Shakespeare Company Deputy Artistic Director Erica Whyman says that although this kind of collaboration 'allows theatres to punch above their weight', the element of compromise makes it more difficult for them to establish a clear identity.[22] In the case of co-productions, one company might have an artistic vision for a production, but their collaborating partner (another company or a venue) might have alternative ideas or might simply make creative contributions that change the nature of the work.

Further reading

The most recent literature on collaborative and devised theatre focuses on the nature and history of different companies, often grouping collaborative and devised work into the same category. In *Making a Performance: Devising Histories and Contemporary Practices* (Routledge, 2007) by Emma Govan, Helen Nicholson and Katie Normington, the authors study the practice and history of devised and collaborative theatre through companies which focus on adaptation, physical theatre, site-specific theatre and political theatre. *Making a Performance* is similar to Deirdre Heddon and Jane Milling's *Devising Performance* (Palgrave Macmillan, 2006) and Alison Oddey's *Devising Theatre: A Practical and Theoretical Handbook* (Routledge, 1994), and it could be perceived as a text that attempts to encompass both previous books' purposes of mapping the history of devised theatre (*Devising Performance*) and introducing a manual for practitioners (*Devising Theatre*). *Devising in Process* (Palgrave Macmillan, 2010), edited by Alex Mermikides and Jackie Smart, is a compilation of case studies chronicled by different writers on the process used by collaborating companies. *Collective Creation in Contemporary Performance* (Palgrave, 2013), edited by Kathryn Mederos Syssoyeva and Scott Proudfit, is a collection of studies that trace the recent history of collaborative theatre companies and practitioners that emerged from European and North American contexts.

There have been a number of books detailing developments in dramaturgical practice published over the last few years that might help the reader consider possibilities for the text but also for how the overall dramatic structure for a production can be authored and shaped. *Dramaturgy in Performance* by Cathy Turner and Synne K. Behrndt (Palgrave Macmillan, 2007) is a history of the practice of dramaturgy and the role of the dramaturg throughout the twentieth and twenty-first centuries in European and North American theatre. The most recent additions to work surrounding new writing and dramaturgical practices are *The Routledge Companion to Dramaturgy* (Routledge, 2014), edited by Magda Romanska – which is a collection of articles, essays and interviews by scholars and practitioners investigating different facets of contemporary dramaturgical practice from a global perspective – and *Dramaturgy in the Making* (Bloomsbury, 2015) by Katalin Trencsényi, a series of studies and interviews with dramaturgs working across theatre and dance practice.

Much of the existing literature on writing for performance focuses on the more traditional elements of playwriting, such as genre, structure and character, but more recent work, such as Fraser Grace and Clare Bayley's *Playwriting: A Writers' and Artists' Companion* (Bloomsbury Academic, 2016), touches on writing within a collaborative or devised context or both contexts. Steve Waters' *The Secret Life of Plays* (Nick Hearn Books, 2010) and David Edgar's *How Plays Work* (Nick Hearn Books, 2009) function as both analyses of the play text and approaches to writing as a solo practice. Although they both place the practice of writing for performance predominantly within the context of live art, John Deeney's *Writing Live: An Investigation of the Relationship Between the Writer and Live Art* (New Playwright's Trust, 1998) and John Freeman's *New Performance/New Writing* (Palgrave Macmillan, 2007) demonstrate the possibilities and the problematics of the role of the writer within more collaborative and less narrative-driven, performance-making contexts.

In terms of creating models and exercises for collaboration, I found Graham and Hoggett's *The Frantic Assembly Book of Devising* (Routledge, 2009) one of the most helpful in understanding the collaborative approach in a step-by-step fashion; the directors explain the process behind each of their productions, including pictures, the backstories, analyses of the processes and practical exercises for the reader. What I have also found useful in terms of understanding how improvisation works is Keith Johnstone's *Impro* (Methuen, 1979) because he organizes the book in terms of the elements essential to improvisation (such as status, spontaneity, masks and narrative skills).

There are a number of books about specific collaborating companies that worked with writers – written by both outsiders and those involved in the companies – that give an overview of historical collaborative practice. However, unless the writer–director relationship within the company was particularly strong, I often found the writer's perspective to be absent from these chronicles. For example, Eileen Blumenthal's *Joseph Chaikin* (Cambridge University Press, 1984) is a comprehensive overview of The Open Theater Artistic Director Joseph Chaikin's development as a director and his relationships with writers' and performers' using an extensive base of material (interviews, play texts, performances analysis and rehearsal documentation). In *Taking Stock: The Theatre of Max Stafford-Clark* (Nick Hern Books, 2007), Stafford-Clark and editor Philip Roberts have collated a series of the director's journal entries and interviews about his career and the evolution of the Joint Stock and Out of Joint theatre companies; Stafford-Clark's notes and later reflections on workshops, rehearsals, performances and critical receptions are organized into case studies on different productions. Another interesting example of a book that documents the work of a single company is *Invisible Things: Documentation from a Devising Process* (Fevered Sleep and The University of Winchester, 2011) by David Harradine, in collaboration with Synne Behrndt, which describes the making of *An Infinite Line: Brighton*, a site-specific performance and film installation created by Fevered Sleep for the 2008 Brighton Festival, focusing on the devising process used, which involved a dramaturg and a writer.

Final reflections

When I first moved to Britain from the United States, an aspiring writer and theatre-maker, I was influenced and excited by a particular kind of theatre I was seeing on London's stages: collaborative, company-driven work that felt both rich and mysterious and was multi-dimensional, filling the space with words, movement, spectacle and sound. I was curious how these kinds of productions – involving both companies and writers – were made. What was written? What was devised? How was the staging composed and constructed? What did the play texts that served as their blueprints look like? Simultaneously, I began to develop my own practice of writing through collaboration, investigating and experimenting with ways to allow the pieces of text I was scripting to inform and be informed by the imaginings of performers, directors and designers. I would sit in rehearsal rooms with pages of dialogue, notebooks, novels, newspaper articles and pictures and persuade per-former friends to take what I was offering them and play. Create. Shape. Debate. Argue. I set out to find ways of making a play text a living, porous thing; receiving and broadcasting ideas; stories and characters bouncing around from person to person. I was hoping to make the kind of collaborative, multi-dimensional work I saw weekly on my nights in the theatres.

When I set out to write *Writing in Collaborative Theatre-Making*, I had intended to try to draw up a series of possible strategies for writ-ers and their collaborators, or perhaps theatre-makers who were not writers but wanted to find new ways of working with text. To inspire people like myself, fascinated by written collaborations and collec-tive work that incorporated writing. I wanted to encourage readers to think of the writer's role as flexible, mouldable to different working situations and different kinds of performance practice. I also wanted to find out about the different ways in which writers became involved in collaborative, company-driven processes. I chose five companies that I believed had distinct collaborative writing practices for me to dissect and explore. I believed that Filter Theatre, Frantic Assembly, Kneehigh, Shared Experience and Teatro Vivo understood the text as a kind of second playing space, open to interventions from the performer, the sound, the body, the audience, the projections and other, extant texts. I cannot pretend the choices in companies is not, in many ways, personal; in addition to four companies that have inspired me with their work for many years, I wanted to write about my own experience as a writer working in collaboration so that I could write from the inside out as well as the outside looking in. Of course there are a number of other possible models of working that I haven't explored in this book, such as group writing, writing in live art practice and writing and dance – to name a few. The pur-pose of this book is to facilitate an insight into and comprehensive understanding of different contemporary and historical models of writer–company collaboration, as well as the advantages, challenges, systems of communication, hierarchies and modes of authorship therein, for practitioners and students alike. Grace argues, 'theatre writing has barely any rules at all, and the most exciting theatre writ-ing arguably thrives on renegotiating whatever rules it began with, finding new ways to break old lore, seemingly with every project.'[23]

It is my hope that those who read *Writing in Collaborative Theatre-Making* will use it as a series of strategies for working as writers and with writers, creating text and engaging with text, as a jumping-off point for finding other possibilities for theatre-making and renegotiating the rules of writing for performance.

Notes

Introduction

1 Chris Goode, speaking on 'The Big Society' panel, *Cutting Edge: British Theatre in Hard Times*, 25 April 2015, Central Saint Martins.

2 As Emma Rice explained to me, 'we haven't created a formula. We try and improve our model every time we do it, but ... the only thing that's a fixture is that the work leads.' Emma Rice, interview with the author, 24 July 2013.

3 'What does collaboration mean in practice? Is it a collaboration on one person's idea, or is it a collaboration from "scratch"? Both of these lead to differing "expectations" being placed upon the writer, which will effect the whole process and therefore the outcome of the project .... What happens to the collaborative relationship between writer, director, designer, composer and lighting designer once the writer is actually alone with the text? Is the writer acting as a documenter and/or dramatist, writing up a series of collective "instructions" for a specific performance? Or is the writer writing a piece of text which will act as a stimulus for a devising rehearsal process? The different expectations can effect the "status" of the writer.' Ruth Ben-Tovim, 'The Writer and the Early Development Stages' in John Deeney (ed.), *Writing Live: An Investigation of the Relationship between Writing and Live Art* (London: New Playwrights Trust, 1998), p.65.

4 John Freeman, *New Performance/New Writing* (Basingstoke: Palgrave Macmillan, 2007), pp.2–3 & 15.

5 Katalin Trencsényi, *Dramaturgy in the Making* (London and New York: Bloomsbury Methuen Drama, 2015), pp.125–126.

6 Fraser Grace and Clare Bayley, *Playwriting: A Writers' and Artists' Companion* (London: Bloomsbury Academic, 2016), pp.65–66.

7 'The show must go on', *The Economist*, 18 February 2012.

8 Michael Billington, *State of the Nation: British Theatre Since 1945* (London: Faber and Faber Limited, 2007), p.392.

9 Tom Morris, 'Without subsidy, our theatres will run out of hits', *The Observer*, 17 June 2012.

10 Alex Sierz, *Rewriting the Nation: British Theatre Today* (London: Methuen Drama, 2011), p.16.

11 'Investigations into new theatre writing in England, 2003–2009', *Arts Council*, www.artscouncil.org.uk/artforms/theatre [Accessed 2 September 2011].

12 Ibid.

13 'New Writing in Theatre 2003–2008: an assessment of new writing within smaller scale in England', commissioned by Arts Council England from

Emma Dunton, Roger Nelson and Hetty Shand (2009) www.artscouncil.org.
uk/publication_archive/new-writing-theatre/. [Accessed 2 September 2011].

14 Ibid.

15 Ibid.

16 Ruth Little and Emily McLaughlin, *The Royal Court Theatre Inside Out* (London: Oberon Books, 2007), p.194.

17 Deirdre Heddon and Jane Milling, *Devising Performance: A Critical History* (Basingstoke: Palgrave Macmillan, 2006), p.2.

18 Occasionally, a performer may contribute written work to the project that s/he has written alone, but in this case, it will be specified.

19 Andy Field, 'All theatre is devised and text-based', *The Guardian* (21 April 2009) www.guardian.co.uk/stage/theatreblog/2009/apr/21/theatre-devised-text-based [Accessed 27 September 2009].

20 Ben Payne, 'Opposing Truths: New Writing and Its Discontents', in John Deeney (ed.), *Writing Live: An Investigation of the Relationship between Writing and Live Art*, p.28.

21 Cathy Turner and Synne K. Behrndt, *Dramaturgy and Performance* (Basingstoke: Palgrave Macmillan, 2008), p.4.

22 Ibid.

23 Ibid., p.98.

Chapter I

1 Jared Diamond, *Guns, Germs and Steel: The Fates of Human Societies*, 3rd ed. (New York: W.W. Norton & Company, Inc., 2005), p.224.

2 In 1962, Piscator wrote, 'The war finally buried bourgeois individualism under a hail of steel and a holocaust of fire. Man, the individual ... revolving egocentrically around the concept of the self, in fact lies buried beneath a marble slab inscribed "The Unknown Soldier"'. Erwin Piscator, *The Political Theatre*, trans. Hugh Rorrison (London: Eyre Methuen Ltd, 1980), p.186.

3 C.D. Innes, *Erwin Piscator's Political Theatre: The Development of Modern German Drama* (Cambridge: Cambridge University Press, 1972), p.68.

4 Cathy Turner and Synne K. Behrndt, *Dramaturgy and Performance* (Basingstoke: Palgrave Macmillan, 2008), p.59.

5 John Willett, *The Theatre of the Weimar Republic* (New York: Holmes and Meier Publishers, Inc., 1988), p.108.

6 Turner and Behrndt, *Dramaturgy and Performance*, p.59.

7 Shomit Mitter and Maria Shevtsova, *Fifty Key Theatre Directors* (London: Routledge, 2005), p.43.

8 Piscator, *The Political Theatre*, p.82.

9 Ibid., p.48

10 Ibid., p.13.

11 In the preface to the epic novel *Tidal Wave* (which he wrote at the same time as the play), Paquet writes, 'It is not the history of a revolution....Not

a picture of Soviet Russia....It was not a matter of copying reality, but of capturing the motive forces of our times in a few figures ... in images which would awaken in us the feelings that reality awoke'. Ibid., p.107.

12 Ibid., pp.110–111.

13 Ibid.

14 In 1963, Piscator wrote about the period of 1926–1928:'my work with actors was very valuable for me ... Gradually the kind of cooperation which my productions required transformed them into a human and artistic, and in a certain sense also a political community'. Ibid., p.120.

15 'This demand for a dramaturg who might "co-operate creatively" was an extension of a role that was usually confined to decisions concerning repertoire, casting and any necessary editing of play texts. It was Piscator ... who developed the model of the "dramaturgical collective"'. Turner and Behrndt, *Dramaturgy and Performance*, p.60.

16 Mitter and Shevtsova, *Fifty Key Theatre Directors*, p.44.

17 Willett, *The Theatre of the Weimar Republic*, p.109.

18 Piscator, *The Political Theatre*, p.259.

19 Willett, *The Theatre of the Weimar Republic*, p.109.

20 Maria-Ley Piscator, *The Piscator Experiment: The Political Theatre* (Carbondale and Edwardsville: Southern Illinois University Press, 1967), p.16.

21 Judith Malina, *The Piscator Notebook* (London: Routledge, 2012), p.12.

22 Nadine Holdsworth, *Joan Littlewood* (London: Routledge, 2006), pp.25–26.

23 'Far from experiencing an overnight revolution in 1956, the British theatre, like society itself, split into opposing camps. The old guard, sensing an external challenge and a shift in attitudes, became ever more protective of its territory and assertive of its values: the West End went on pumping out right-wing propaganda and peddling cosy reassurance. At the same time, a radical generation, principally though not exclusively young, acquired a new militancy and authority.' Michael Billington, *State of the Nation: British Theatre Since 1945* (London: Faber and Faber, 2007), p.93.

24 Emma Govan, Helen Nicholson and Katie Normington, *Making a Performance: Devising Histories and Contemporary Practices* (Abington: Routledge, 2007), p.48.

25 Joan Littlewood, *Joan's Book: Joan Littlewood's Peculiar History as She Tells It* (London: Methuen, 1994), p.669.

26 Peter Rankin, *Joan Littlewood: Dreams and Realities – The Official Biography* (London: Oberon Books Ltd, 2014), p.147.

27 John Elsom, *Post-War British Theatre* (London: Routledge and Kegan Paul Ltd., 1976), p.86.

28 Govan, Nicholson and Normington, *Making a Performance*, p.48.

29 'Sometimes you could come up with something that was rejected, and sometimes you'd come up with an idea that would be incorporated. It was always her editing. She used to say, I'm a concierge. She'd say, I'd sit there and watch things go past and I'd say no to some and yes to others. A bit more complicated than that, but she never liked being called a director. She'd say, I'm a saboteur or something or other, but never a director.' Peter Rankin, personal interview with the author, 29 November 2007.

30 Ibid.
31 Ibid.
32 Ibid.
33 Ibid.
34 Ibid.
35 Littlewood, *Joan's Book*, p.683.
36 Ibid.
37 Anthony Frost and Ralph Yarrow, *Improvisation in Drama* (Basingstoke: Macmillan, 1990), p.694.
38 Ibid.
39 Of John McGrath, Maria Di Cenzo notes, that he was 'part of a generation of theatregoers/makers whose conception of theatre's form and function was being changed by the work of Joan Littlewood'. Maria Di Cenzo, *The Politics of Alternative Theatre in Britain, 1968–1990: The case of 7:84 (Scotland)* (Cambridge: Cambridge University Press, 1996), p.153.
40 Megan Terry, *Viet Rock and Other Plays* (New York: Simon and Schuster, 1966), p.9.
41 Kathryn Mederos Syssoyeva and Scott Proudfit (eds), *A History of Collective Creation* (New York: Palgrave Macmillan, 2013), p.1.
42 Robert Baker-White, *The Text in Play: Representations of Rehearsal in Modern Drama* (London: Associated University Press, 1999), p.174.
43 Helen Krich Chinoy and Linda Walsh Jenkins (eds), *Women in American Theatre: Revised and Expanded Edition* (New York: Theatre Communications Group, Inc., 1981), p.329.
44 'This interest in childhood, games and the influence of developmental psychology was reflected in the content of many of the devised performances of the 1960s and 1970s, such as The Open Theater's *Mutation Show*'. Deirdre Heddon and Jane Milling, *Devising Performance: A Critical History* (Basingstoke: Palgrave Macmillan, 2006), p.34.
45 Theodore Shank, *American Alternative Theatre* (London: Macmillan, 1982), p.38.
46 Stephen J. Bottoms, *Playing Underground: A Critical History of the 1960s Off-Off-Broadway Movement* (Ann Arbor, MI: University of Michigan Press, 2004), pp.176–177.
47 Robert Pasolli, *A Book on The Open Theater* (New York: The Bobbs-Merrill Company, Inc., 1970), p.80.
48 Ibid.
49 '*Viet Rock* fully embodied The Open Theater's conviction that actors were creative artists rather than mere interpreters of a playwright's word; but that a playwright was also needed to give form and voice to their experiments.' Bottoms, *Playing Underground*, p.179.
50 Ibid.
51 Ibid.
52 Ibid., p.180.
53 Mederos Syssoyeva and Proudfit, *A History of Collective Creation*, p.4.
54 Shank, *American Alternative Theatre*, p.49.

55 Pasolli, *A Book on The Open Theater*, pp.10–11.
56 Ibid., p.36.
57 Ibid.
58 William Gaskill, *A Sense of Direction: Life at the Royal Court* (London: Faber and Faber Limited, 1988), p.141.
59 'The whole area of performance art and non-literary theatre is something else. If all writers were qualified directors we would cease to exist.' Ibid., p.140.
60 Philip Roberts and Max Stafford-Clark, *Taking Stock: The Theatre of Max Stafford-Clark* (London: Nick Hern Books, 2007), p.31.
61 Ruth Little and Emily McLoughlin, *The Royal Court Theatre Inside Out* (London: Oberon Books, 2007), p.106.
62 Roberts and Stafford-Clark, *Taking Stock*, p.286.
63 Catherine Itzin, *Stages in the Revolution: Political Theatre in Britain Since 1968* (London: Eyre Methuen, 1980), p.287.
64 Billington comments on Brecht's Berliner Ensemble's visit to London in 1956 and the lasting effect it had on Gaskill: 'But no one has caught better than William Gaskill the adrenalin buzz created by the Ensemble's visit, which, he says, changed his life....And Brecht's notion of Epic Theatre – with its emphasis on discrete narrative, its use of theatrical montage, its appeal to reason rather than to feelings – had a huge effect on British dramaturgy.' Michael Billington, *State of the Nation: British Theatre Since 1945* (Faber and Faber: London, 2007), p.95.
65 Ibid., p.267.
66 Simon Callow, *Being an Actor* (London: Methuen, 1984), p.64.
67 Patterson, p.164.
68 Ibid.
69 Roberts and Stafford-Clark, *Taking Stock*, p.89.
70 Di Cenzo, *The Politics of Alternative Theatre in Britain*, p.93.
71 Gillian Hanna (ed.), *Monstrous Regiment: Four Plays and a Collective Celebration* (London: Nick Hearn Books, 1991), p.xxxiii.

Chapter 2

1 Shared Experience, *Arts Council England* (2011) www.artscouncil.org.uk/rfo/shared-experience/ [Accessed 10 March 2011].
2 Kristen Crouch, 'Expressions of "Lust and Rage": Shared Experience Theatre's Adaptation of *Jane Eyre*', in Sharon Friedman (ed.), *Feminist Theatrical Revisions of Classical Works: Critical Essays* (Jefferson: McFarland and Company Inc., Publishers, 2009), p.202.
3 Theo Herdman, email correspondence with the author, 10 May 2011.
4 Polly Teale, interview with the author, 15 March 2011.
5 Helen Krich Chinoy and Linda Walsh Jenkins (eds), *Women in American Theatre: Revised and Expanded Edition* (New York: Theatre Communications Group, Inc., 1981), p.329.

6 Catherine Itzin, *Stages in the Revolution: Political Theatre in Britain Since 1968* (London: Eyre Methuen, 1980), p.287.

7 Ibid.

8 Ibid.

9 Liz Ranken, interview with the author, 28 June 2011.

10 Ibid.

11 Ibid.

12 Helen Edmundson, interview with the author, 19 May 2008.

13 Ibid.

14 Ibid.

15 Ibid.

16 Ibid.

17 Ibid.

18 Ibid.

19 Polly Teale, interview with the author, 15 March 2011.

20 Helen Edmundson, interview with the author, 19 May 2008.

21 Helen Edmundson, *War and Peace* (London: Nick Hearn Books, 2008), p.v.

22 Helen Edmundson, interview with the author, 19 May 2008.

23 Ibid.

24 Nancy Meckler, personal interview, 9 July 2009.

25 Leo Tolstoy, *War and Peace*, trans. Constance Garnett (New York and Toronto: Modern Library Paperback Edition, 2002), p.1027.

26 Edmundson, *War and Peace*, p.91.

27 Ibid., p.142.

28 Gillian King, Shared Experience education pack for *War and Peace* by Helen Edmundson (2008) www.sharedexperience.org.uk/media/education/war-and-peace_edpack.pdf [Accessed 2 August 2011].

29 Liz Ranken, interview with the author, 28 June 2011.

30 Helen Edmundson, interview with the author, 19 May 2008.

31 Ibid.

32 Ibid.

33 Helen Manful, *Taking Stage: Women Directors on Directing* (London: Methuen, 1999), p.168.

34 Theo Herdman, email correspondence with the author, 10 May 2011.

35 Scott Graham, email correspondence with the author, 13 April 2010.

36 Scott Graham and Steven Hoggett, interview with Aleks Sierz, 19 February 2004. Email correspondence with the author, 15 April 2010.

37 Scott Graham, email correspondence with the author, 13 April 2010.

38 Scott Graham and Steven Hoggett, interview with Aleks Sierz, 19 February 2004. Email correspondence with the author, 15 April 2010.

39 Steven Hoggett, interview with the author, 11 October 2010.

40 Ibid.

41 Ibid.

42 Ibid.

43 Scott Graham and Steven Hoggett, interview with Aleks Sierz, 19 February 2004. Email correspondence with the author, 15 April 2010.

44 Ibid.
45 Steven Hoggett, interview with the author, 11 October 2010.
46 Ibid.
47 Bryony Lavery, interview with the author, 30 April 2009.
48 Steven Hoggett, interview with the author, 11 October 2010.
49 Ibid.
50 Bryony Lavery, interview with the author, 30 April 2009.
51 Ibid.
52 Steven Hoggett, interview with the author, 11 October 2010.
53 Scott Graham, email correspondence with the author, 13 April 2010.
54 Ibid.
55 Steven Hoggett, interview with the author, 11 October 2010.
56 Scott Graham and Steven Hoggett, *The Frantic Assembly Book of Devising Theatre* (Abington: Routledge, 2009), p.170.
57 Regarding the relationship between spoken dialogue and physicality, Hoggett explains, 'Physicality … at its best … is counterpoint or it's subversive to what is being spoken … . [I]t's where we think the heart of our intention for physical work rests'. Steven Hoggett, interview with the author, 11 October 2010.
58 Ibid.
59 'We tend to team tag. When one is flagging the other steps in. We both direct and choreograph. We communicate very quickly, some would say imperceptibly. That is not to say we always agree.' Scott Graham, email correspondence with the author, 13 April 2010.
60 Samuel James, interview with the author, 26 March 2008.
61 Ibid.
62 'By choreography we mean any formalized movements that become set and can be repeated'. Graham and Hoggett, *The Frantic Assembly Book of Devising Theatre*, p.125.
63 James commented, 'we would look at sequences, an idea of movement or an idea of a theme of movement … . We're going to look at the idea that you're on the floor or we're going to look at the idea of stopping … . It was very much, these are your boundaries that we're looking for. … [I]t was never necessarily sort of placed in the exploration of the sequence – it was never given a specific place within the script'. Samuel James, interview with the author, 26 March 2008.
64 'All of our devising is broken down into tasks. … They never set out to encapsulate the whole production idea or solve the entire demands of the text. … By setting tasks you allow your performers to offer much creative input into the devising of choreography without burdening them with the responsibility of creating the whole show. … The shaping of theatre and choreography requires an outside eye and it is this objective influence that can liberate the performer to be brace, take risks and try things new. We, as the directors/choreographers, are liberated too as the performer is now providing a palette so much larger and richer than our own imaginations could provide.' Graham and Hoggett, *The Frantic Assembly Book of Devising Theatre*, p.7.
65 Nina Steiger, 'Absolute immediacy: A conversation with Scott Graham', *Contemporary Theatre Review*, 16:3, 2006, p.313.

66 Graham and Hoggett, *The Frantic Assembly Book of Devising Theatre*, p.170.
67 Scott Graham and Steven Hoggett, interview with Aleks Sierz, 19 February 2004. Email correspondence with the author, 15 April 2010.
68 Steven Hoggett, interview with the author, 11 October 2010.
69 Bryony Lavery, *Stockholm* (London: Oberon Modern Plays, 2007), p.50.
70 Graham and Hoggett, *The Frantic Assembly Book of Devising Theatre*, p.84.
71 Lavery, *Stockholm*, pp.65–66.
72 Ibid.
73 Helen Freshwater, 'Fingers on the Collective Pulse?', *Performance Research*, 9:3, 2004, p.34.
74 Samuel James, interview with the author, 26 March 2008.
75 Graham and Hoggett, *The Frantic Assembly Book of Devising Theatre*, p.169.
76 Ibid., p.197.
77 Ibid.
78 Aleks Sierz, *Rewriting the Nation: British Theatre Today* (London: Methuen Drama, 2011), p.4.
79 Bryony Lavery, interview with the author, 30 April 2009.
80 Graham and Hoggett, *The Frantic Assembly Book of Devising*, Theatre, p.6.

Chapter 3

1 Filter Theatre, *British Council*, *Arts*, (2010) www.britishcouncil.org/arts-performanceinprofile-2009-british_council-filter_theatre.htm [Accessed 25 May 2010].
2 Ferdy Roberts, interview with the author, 31 July 2008.
3 Ibid.
4 Oliver Dimsdale, interview with the author, 23 July 2008.
5 Guy Retallack, interview with the author, 9 April 2009.
6 Cathy Turner and Synne K. Behrndt, *Dramaturgy and Performance* (Basingstoke: Palgrave Macmillan, 2008), p.172.
7 Ibid., p.150.
8 Ferdy Roberts, interview with the author, 31 July 2008.
9 Guy Retallack, interview with the author, 9 April 2009.
10 Turner and Behrndt, *Dramaturgy and Performance*, p.171.
11 Guy Retallack, interview with the author, 9 April 2009.
12 Ibid.
13 Joan Schirle, 'Potholes in the Road to Devising', *Theatre Topics*, 15:1, 2005, p.91.
14 Ibid.
15 Dawn King, interview with the author, 3 September 2009.
16 Tim Phillips, interview with the author, 19 January 2008.
17 Margaret Atwood, *Negotiating with the Dead: A Writer on Writing* (London: Virago Press, 2003), p.4.
18 Dawn King, interview with the author, 3 September 2009.

19 Ibid.

20 Tim Phillips, interview with the author, 19 January 2008.

21 It should be noted that the character names correspond with the actors who created them in rehearsal and performed them in scratch and final performances. The changes in characters and character names may have been a result of relative availability of the performers at the time, certain people having been able to be involved for certain stages of the devising process.

22 Dawn King, personal interview, 3 September 2009.

23 King said, 'I think that that was one of the things that they were asking is, how can we get more of the book in?' Ibid.

24 Filter Theatre, Dawn King and Ollie Wilkinson, *Faster*, Draft Two, unpublished (2002), p.29.

25 Ibid.

26 Ferdy Roberts, interview with the author, 31 July 2008.

27 Stephen Brown, interview with the author, 19 February 2008.

28 Ibid.

29 It is important to note that not only was Brown a more experienced writer than King or Wilkinson and had a closer working relationship with the company, but he also had the additional support in the form of dramaturgical advice from McGrath. McGrath was not, however, present when King and Wilkinson were composing material. One could assume that this change was a result of the difficulty the company previously experienced in stage two of the process. Dawn King, interview with the author, 3 September 2009.

30 Stephen Brown, interview with the author, 19 February 2008.

31 Turner and Behrndt, *Dramaturgy and Performance*, p.156.

32 Emma Govan, Helen Nicholson and Katie Normington, *Making a Performance: Devising Histories and Contemporary Practices* (Abington: Routledge, 2007), p.100.

33 Filter Theatre and Stephen Brown, *Filter*, final version, unpublished (2003), p.13.

34 Ibid., p.14.

35 Guy Retallack, interview with the author, 9 April 2009.

36 Rachel Halliburton, review of *Faster* by Filter and Stephen Brown, *The Evening Standard*, 8 April 2003.

37 Ferdy Roberts, interview with the author, 31 July 2008.

38 Stephen Brown, interview with the author, 19 February 2008.

39 Guy Retallack, interview with the author, 9 April 2009.

40 Ibid.

41 It should be noted that even though Dimsdale, Roberts and Phillips are the artistic directors of Filter, they are also performers. Dimsdale and Roberts perform as actors and Phillips as a musician in each production. Accordingly, the three may be referred to as directors and also as performers. If there is a reference to a production director hired by the company to direct a project or to other performers, it will be specified.

Chapter 4

1 Polly Teale, interview with the author, 15 March 2011.
2 Ibid.
3 Angela Simpson, interview with the author, 5 December 2009.
4 Ibid.
5 Polly Teale, interview with the author, 15 March 2011.
6 Ibid.
7 Polly Teale, 'Three sisters', *The Guardian* (2005) www.guardian.co.uk/stage/2005/aug/13/theatre.classics [Accessed 3 August 2011].
8 Ibid.
9 Liz Ranken, interview with the author, 28 June 2011.
10 Polly Teale, interview with the author, 10 July 2008.
11 Polly Teale, interview with the author, 15 March 2011.
12 Ibid.
13 Gillian King. Shared Experience education pack: *After Mrs. Rochester*. www.sharedexperience.org.uk/media/education/after-mrs-rochester_edpack.pdf [Accessed 13 May 2014].
14 Liz Ranken, interview with the author, 28 June 2011.
15 Ibid.
16 Ibid.
17 Polly Teale, interview with the author, 15 March 2011.
18 Polly Teale, 'Three sisters', *The Guardian* (2005) www.guardian.co.uk/stage/2005/aug/13/theatre.classics [Accessed 3 August 2011].
19 Polly Teale, *Brontë* (London: Nick Hearn Books, 2005), p.13.
20 Polly Teale, 'Three sisters', *The Guardian* (2005) www.guardian.co.uk/stage/2005/aug/13/theatre.classics [Accessed 3 August 2011].
21 Teale, *Brontë* (2005), p.72.
22 Polly Teale, interview with the author, 15 March 2011.
23 Ibid.
24 Teale, *Brontë* (2005), p.51.
25 Ibid.
26 Polly Teale, *Brontë* (London: Nick Hearn Books, 2011), p. ix.
27 Ibid., p.38.
28 Muriel Spark (ed.), *The Brontë Letters* (London: Macmillan, 1954), p.118.
29 Teale, *Brontë* (2011), p.38.
30 Ibid.
31 Ibid.
32 Charlotte Brontë, *Jane Eyre* (London: Macdonald and Co., Ltd., 1955), pp.326–327.
33 Teale, *Brontë* (2011), p.ix.
34 Govan, Nicholson and Normington, *Making a Performance: Devising Histories and Contemporary Practices* (Abington: Routledge, 2007), pp.100–101.
35 Ibid.
36 Polly Teale, interview with the author, 15 March 2011.

37 Liz Ranken, interview with the author, 28 June 2011.

38 Later on, after *Water* was finished, Farr and Filter agreed that any royalties would be split between the four of them. There were also separate fees and contracts for each Filter member as performers in addition to the writing contract. David Farr, interview with the author, 2 July 2009.

39 Tim Phillips, interview with the author, 19 January 2008.

40 Cathy Turner and Synne K. Behrndt, *Dramaturgy and Performance* (Basingstoke: Palgrave Macmillan, 2008), p.162.

41 Tim Phillips, interview with the author, 19 January 2008.

42 Ibid.

43 Turner and Behrndt, *Dramaturgy and Performance*, p.163.

44 Oliver Dimsdale, interview with the author, 23 July 2008.

45 Ferdy Roberts, interview with the author, 31 July 2008.

46 Govan, Nicholson and Normington, *Making a Performance*, p.62.

47 Filter Theatre and David Farr, *Water*, final version, unpublished (2007), p.2.

48 David Farr, interview with the author, 2 July 2009.

49 Ibid.

50 Turner and Behrndt, *Dramaturgy and Performance*, p.156.

51 David Farr, interview with the author, 2 July 2009.

52 Govan, Nicholson and Normington, *Making a Performance*, pp.194–195.

53 Tim Phillips, interview with the author, 19 January 2008.

54 Farr explained,' I would go away and write some of the political scenes between ... Victoria's character [Claudia] and her political boss.... [T]here are certain things an actor cannot improvise. They can't improvise knowing stuff about political things. If they don't know it, they don't know it. And so you have to go away and actually write it. They can always improvise in relationships. Of course it's something we all have contact with'. David Farr, interview with the author, 2 July 2009.

55 Ibid.

56 Ibid.

57 'I'm a very good storyteller and a good linguist....I know something visual when I see it, but ... I don't create visually. ... So I'm always keen to collaborate with people who do that.' Ibid.

58 Filter Theatre and David Farr, *Water*, final version, unpublished (2007), p.14.

59 Anne Bogart, *And Then, You Act: Making Art in an Unpredictable World* (New York: Routledge, 2007), p.37.

60 Tim Phillips, interview with the author, 19 January 2008.

Chapter 5

1 Catherine Love and Diana Damian, 'Kneehigh', *Exeunt Magazine* (2012) exeuntmagazine.com/features/kneehigh/ [Accessed 18, November 2014]

2 Duška Radosavljević (ed.), *The Contemporary Ensemble: Interviews with theatremakers* (London and New York: Routledge, 2015), pp.18–19.

3 Ibid., pp.11–12.
4 Emma Rice, interview with the author, 24 July 2013.
5 Emma Rice, 'From a community to the West End', interview by Duška Radosavljević in Radosavljević, *The Contemporary Ensemble*, p.101.
6 Carl Grose, interview with the author, 27 March 2013.
7 Joanna Holden, 'On being an ensemble actor in the UK' interview by Duška Radosavljević in Radosavljević, *The Contemporary Ensemble*, pp.110–111.
8 Rice in Radosavljević, *The Contemporary Ensemble*, p.103.
9 Anna Maria Murphy, email correspondence with the author, 25 November 2014.
10 Anna Maria Murphy, interview with the author, 21 March 2013.
11 Stuart McLoughlin, interview with the author, 11 December 2007.
12 Carl Grose, 'Writing Tristan and Yseult: An interview with Carl Grose', Kneehigh Theatre website www.kneehigh.co.uk/list/carl-grose-TY.php [Accessed 19 November 2014].
13 Kneehigh Theatre website www.kneehigh.co.uk/show/tristan_yseult.php>[Accessed 17 February 2015].
14 Carl Grose, interview with the author, 27 March 2013.
15 Ibid.
16 Carl Grose, 'Writing *Tristan and Yseult*: An interview with Carl Grose', interview with Kneehigh Theatre, Kneehigh Theatre website www.kneehigh.co.uk/list/carl-grose-TY.php [Accessed 19 November 2014].
17 Anna Maria Murphy, interview with the author, 21 March 2013.
18 Ibid.
19 Carl Grose, Anna Maria Murphy and Emma Rice, 'Tristan & Yseult', in *The Kneehigh Anthology: Volume 1: Tristan & Yseult / The Bacchae / The Wooden Frock / The Red Shoes* (London: Oberon Books, Ltd, 2005, 2011), p.21.
20 Anna Maria Murphy, interview with the author, 21 March 2013.
21 Emma Rice, Mike Shepherd, Ian Ross and Carl Grose, 'A Conversation with Some of *Tristan & Yseult*'s creators and artists', interview with the Chicago Shakespeare Theater, Chicago Shakespeare Theater website www.chicagoshakes.com/plays_and_events/tristan/tristanconversation [Accessed 25 Nov 2014].
22 Emma Rice, Kneehigh Theatre website www.kneehigh.co.uk/page/making_a_show.php [Accessed 25 March 2013].
23 Emma Rice, interview with the author, 24 July 2013.
24 Carl Grose, interview with the author, 27 March 2013.
25 Emma Rice, Kneehigh Theatre website www.kneehigh.co.uk/page/making_a_show.php [Accessed 25 March 2013].
26 Emma Rice, interview with the author, 24 July 2013.
27 Grose, Murphy and Rice, *The Kneehigh Anthology*, p.37.
28 Ibid.
29 Video recording of *Tristan and Yseult* by Kneehigh Theatre, performed on 12 April 2005 at the National Theatre, CPA2/17, Kneehigh Archive, Archives and Special Collections, Falmouth University and University of Exeter Penryn Campus.
30 Ben Brantley, review of *Tristan and Yseult* by Kneehigh Theatre, *New York Times*, 24 November 2014 www.nytimes.com/2014/11/25/theater/kneehigh-theaters-tristan-yseult.html?_r=0 [Accessed 23 February 2015].

31 Anna Maria Murphy, interview with the author, 21 March 2013.
32 Ibid.
33 Carl Grose, email correspondence with the author, 24 November 2014.
34 Emma Rice, Mike Shepherd, Ian Ross and Carl Grose, 'A Conversation with Some of *Tristan & Yseult*'s creators and artists', interview with the Chicago Shakespeare Theater, Chicago Shakespeare Theater website www.chicagoshakes.com/plays_and_events/tristan/tristanconversation [Accessed 25 November 2014].
35 Carl Grose, 'Writing *Tristan and Yseult*: An interview with Carl Grose', Kneehigh Theatre website www.kneehigh.co.uk/list/carl-grose-TY.php [Accessed 19 November 2014].
36 Grose, Murphy and Rice, *The Kneehigh Anthology*, pp.22–23.
37 Anna Maria Murphy, interview with the author, 21 March 2013.
38 Grose, Murphy and Rice, *The Kneehigh Anthology*, p.58.
39 Ibid.
40 Carl Grose, interview with the author, 27 March 2013.
41 Ibid.
42 Ibid.
43 Claire MacDonald, 'Conducting the flow: Dramaturgy and writing', *Studies in Theatre and Performance*, 30:1, 2010, p.94.
44 Carl Grose, interview with the author, 27 March 2013.
45 Carl Grose, 'Writing *Tristan and Yseult*: An interview with Carl Grose', Kneehigh Theatre website www.kneehigh.co.uk/list/carl-grose-TY.php [Accessed 19 November 2014].
46 Carl Grose, interview with the author, 27 March 2013.
47 Anna Maria Murphy, interview with the author, 21 March 2013
48 Ibid.
49 Emma Rice, interview with the author, 24 July 2013.
50 Ibid.
51 Ibid.
52 Ibid.
53 Sebastian Born, interview with the author, 6 June 2014.
54 Ibid.
55 Carl Grose, email correspondence, 30 March 2013.

Chapter 6

1 Teatro Vivo website www.teatrovivo.co.uk/about-us/ [Accessed 30 March 2015].
2 Duška Radosavljević (ed.), *The Contemporary Ensemble: Interviews with theatre-makers*, London and New York: Routledge, 2015, pp.18–19.
3 Ibid., pp.11–12.
4 Ibid., p.11.
5 Mike Pearson, *Site-Specific Performance* (Basingstoke: Palgrave Macmillan, 2010), p.19.

212 *Notes*

6 Mark Stevenson, email correspondence with the author, 24 April 2015.
7 Teatro Vivo website www.teatrovivo.co.uk/the-odyssey-2/ [Accessed 31 March 2015].
8 Sophie Austin, email correspondence with the author, 30 April 2013.
9 Mark Stevenson, email correspondence with the author, 24 April 2015.
10 Sophie Austin, email correspondence with the author, 30 April 2013.
11 Ibid.
12 Ibid.
13 Katalin Trencsényi, *Dramaturgy in the Making* (London and New York: Bloomsbury Methuen Drama, 2015), p.xxi.
14 Michael Wagg, email correspondence with the author, 12 September 2013.
15 Vic Bryson, email correspondence with the author, 5 May 2013.
16 Michael Wagg, email correspondence with the author, 12 September 2013.
17 Sophie Austin, email correspondence with the author, 30 April 2013.
18 Vic Bryson, email correspondence with the author, 5 May 2013.
19 Rose Burnett Bonczek and David Storck, *Ensemble Theatre Making: A Practical Guide* (London and New York: Routledge, 2013), p.5.
20 Sophie Austin, email correspondence with the author, 3 January 2012.
21 Trencsényi, *Dramaturgy in the Making*, p.102.
22 Milan Zvada, 'Dramaturgy as a way of looking into the spectator's aesthetic experience', in Magda Romanska (ed.), *The Routledge Companion to Dramaturgy* (London and New York: Routledge, 2015), pp.203–204.
23 Pearson, *Site-Specific Performance*, p.155.
24 Ibid., p.156.
25 Ibid., p.166.
26 Dramaturgy at Work website <https://dramaturgyatwork.wordpress.com/about-2/london-a-feb-2014/> [Accessed 11 August 2015].
27 Vic Bryson, email correspondence to Sophie Austin, Catherine Hooper, Michael Wagg and the author, 18 January 2012.
28 Ibid.
29 Sarah Sigal, email correspondence with Sophie Austin, Vic Bryson, Catherine Hooper and Michael Wagg, 19 January 2012.
30 Michael Wagg, email correspondence with the author, 12 September 2013.
31 Claire MacDonald, 'Conducting the flow: Dramaturgy and writing', *Studies in Theatre and Performance*, 30:1, 2010, pp.92–93.
32 Vic Bryson, email correspondence with the author, 5 May 2013.
33 Sophie Austin, email correspondence with the author, 28 March 2013.
34 This is not to say, however, that every incarnation of a multiple writer approach to collaborative work will face this particular challenge as not all processes involving multiple writers necessitate devising and/or performer-centred creation.
35 Michael Wagg, email correspondence with the author, 12 September 2013.
36 Mark Stevenson, email correspondence with the author, 24 April 2015.
37 Trencsényi, *Dramaturgy in the Making*, p.xxii.
38 Mark Stevenson, email correspondence with the author, 24 April 2015.
39 Sophie Austin, email correspondence with the author, 28 March 2013.

40 Ibid.
41 Ibid.
42 Mark Stevenson, email correspondence with the author, 24 April 2015.
43 Josephine Machon, *Immersive Theatres: Intimacy and Immediacy in Contemporary Performance* (Basingstoke: Palgrave Macmillan, 2013), p.57.
44 Mark Stevenson, email correspondence with the author, 24 April 2015.
45 Vic Bryson, email correspondence with the author, 5 May 2013.
46 Burnett Bonczek and Storck, *Ensemble Theatre Making*, p.66.
47 Vic Bryson, email correspondence, 5 May 2013.
48 Teresa Stankiewicz, 'Who is the dramaturg in devised theatre?', in *The Routledge Companion to Dramaturgy*, Romanska, p.195.
49 Sophie Austin, email correspondence with the author, 28 March 2013.
50 Michael Wagg, 'Homer in Deptford', blog, *Duck Song*, 2012 <https://ducksong.wordpress.com/prose/> [Accessed 11 August 2015].
51 Ibid.

Conclusion

1 Claire MacDonald, 'Conducting the flow: Dramaturgy and writing', *Studies in Theatre and Performance*, 30:1, 2010, p.100.
2 Stephen Brown, interview with the author, 19 February 2008.
3 Ben Power, email correspondence with the author, 7 October 2013.
4 Grace and Bayley, *Playwriting*, p.86.
5 Oliver Dimsdale, interview with the author, 23 July 2008.
6 Emma Rice, interview with the author, 24 July 2013.
7 Vic Bryson, email correspondence with the author, 5 May 2013.
8 Ibid.
9 Emma Rice, interview with the author, 24 July 2013.
10 Joan Schirle, 'Potholes in the Road to Devising', *Theatre Topics*, 15:1, 2005, p.91.
11 Grace and Bayley, *Playwriting*, p.85.
12 Ibid., p.85.
13 Fraser Grace and Clare Bayley, *Playwriting: A Writers' and Artists' Companion* (London: Bloomsbury Academic, 2016), p.5.
14 Fin Kennedy, 'In Battalions', www.scribd.com/doc/126273288/In-Battalions [Accessed 21 December 2015].
15 *Arts Index: England 2007–2014*, published by National Campaign for the Arts. Distributed by *The Guardian* and Culture Professionals Network, p.3.
16 Ibid., p.74.
17 Alex Mermikides and Jackie Smart (eds), *Devising in Process* (Basingstoke: Palgrave Macmillan, 2010), p.15.
18 Joe Sumison speaking on the 'All in it together?' panel, *Cutting Edge: British Theatre in Hard Times*, 25 April 2015, Central Saint Martins.
19 'We all know that the biggest subsidisers of the arts are those who work in the arts. Very little work would ever make it to the stage if it was not for

people giving their labour away for free, or being paid very poorly for what they do.' Lyn Gardner, 'Love your arts job? It doesn't mean you shouldn't be properly paid', *The Guardian*, 13 July 2015. www.theguardian.com/stage/theatreblog/2015/jul/13/love-your-arts-job-it-doesnt-mean-you-shouldnt-be-properly paid?CMP=Share_iOSApp_Other [Accessed 14.7.15].

20 Elizabeth Newman speaking on the 'All in it together?' panel, *Cutting Edge: British Theatre in Hard Times*, 25 April 2015, Central Saint Martins.
21 Ibid.
22 Erica Whyman speaking during the keynote speech, *Cutting Edge: British Theatre in Hard Times*, 25 April 2015, Central Saint Martins.
23 Grace and Bayley, *Playwriting*, p.3.

Bibliography

Books

Arts Index: England 2007–2014, published by National Campaign for the Arts. Distributed by *The Guardian* and Culture Professionals Network.

Baker-White, Robert, *The Text in Play: Representations of Rehearsal in Modern Drama*, London: Associated University Press, 1999.

Billington, Michael, *State of the Nation: British Theatre Since 1945*, London: Faber and Faber Limited, 2007.

Bogart, Anne, *And Then, You Act: Making Art in an Unpredictable World*, New York: Routledge, 2007.

Bottoms, Stephen J., *Playing Underground: A Critical History of the 1960s Off-Off-Broadway Movement*, Ann Arbor, MI: University of Michigan Press, 2004.

Brontë, Charlotte, *Jane Eyre*, London: Macdonald and Co., Ltd., 1955.

Burnett Bonczek, Rose and David Storck, *Ensemble Theatre Making: A Practical Guide*, London and New York: Routledge, 2013.

Callow, Simon, *Being an Actor*, London: Methuen, 1984.

Deeney, John (ed.), *Writing Live: An Investigation of the Relationship between Writing and Live Art*, London: New Playwrights Trust, 1998.

Di Cenzo, Maria, *The Politics of Alternative Theatre in Britain, 1968–1990: The case of 7:84 (Scotland)*, Cambridge: Cambridge University Press, 1996.

Diamond, Jared, *Guns, Germs and Steel: The Fates of Human Societies*, 3rd ed., New York: W.W. Norton & Company, Inc., 2005.

Elsom, John, *Post-War British Theatre*, London: Routledge and Kegan Paul Ltd., 1976.

Freeman, John, *New Performance/New Writing*, Basingstoke: Palgrave Macmillan, 2007.

Friedman, Sharon (ed.), *Feminist Theatrical Revisions of Classical Works: Critical Essays*, Jefferson: Macfarland and Company Inc., Publishers, 2009.

Frost, Anthony and Ralph Yarrow, *Improvisation in Drama*, Basingstoke: Macmillan, 1990.

Gaskill, William, *A Sense of Direction: Life at the Royal Court*, London: Faber and Faber Limited, 1988.

Gleick, James, *Faster: The Acceleration of Just About Everything*, London: Abacus, 1999.

Govan, Emma, Helen Nicholson and Katie Normington, *Making a Performance: Devising Histories and Contemporary Practices*, Abington: Routledge, 2007.

Grace, Fraser and Clare Bayley, *Playwriting: A Writers' and Artists' Companion*, London: Bloomsbury Academic, 2016.

Graham, Scott and Steven Hoggett, *The Frantic Assembly Book of Devising Theatre*, Abington: Routledge, 2009.

Heddon, Deirdre and Jane Milling, *Devising Performance: A Critical History*, Basingstoke: Palgrave Macmillan, 2006.

Holdsworth, Nadine, *Joan Littlewood*, London: Routledge, 2006.

Innes, C.D., *Erwin Piscator's Political Theatre: The Development of Modern German Drama*, Cambridge: Cambridge University Press, 1972.

Itzin, Catherine, *Stages in the Revolution: Political Theatre in Britain Since 1968*, London: Eyre Methuen, 1980.

Krich Chinoy, Helen and Linda Walsh Jenkins (eds), *Women in American Theatre: Revised and Expanded Edition*, New York: Theatre Communications Group, Inc., 1981.

Lane, David, *Contemporary British Drama*, Edinburgh: Edinburgh University Press, 2010.

Little, Ruth and Emily McLaughlin, *The Royal Court Theatre Inside Out*, London: Oberon Books, 2007.

Littlewood, Joan, *Joan's Book: Joan Littlewood's Peculiar History as She Tells It*, London: Methuen, 1994.

Malina, Judith, *The Piscator Notebook*, London: Routledge, 2012.

Manful, Helen, *Taking Stage: Women Directors on Directing*, London: Methuen, 1999.

Machon, Josephine, *Immersive Theatres: Intimacy and Immediacy in Contemporary Performance*, Basingstoke: Palgrave Macmillan, 2013.

Mederos Syssoyeva, Kathryn and Scott Proudfit (eds), *A History of Collective Creation*, New York: Palgrave Macmillan, 2013.

Mermikides, Alex and Jackie Smart (eds), *Devising in Process*, Basingstoke: Palgrave Macmillan, 2010.

Mitter, Shomit and Maria Shevtsova, *Fifty Key Theatre Directors*, London: Routledge, 2005.

Pasolli, Robert, *A Book on The Open Theater*, New York: The Bobbs-Merrill Company, Inc., 1970.

Pearson, Mike, *Site-Specific Performance*, Basingstoke: Palgrave Macmillan, 2010.

Piscator, Erwin, *The Political Theatre*, trans. Hugh Rorrison, London: Eyre Methuen Ltd, 1980.

Piscator, Maria-Ley, *The Piscator Experiment: The Political Theatre*, Carbondale and Edwardsville: Southern Illinois University Press, 1967.

Radosavljević, Duška (ed.), *The Contemporary Ensemble: Interviews with theatre-makers*, London and New York: Routledge, 2015.

Rankin, Peter, *Joan Littlewood: Dreams and Realities – The Official Biography*, London: Oberon Books, 2014.

Roberts, Philip and Max Stafford-Clark, *Taking Stock: The Theatre of Max Stafford-Clark*, London: Nick Hern Books, 2007.

Romanska, Magda (ed.), *The Routledge Companion to Dramaturgy*, London and New York: Routledge, 2015.

Shank, Theodore, *American Alternative Theatre*, London: Macmillan Press, 1982.

Sierz, Alex, *Rewriting the Nation: British Theatre Today*, London: Methuen Drama, 2011.

Spark, Muriel (ed.), *The Brontë Letters*, London: Macmillan, 1954.

Tolstoy, Leo, *War and Peace*, trans. Constance Garnett, New York and Toronto, ON: Modern Library Paperback Edition, 2002.

Trencsényi, Katalin, *Dramaturgy in the Making*, London and New York: Bloomsbury Methuen Drama, 2015.

Turner, Cathy and Synne K. Behrndt, *Dramaturgy and Performance*, Basingstoke: Palgrave Macmillan, 2008.

Willett, John, *The Theatre of the Weimar Republic*, New York: Holmes and Meier Publishers, Inc., 1988.

Articles

Brantley, Ben, review of *Tristan and Yseult* by Kneehigh Theatre, *New York Times*, 24 November 2014 <http://www.nytimes.com/2014/11/25/theater/kneehigh-theaters-tristan-yseult.html?_r=0> [Accessed 23 February 2015].

Field, Andy, 'All theatre is devised and text-based', *The Guardian* (2009) <http://www.guardian.co.uk/stage/theatreblog/2009/apr/21/theatre-devised-text-based> [Accessed 27 September 2009].

Freshwater, Helen, 'Fingers on the Collective Pulse?', *Performance Research*, 9:3, 2004.

Gardner, Lyn, 'Love your arts job? It doesn't mean you shouldn't be properly paid', *The Guardian*, 13 July 2015. <http://www.theguardian.com/stage/theatreblog/2015/jul/13/love-your-arts-job-it-doesnt-mean-you-shouldnt-be-properly paid?CMP=Share_iOSApp_Other> [Accessed 14 July 2015].

Grose, Carl, 'Writing Tristan and Yseult: An interview with Carl Grose', Kneehigh Theatre website <http://www.kneehigh.co.uk/list/carl-grose-TY.php> [Accessed 19 November 2014].

Halliburton, Rachel, review of *Faster* by Filter and Stephen Brown, *The Evening Standard*, 8, April 2003.

Love, Catherine and Diana Damian, 'Kneehigh', *Exeunt Magazine* (2012) <http://exeuntmagazine.com/features/kneehigh/> [Accessed 18 November 2014].

MacDonald, Claire, 'Conducting the flow: Dramaturgy and writing', *Studies in Theatre and Performance*, 30:1, 2010.

Morris, Tom, 'Without subsidy, our theatres will run out of hits', *The Observer*, 17 June 2012.

Schirle, Joan, 'Potholes in the Road to Devising', *Theatre Topics*, 15:1, 2005.

Steiger, Nina, 'Absolute immediacy: A conversation with Scott Graham', *Contemporary Theatre Review*, 16:3, 2006.

Teale, Polly, 'Three sisters', *The Guardian*, 13 August 2005 <http://www.guardian.co.uk/stage/2005/aug/13/theatre.classics> [Accessed 3 August 2011].

'The show must go on', *The Economist*, 18 February 2012.

Plays

Edmundson, Helen, *War and Peace*, London: Nick Hearn Books, 2008.
Grose, Carl, Anna Maria Murphy and Emma Rice, 'Tristan & Yseult', in *The Knee-high Anthology: Volume 1: Tristan & Yseult / The Bacchae / The Wooden Frock / The Red Shoes*, London: Oberon Books, 2005, 2011.
Hanna, Gillian (ed.), *Monstrous Regiment: Four Plays and a Collective Celebration*, London: Nick Hearn Books, 1991.
Teale, Polly, *Brontë*, London: Nick Hearn Books, 2005.
Teale, Polly, *Brontë*, London: Nick Hearn Books, 2011.
Terry, Megan, *Viet Rock and Other Plays*, New York: Simon and Schuster, 1966.

Interviews

Born, Sebastian, interview with the author, 6 June 2014.
Brown, Stephen, interview with the author, 19 February 2008.
Dimsdale, Oliver, interview with the author, 23 July 2008.
Edmundson, Helen, interview with the author, 19 May 2008.
Farr, David, interview with the author, 2 July 2009.
Graham, Scott and Steven Hoggett, interview with Aleks Seirz, 19 February 2004. Email correspondence with the author, 15 April 2010.
Grose, Carl, interview with the author, 27 March 2013.
Hoggett, Steven, interview with the author, 11 October 2010.
James, Samuel, interview with the author, 26 March 2008.
King, Dawn, interview with the author, 3 September 2009.
Lavery, Bryony, interview with the author, 30 April 2009.
McLoughlin, Stuart, interview with the author, 11 December 2007.
Meckler, Nancy, interview with the author, 9 July 2009.
Murphy, Anna Maria, interview with the author, 21 March 2013.
Phillips, Tim, interview with the author, 19 January 2008.
Ranken, Liz, interview with the author, 28 June 2011.
Rankin, Peter, interview with the author, 29 November 2007.
Retallack, Guy, interview with the author, 9 April 2009.
Rice, Emma, interview with the author, 24 July 2013.
Rice, Emma, Mike Shepherd, Ian Ross and Carl Grose, 'A Conversation with Some of *Tristan & Yseult*'s creators and artists', interview with the Chicago Shakespeare Theater, Chicago Shakespeare Theater website <http://www.chicagoshakes.com/plays_and_events/tristan/tristanconversation> [Accessed 25 November 2014].
Roberts, Ferdy, interview with the author, 31 July 2008.
Simpson, Angela, interview with the author, 5 December 2009.
Teale, Polly, interview with the author, 10 July 2008.
Teale, Polly, interview with the author, 15 March 2011.

Emails

Austin, Sophie, email correspondence with the author, 30 April 2013.
Bryson, Vic, email correspondence to Sophie Austin, Catherine Hooper, Michael Wagg and the author, 18 January 2012.
Bryson, Vic, email correspondence with the author, 5 May 2013.
Graham, Scott, email correspondence with the author, 13 April 2010.
Grose, Carl, email correspondence with the author, 24 November 2014.
Herdman, Theo, email correspondence with the author, 10 May 2011.
Murphy, Anna Maria, email correspondence with the author, 25 November 2014.
Power, Ben, email correspondence with the author, 7 October 2013.
Sigal, Sarah, email correspondence with Sophie Austin, Vic Bryson, Catherine Hooper and Michael Wagg, 19 January 2012.
Stevenson, Mark, email correspondence with the author, 24 April 2015.
Wagg, Michael, email correspondence with the author, 12 September 2013.

Websites

Dramaturgy at Work website <https://dramaturgyatwork.wordpress.com/about-2/london-a-feb-2014/> [Accessed 11 August 2015].
Filter Theatre, *British Council, Arts*, (2010) <http://www.britishcouncil.org/arts-performanceinprofile-2009-british_council-filter_theatre.htm> [Accessed 25 May 2010].
'Investigations into new theatre writing in England, 2003–2009', *Arts Council*, <http://www.artscouncil.org.uk/artforms/theatre> [Accessed 2 September 2011].
Kennedy, Fin, 'In Battalions', <http://www.scribd.com/doc/126273288/In-Battalions> [Accessed 21 December 2015].
King, Gillian, Shared Experience education pack: *After Mrs. Rochester.* <http://www.sharedexperience.org.uk/media/education/after-mrs-rochester_edpack.pdf> [Accessed 13 May 2014].
King, Gillian, Shared Experience education pack for *War and Peace* by Helen Edmundson (2008) <http://www.sharedexperience.org.uk/media/education/war-and-peace_edpack.pdf> [Accessed 2 August 2011].
Kneehigh Theatre website <http://www.kneehigh.co.uk/show/tristan_yseult.php> [Accessed 17 February 2015].
'New Writing in Theatre 2003–2008: an assessment of new writing within smaller scale in England', commissioned by Arts Council England from Emma Dunton, Roger Nelson and Hetty Shand (2009) <http://www.artscouncil.org.uk/publication_archive/new-writing-theatre/> [Accessed 2 September 2011].
Rice, Emma, Kneehigh Theatre website <http://www.kneehigh.co.uk/page/making_a_show.php> [Accessed 25 March 2013].
Shared Experience, *Arts Council England* (2011) <http://www.artscouncil.org.uk/rfo/shared-experience/> [Accessed 10 March 2011].

Shared Experience website (2011) <http://www.sharedexperience.org.uk/company.html> [Accessed 10 March 2011].

Teatro Vivo website <http://www.teatrovivo.co.uk/about-us/> [Accessed 30 March 2015].

Blogs

Wagg, Michael, 'Homer in Deptford', blog, *Duck Song*, 2012 <https://ducksong.wordpress.com/prose/> [Accessed 11 August 2015].

Conferences

Cutting Edge: British Theatre in Hard Times, 25 April 2015, Central Saint Martins.

Performances

Video recording of *Tristan and Yseult* by Kneehigh Theatre, performed on 12 April 2005 at the National Theatre, CPA2/17, Kneehigh Archive, Archives and Special Collections, Falmouth University and University of Exeter Penryn Campus.

Unpublished manuscripts

Filter Theatre and David Farr, *Water*, final version, unpublished (2007).

Filter Theatre, Dawn King and Ollie Wilkinson, *Faster*, Draft Two, unpublished (2002).

Filter Theatre and Stephen Brown, *Filter*, final version, unpublished (2003).

Index